THE STRUCTURE
OF
METAPHYSICS

International Library of Psychology Philosophy and Scientific Method

GENERAL EDITOR   C. K. OGDEN, M.A. (*Magdalene College, Cambridge*)

**Asterisks denote that other books by the same author are included in this series.
A complete list will be found at the end of the volume.*

THE STRUCTURE
OF
METAPHYSICS

by

MORRIS LAZEROWITZ
Professor of Philosophy, Smith College

With a Foreword by

JOHN WISDOM
Professor of Philosophy in the University of Cambridge

ROUTLEDGE AND KEGAN PAUL

London

First published 1955
by Routledge & Kegan Paul Ltd.
Broadway House, Carter Lane, E.C.4
Printed in Great Britain
by W. & J. Mackay & Co. Ltd.
Chatham, Kent

To Alice

CONTENTS

NOTE

Those papers in this volume which have previously been published, originally appeared as follows:—

FOREWORD
By JOHN WISDOM

A breeze blows through these pages. You may think it blows away not only dust. You may think Professor Lazerowitz makes too light of philosophical problems, or of some of them. But even if he does I am glad of the air. After all it is open to any one to go through the rooms again and replace any valuable antiques for which he thinks Professor Lazerowitz has not shown a proper care. For my part, as I have said, I am glad of the air. For in philosophy the atmosphere too often reminds me of a house the inmates of which are for ever debating whether, when, and how they could, or should, go out, but never in fact do go out. Professor Lazerowitz would be sure to ask them whether they really *want* to go out. What an insufferable question!

I know it is easy to fail to bring out philosophical difficulties. But it is also easy to make sure that one never clears them up, never sees what the other man means and what he *doesn't* mean, never even makes an advance in a dialectic progress.

What does Professor Lazerowitz do in this book? Three things. First, he brings before us, in his own specially clear and crisp way, that change which has come over philosophy as we have come to realize how very strange philosophical questions are, and presents a certain new view of philosophy and its associated new philosophical procedure. Second, he takes up certain typical philosophical disputes and in doing so illustrates the new procedure. He asks what has led philosophers to say the extraordinary things they have said. At this stage he aims to carry this inquiry only far enough to reveal some of the confusions, excuses and reasons behind philosophical doctrines. Third, he carries the inquiry further and submits that there are often causes for adherence to a philosophical theory, deeper than those which appear when we ask the reasons for the theory. In illustration of this he ventures in outline a surmise as to one of the deeper sources which lie behind the old and phoenix-like paradox 'Change is unreal'. It is my belief that he is right in this surmise.

I would like to say a few words about these three themes in Professor Lazerowitz's book. A philosophical paradox, such as 'Mind does not exist', or 'The Past does not exist', appears at first to be an alarming statement as to a matter of fact, or a denial that any statement of a certain type, for instance one about minds, or one about the past, is true. However, such paradoxes are often soon modified, so that they appear not as statements to the effect that all statements of a certain type are false, but as statements to the effect that what we have thought to be adequate reasons for these statements are not adequate, or not even reasons at all. At once philosophical disputes look less like disputes as to matters of fact and more like logical disputes as to whether certain premises are or are not good reasons for certain conclusions. They retain, however, the appearance of a conflict between a sceptical paradox and a common-sense platitude. At this point a curious change of sides often takes place. For those philosophers who, in opposition to sceptics, support the seemingly common sense and platitudinous claim that the premises we have so long accepted as adequate for our conclusions *are* adequate, often support this claim and oppose the sceptics by insisting that our conclusions are deducible from, reducible to, our premises. For instance such a philosopher, in opposition to a sceptic who insists that our reasons for the statements we make about the past are no good because our premises are all about the present or the future, will insist that statements about the past are analysable into, are nothing but, statements about the present and the future. He will say that sentences about the past can be translated into sentences descriptive of that about the present and the future which makes us say what we do about the past. At once philosophy appears as a matter of logical analysis, of definitions, of equations, of translations.

Those of us who came to view philosophy as a matter of logical analysis or definition were able to explain to ourselves the hitherto curious and obstinate character of philosophical disputes, by saying that philosophers had been hindered by misunderstanding the

general nature of their disputes. What became disturbing was the
fact that philosophical problems, when re-presented as problems
of definitions, of equations, retained their curious chronic character. As we all know, it was at this juncture that Wittgenstein
compared philosophical questions to questions which have no
answers, Yes or No. He compared them to questions the rival
answers to which present now these, now those, features of a
situation which we haven't a word for. He compared them to
questions the answers to which introduce, and so recommend, a
certain mode of description, a certain projection, a certain notation for viewing that which we wish to view.

In metaphysical philosophy what we wish to view are certain
old and puzzling features of the ways in which we settle questions
of different types, for instance moral questions, questions about
minds, questions about material things. Our difficulty in philosophy, Wittgenstein said, arises from the idea that our language
is a simpler calculus than it is, from a craving for definition. If
only we could say that statements of a given type, for instance
statements about the past, are *reducible to* those upon which they
appear to be based, for instance statements about the present
'evidences' of the past, then we could say that statements of the
given type are *deducible from* those upon which they appear to be
based. But statements of a given type are never reducible to statements of another type. All statements, which are reducible to
statements about the present, are statements about the present,
and not about the past. Philosophers are not interested in a class
of statements unless statements of that class cannot be defined in
terms of statements which are not of that class. No wonder our
definition programme broke down. But the break down is more
profound than at first appears. For not only is it the case that
statements of a given type are not reducible to those of another
type as statements within a type may be reducible to one another,
it is also the case that statements of a given type are not *not*
reducible to statements of another type in the way in which statements within a type may be not reducible to each other. For instance, a statement of logical necessity is not not deducible from
a statement about words in the way in which the statement 'The
word "four" may always be substituted for the phrase "two and
two" is not deducible from' 'The word "two" may always be

substituted for the phrase "one and one".' No wonder Wittgenstein so often *at the end* of a philosophical discussion would say,
'Say which you like'.

It is my belief that here is one of those great flashes of insight
with which Wittgenstein illuminated philosophy itself and those
things which philosophy should illuminate, for instance the character of statements, which, if true, are necessarily true, and the
character of statements about minds, and the character of statements about the past, and so on. Nor did Wittgenstein strike a
light and then fail to show how it may be used. Far from it. At the
same time it is, I believe, a fact that when people listened to Wittgenstein they often found it difficult to get a steady light giving
an ordered view of what they wished to see and that when they
now read him they still have this difficulty. Yet such a steady light
and ordered view is needed.

Now when Professor Lazerowitz introduces to us the contention that philosophical theories are notational innovations he does
so in a certain way. He introduces it as a result which we obtain
when we seek to explain the phenomena of philosophical dis-
putations. At once it appears as an account, one might almost
say as a hypothesis, the adequacy of which as compared with that
of other accounts, other hypotheses, is to be judged by the way it
covers the phenomena to be explained. At once the light becomes
steadier, at once we can more readily use it to obtain a coherent
view of philosophy and of what philosophy reviews.

Second, having introduced in this particular manner this account of philosophical theories as being the introduction and
recommendation of certain modes of presenting the logical character of classes of statements, Professor Lazerowitz also in the
same, as one might say scientific, manner, applies this account of
philosophy in the consideration of certain traditional philosophical
questions—for instance the question of the existence of universals
and the question of the nature of logical necessity. It seems to me
that as he proceeds the character of these old and mysterious disputes becomes vastly plainer and that the value of the new
account of philosophy is thus brought out.

This new account of philosophy is, I submit, itself a philosophical 'theory', a 'theory' as to the nature of philosophical
statements as opposed to a 'theory' of the nature of, for instance,

mathematical statements, or moral statements. And it has its dangers. For one may forget that a philosophical 'theory' is, or should be, a verbal recommendation made not with a view to convenience, but with a view to illuminating the facts, the facts as to the way we verify statements of this sort, or of that. A philosopher who declares that we have no knowledge of material things is not declaring that it would be more convenient never to use the word 'knowledge' in connection with material things. He is recommending to us that new view of the verification of statements about material things which we may gain if for a moment we call all such statements 'hypotheses' and draw the line for applying the word 'knowledge' here.

Professor Lazerowitz does not deny this. It may be that at times in his efforts to bring out how close are philosophical theories to verbal innovations, he does not emphasize the way these innovations may illuminate and distort the modes of verification proper to the types of statement with which the philosopher is concerned. But anyone who reads these essays carefully cannot but notice that Professor Lazerowitz not also says that a notational innovation may show us, or obscure from us, some continuity or contrast we have missed, but also gives examples of this. For instance, he does this in the essay on universals. Besides he certainly shows that if we call philosophical theories not 'theories', 'but verbal innovations', then this innovation puts philosophical disputation in a new light. Indeed this innovation, this new name, may influence the way in which we conduct philosophical inquiry in a degree which is much more marked than the influence on physical inquiry of the innovations suggested by one who refuses to speak of knowledge of the external world, or the influence on mathematical and logical inquiry of the innovation suggested by one who says that mathematical and logical statements are statements as to the usage of words.

If we say then that Professor Lazerowitz takes the view that philosophical theories are verbal innovations, we must remember first that he is of course aware that they are not consciously proffered as verbal innovations, and second that he is aware that such innovations may illuminate or distort, or both illuminate and distort what the metaphysical philosopher is concerned with, namely the mode of verification proper to some class of statements.

The more clearly we grasp the fact that in introducing and recommending a notation a philosopher aims not at a more convenient or expedient form of expression, but at one which will help us to realize what we may have failed to realize, even though it has been before us, the more we understand why philosophers show concern, excitement, pleasure and vexation as they argue for their views. At the same time we may feel that the very passionate concern which philosophers feel about their views suggests that there are *other* forces at work beside the desire to grasp the logical character of a class of statements or questions.

And the third thing which Professor Lazerowitz does is to submit that this in fact is so, that there are causes encouraging, driving a philosopher to speak in the way he recommends other than those he mentions under the guise of reasons for his view, causes much more hidden. No doubt such unconscious causes may play a part in our acceptance or rejection of certain answers to questions which are not philosophical but, for instance, political, historical, or scientific. But the more a question is finally settled by observation and, or, calculation on well established lines, the less scope have unconscious causes. When the matter is one of adopting a way of presenting things which shall put certain things in a certain light and others in another light, then unconscious causes have much greater scope. We can't do without these sources of light and energy. But concealed lighting can make things look very different from what they are. Why not pull the curtains and open the windows? The light will be better, the air will be fresher, and we shall be freer.

PREFACE

In these papers I have tried to win my way to an understanding of the nature of metaphysics, and I am only too well aware of the difficulty and uncertainty with which I proceed and of how far I fall short of my goal. Although these papers have a unity of purpose, each paper represents a fresh start and was written without a cautious eye to what I had already said elsewhere. Circumspect consistency has been no part of my aim. The attentive reader is certain, thus, to discover not only clumsy and misleading exposition, which first attempts to view a complex subject through a new medium make inevitable, but also inconsistencies. My hope is that these will serve to stimulate him to do further work in a field in which too little is being done. He will also see that I return a number of times to the question as to the nature of *a priori* necessity. I do this because, in my opinion, getting clear on this question is of first importance to the understanding of metaphysics.

Three of the essays in the present collection (II, X and XII) have not appeared before in print. For permission to reprint the other essays it is my pleasant duty to thank the editors of the following journals and books:—

Analysis, Mind, The Philosophical Review, Proceedings of the Aristotelian Society.

Philosophical Analysis, Cornell University Press; *The Philosophy of G. E. Moore,* The Library of Living Philosophers, Vol. IV.

Northampton, Massachusetts,   MORRIS LAZEROWITZ

January 1955.

I

MOORE'S PARADOX

IT has frequently happened that philosophers have held seriously views which seem to go completely counter to ever so many beliefs of common sense. Different philosophers have said, with the assured air of stating incontrovertible fact, that

(1) Physical objects exist only while being perceived;
(2) Material bodies are unreal;
(3) Time is unreal;
(4) Space is unreal;
(5) No one can know with certainty that any other person exists.

These theories, and many others like them, appear to be about matters of fact, open to establishment or disestablishment by observation and experimentation. In this respect they resemble propositions found in ordinary science text-books, e.g., the proposition, which parallels (1), that mercury exists in a solid state only at a temperature less than 38.86 degrees below zero Fahrenheit, or the proposition, which parallels (5), that human beings cannot hear sounds of high pitch readily audible to dogs. And by backing these theories with proof philosophers give the impression of destroying the most assured beliefs of ordinary life, of being like scientists who demonstrate facts, e.g., that the speed with which an object falls does not depend upon its weight, which reduce some of our strongest convictions to mere superstitions. All these philosophical theories have this in common, that from each of them it seems to follow that *no* propositions of very large classes of propositions of ordinary discourse are *ever* true; and some of these propositions each of us, ordinary people as well as scientists, should unhesitatingly say we know to be true. From (1), namely, that physical objects exist only while being perceived, the shocking consequence seems to follow that every proposition asserting the existence of an object which happens not to be perceived by anyone, e.g., the film inside my camera, is always false. From the view (2) that material bodies are unreal the equally shocking consequence seems to follow that every proposition stating the existence of material objects, e.g., the proposition that I have a pen right now in my hand or the proposition that I have a hand, is always false. And the views (3), (4) and (5) appear to have similar consequences with regard to all propositions of the classes of temporal propositions, spatial propositions, and propositions about our knowledge of other selves, namely, that none of them is ever true.

These views and many others in philosophy should consequently be cause for serious concern, since so much of what we take as absolutely unquestionable, not only in ordinary life but in scientific investigation, is apparently brought into question. Professor G. E. Moore has taken this as a cause for concern, and has made it one of his main objects to combat such views and to defend Common Sense against their consequences. Against them he has maintained that many propositions of the classes which, according to these views, never contain true propositions *are* often true; i.e., that there are many true temporal and spatial propositions, many true propositions stating the existence of unperceived physical objects, many true propositions with regard to our knowledge of other selves. In proof of this, and consequently in refutation of these views, he has contended that he knows, and similarly for everyone else, that:—

There exists at present a living human body, which is *my* body. This body was born at a certain time in the past, and has existed continuously ever since . . . and, at every moment since it was born, there have also existed many other things, having shape and size in three dimensions (in the same familiar sense in which it has), from which it has been *at various distances* (in the familiar sense in which it is now at a distance both from that mantelpiece and from that book-case, and at a greater distance from the book-case than it is from the mantelpiece) . . . And, just as my body has been the body of a human being, namely myself

. . . so, in the case of very many of the other human bodies which have lived upon the earth, each has been the body of a different human being . . .[1]

It is plain that an important part of what Moore does in attempting to refute philosophical theories from which it follows, or at any rate seems to follow, that no propositions of certain classes of propositions expressed in ordinary discourse are ever true, is to refer to plain matters of fact which it would simply be a farce to deny. Thus, for example, against the views that space and time are unreal he cites such facts as those to the effect that he was 'born at a certain time in the past' and that he has a body. Obviously, similar facts hold for anyone who ever held that space and time are unreal, and are, furthermore, perfectly well *known* by those who hold these views. A peculiar feature of such views, which immediately becomes evident from Moore's refutations, is that phenomena of the sort the existence of which they deny are so plainly before all our noses that it is startling to have them referred to in refutation of important philosophical views. This is what Moore often does; he calls attention to facts which make important philosophical views look ridiculous. The strange thing, if we stop to think of it, is not that anyone who has been taken in by these views has overlooked what is so obvious, but that he should have accepted or even been troubled by views which go against what he has *not* overlooked. It leads us, furthermore, to wonder what could ever have made anyone formulate them.

Demonstrations of the sort Moore uses against them would, in ordinary life as well as in science, be absolutely conclusive, to see which requires no special training. They are of the form '*a* is a *fact*; theory T is logically inconsistent with *a*; therefore T is false'. In ordinary life, as well as in science, we *give up* theories which are logically inconsistent with facts which we *know*. In philosophy, however, as Moore has pointed out, this frequently does *not* happen. In connexion with philosophical theories which seem obviously inconsistent with innumerable propositions expressed, or implied, in scientific and ordinary discourse, Moore has formulated what is one of the most important paradoxes in philosophy. He has pointed out that philosophers '. . . have been

[1] 'A Defence of Common Sense', *Contemporary British Philosophy*, v. II, pp. 194-5.

able to hold sincerely, as part of their philosophical creed, propositions inconsistent with what they themselves *knew* to be true, and . . . this has really frequently happened'.[1] This is an astonishing paradox; and by expressing it Moore brings to sharp focus a discontent with philosophy which ever so many people have felt but have never been able to express in any clear way. It may be recalled that Professor Broad, for example, felt it necessary to defend philosophy against the vague charge that it is 'moonshine'.[2] Moore's refutations show that a great deal of philosophy is 'moonshine' *of some sort*. They bring out a likeness between many philosophical views and grotesque fiction, a likeness between them and stories like that of the hunter whose reply to the question as to how he had escaped from wild beasts which had completely surrounded him, was, 'I didn't escape; they ate me up'. Moore's paradox makes this likeness even stronger; but, what is perhaps more important, it brings out a marked difference between them: the difference, namely, that philosophers who express views inconsistent with what they know nevertheless hold those views *sincerely*. It thus sobers us and addresses our attention to the problem as to what makes this *possible*. This, it seems to me, is the *real* problem: to see what it is about the *nature* of the views and the arguments used in their support that makes it possible for philosophers to hold them in the face of plain matter of fact, with which, as seems to be the case, the views are inconsistent. And it is my present purpose to consider this problem.

If the refutations Moore formulates are looked at in conjunction with his paradox a fact appears which may seem as surprising as the views against which they are brought. Moore attempts to confute philosophers by calling attention to facts of a sort which, according to his paradox, they already know and therefore have not overlooked or ignored. Now, we may say that a necessary condition which a fact *a* must satisfy in order to establish the falsity of a proposed theory T is that a person who holds T will give it up on getting to know *a*, given both that the person holding T is sincere and also that the inconsistency between *a* and T is absolutely obvious, requiring no process of ratiocination in addition to looking at both in juxtaposition. Facts of the sort

[1] 'A Defence of Common Sense', *Contemporary British Philosophy,* v. II, p. 203.
[2] C. D. Broad, *Scientific Thought,* p. 11.

Moore directs attention to in attempting to confute certain philosophers are, if inconsistent with their theories, *obviously* inconsistent with them; nothing, for example, could be more obvious than the inconsistency, if there is one, between a fact of the form 'I have a body' and the view that there are no material bodies. In spite of such facts being perfectly well known by them, philosophers nevertheless persist in holding their views. That is, *knowing* such facts does not make them *give up* their views; and the only conclusion possible, it seems to me, is that such facts are not inconsistent with *their* views, however incomprehensible this may seem. Thus, as I shall try to show, Moore's paradox, according to which they *do* know such facts, leads to the conclusion that his 'refutations' are not refutations.

It may be pointed out in this connexion that conflicting attitudes on the part of Moore himself can be detected, that his attitude toward his own refutations is ambiguous. The sort of facts to which he refers in demonstrating the falsity of philosophical views like (1)–(5) creates the impression that the views are so patently false as to make it completely unaccountable how anyone could ever hold them. And one can only gather that his attitude regarding them is that they are not worthy of serious concern. He has, as a matter of fact, given expression to this attitude:—

This, after all, you know, really is a finger: there is no doubt about it: I know it, and you all know it . . . The questions whether we do ever know such things as these, and whether there are any material things, seem to me, therefore, to be questions *which there is no need to take seriously*: they are questions which it is quite easy to answer, with certainty, in the affirmative.[1]

Moore does, however, take such questions quite seriously; he has written and continues to write on them.[2] In spite of his contention that 'they are questions which it is quite easy to answer, with certainty, in the affirmative' he has thought answers in the negative, i.e., views such as that time is unreal and that material bodies are unreal, to be sufficiently important to *defend* Common Sense against them. This, it seems to me, reasonably leads to the

[1] *Philosophical Studies,* 'Some Judgments of Perception', p. 228. Italics my own.
[2] Cf. his 'Proof of an External World', Annual Philosophical Lecture, Henriette Hertz Trust, *Proc. Brit. Acad.,* Vol. XXV (1939).

supposition that he grants them an importance which is precluded by the attitude evinced by his refutations. His constant concern to refute them shows his attitude to be that they *are* important. If, consequently, this concern is taken seriously, as it should be, it must be concluded that his attitude with regard to his refutations is ambivalent. It must be supposed that he himself, in a concealed way, is uneasy as to whether his 'refutations' are refutations.

In this study I wish to show that his 'refutations' are not refutations, and also, more generally, that the views the falsity of which they are designed to establish, *have no refutations*. I wish to show how his paradox together with his refutations throw light on the *nature* of the views, so that it can be seen that those views have no refutations.

Moore is unquestionably right in saying that philosophers *know* facts of the sort he uses to confute them, e.g., facts to the effect that they were born at a certain time in the past, have bodies, own things which at various times are perceived by no one. In case it is thought that what Moore says is doubtful, a good way to test a person who makes academic assertions which are inconsistent with what we think he knows all along is to observe how he acts in relevant situations. We take as a criterion of a person's knowledge with regard to various matters of fact, not only his academic claims, but also his behaviour in the presence of such facts; and if his behaviour is and continues to be incompatible with his claims, we discount them as *just talk* and accept his behaviour as indicative of what he *really* knows. For example, if an entirely competent and honest doctor were persistently to say that no disease is incurable, and nevertheless continued to treat cases, say, of leprosy the way other competent doctors treat them, as cases of a disease which cannot, as yet at any rate, be cured, we should reject what he says, regardless of his sincerity, as puzzling talk and be perfectly certain that he *knows* that leprosy is an incurable disease.

The views with regard to space, time, material bodies, etc., against which Moore defends Common Sense, give rise to the idea that *ordinary* behaviour is inappropriate to reality, and that if people only knew better they would change their behaviour to suit the facts—this would seem to be the practical consequence of establishing such views. It is consequently to be expected that philosophers who hold such views will act differently. It is to be expected that philosophers who hold that no one can know with certainty that any other person exists will greet their friends with at least *some* hesitance, with the mental aside, 'For all I know, this may be nothing but a subjective show; after all, I don't really know that other people exist'. The idea of travelling in trains should immediately bring up a picture of certain disaster in the mind of anyone who held that physical objects exist only while being perceived, because 'a railway train would only have wheels when it is not going, since, while it is going, the passengers cannot see them',[1] When one considers how people would behave if the conductor were suddenly to shout that the train, in which they were going at sixty miles an hour, no longer had its wheels, it might well be expected that some philosophers would never leave home.

It would seem reasonable to expect *some* difference in behaviour on the part of philosophers who sincerely hold views like (1)–(5). None, of course, as Moore's paradox anticipates, is discernible. It is a fact that the superior knowledge which philosophers give the impression of having results in no different behaviour from that met with in ordinary life. Despite a philosopher's unquestionably sincere claim to have demonstrated the unreality of time, like any other person he consults his watch, hurries to an appointment, and apologizes for being late. Despite his view about the unreality of space, he complains that the distance from his home to his lecture room is too much for him to walk of a morning or that an ugly building is between his study window and a fine view. Despite his view about the unreality of material objects, he is as careful as any normal person to avoid oncoming cars when crossing the street and remarks with satisfaction on the thickness of the steel door of the bank vault in which his valuables are kept. And, apart from the fact that no uncertainty whatever can be detected in his behaviour, it is a safe bet that he does not make any mental aside about the possible non-existence of other people when he hails his friend, accepts his offer of a cigarette, and walks down the street with him. For he fails to show the slightest signs of doubt in circumstances which should bring out his doubt in its most acute form, namely, when he tries to convince others of the correctness of

[1]Moore's example, used by B. Russell in *The Analysis of Matter*, p. 210.

the view that no one can know with certainty that other people exist.

On the contrary, circumstances can easily be imagined in which such views could be used to *reassure* a philosopher who is in *real* doubt or in some actual state of anxiety about ordinary situations. If, for example, we were to tell him that the automobile which he had locked in his garage has vanished, that it is no more, he would behave like any ordinary person: he very naturally would be upset, want to notify the police, certainly regret that he had not insured it. If, in answer to his question as to what had happened, whether it had burnt, or been struck by lightning, we say it was none of these but only that it was locked in the garage and so was not being perceived, there is no question but that he would be relieved. That is, when he understands that the only reason for our saying his automobile is no more is his own philosophical view that physical objects exist only while being perceived, he is reassured that his automobile *does exist*. Similar situations can be imagined in connexion with the other views. For example, when he begins to apologize for having come a half-hour late to dinner and we insist he is not late, like any other person he expresses relief and wonders what is wrong with his watch. When we go on to explain that he could not have come late because, according to his own view, time is unreal, he thinks we are good-natured about the whole thing and goes on with his explanation as to why he *was* late. It is a curious feature of views like (1)–(5) that, if they are given as reasons for statements with regard to ordinary matters of fact, they are treated as *jokes*.

It is clear that Moore is entirely right in saying that philosophers who hold these views *know* facts of the sort which by their views they seem plainly to deny. Their ordinary behaviour shows this. Even their academic talk frequently shows this, as he has pointed out:—

> . . . all philosophers who have held such views have repeatedly, even in their philosophical works, expressed other views inconsistent with them: i.e., no philosopher has ever been able to hold such views consistently. One way in which they have betrayed this inconsistency, is by alluding to the existence of other philosophers. Another way is by alluding to the existence of the human race, and in particular by using 'we' . . .[1]

[1]'A Defence of Common Sense', pp. 202–3.

8

And they are not struck by the absurdity of saying 'none of *us* can ever really know that any human being besides himself exists', or of starting a lecture with the statement, 'In the course of this lecture I propose to demonstrate the unreality of time', because not for a moment is the existence of other people or of temporal phenomena in question. If they were in question the proponents of the views could not fail to *see* the absurdity. Regardless of what they hold academically, such facts are never *really* in question; everything goes to show that philosophers know them *even while* expressing their views.

This makes it look as though holding such views and attempting to 'prove' them is nothing but a solemn pretence, a sort of intellectual game of make-believe which many adults like to play. But to suppose this is as far from the truth as anything could be. Moore is certainly right when as part of his paradox he states that philosophers hold such views 'sincerely'. Their behaviour shows this as clearly as it shows that they know facts which seem to be in obvious contradiction to their views. Undoubtedly they hold their views sincerely, and undoubtedly they know facts which appear to render their views false. Consequently, it is, so far as I can see, a correct paraphrase of Moore's paradox that philosophers have held '. . . sincerely, as part of their philosophical creed, propositions inconsistent with what they themselves knew to be true', to say that philosophers have held '*sincerely,* as part of their philosophical creed, propositions which they *knew to be false*'. And if his 'refutations' are refutations, then philosophers *have* held views they knew to be false. This is impossible, and the only conclusion, it seems to me, is that his 'refutations' are not refutations of their views. To see this it is first necessary to see that views like (1)–(5) are not empirical.

It is in the first place natural to look on the disputes between Moore and other philosophers as being empirical. The views, by the way they are expressed, seem for one thing to imply the falsity of ordinary *empirical* propositions, such as the proposition that in 1893 F. H. Bradley published arguments for the unreality of time. And if they did imply the falsity of propositions which are such that they could logically have a truth-value other than the one they in fact have, they would themselves have to be empirical, be such that they could logically have a truth-value other than the one they have. For another thing, Moore actually adds to the illusion that the disputes are with regard to matters of fact. The manner in which he expresses his demonstrations, viz., *a* is a fact, *a* is inconsistent with T, therefore T is false, does this. I.e., he uses language which gives the impression that he brings empirical facts to bear against the views; and since only empirical propositions can be inconsistent with such facts, or have implications with regard to them, the impression is naturally created that the disputes are about empirical facts.

Looked at in this way, however, the disputes between Moore and other philosophers become completely incomprehensible: for they *remain unresolved*. When in ordinary life an empirical theory is in question recourse to the facts, if they are available, will settle the matter. This seldom, if ever, happens in philosophy. There is a story that once, when Zeno propounded his theory about the impossibility of motion, Diogenes, in refutation of the view, stood up and walked several times across the room. But there is no story of Zeno having given up his view, nor, so far as is known, of Bradley having given up his. In ordinary life, having one's attention called to facts which are incompatible with a given view makes one discard it. This, as is to be expected from Moore's paradox, does not happen in philosophy. For, since philosophers hold their views *while* (and in spite of) *knowing such facts,* recourse to the facts will not result in the views being given up. Consequently the disputes cannot be looked upon as empirical. To do so leads to the self-contradictory conclusion that philosophical disputes with regard to matters of fact *cannot* be settled empirically. The only way to avoid this contradiction is to say that the disputes are not empirical. The following considerations show this most plainly.

Let us examine the statement, 'Time is unreal'. If, to use Moore's expression, it is translated 'into the concrete',[1] it looks as though what a philosopher who makes it means to assert is that '. . . . nothing ever happens before or after anything else; nothing is ever simultaneous with anything else; it is never true that anything is past; never true that anything will happen in the future; never true that anything is happening now; and so on'.[2] 'Time is unreal' means the same as 'There are no temporal facts'.

[1] *Philosophical Studies,* 'The Conception of Reality', p. 209.
[2] *Ibid.,* p. 210.

Parenthetically, it may be remarked that translating philosophical views into the concrete is an important part of Moore's technique; for by it he gets rid of misleading pictures which are naturally associated with the views, e.g., the picture of time as a sort of mysterious object.[1] It is such pictures, the empirical counterparts of philosophical statements, that in part make the views so intriguing and at the same time prevent one from seeing what they actually come to. By removing the pictures he deprives the views of an important part of their mystification. But to do this is not enough. To return from the digression, if 'Time is unreal' is taken to mean that there are no temporal facts, the view looks plainly to be empirical: 'There are no temporal facts' bears a great similarity to 'There are no centaurs'. But the empirical look is a deceptive feature, both of the view and of its translation. If the attention of a philosopher who holds the view and grants the translation is called to various events that just took place and are now taking place, he will continue to maintain that there are no temporal facts, and perhaps repeat his argument for maintaining the view. It looks as though he wishes to deny the facts. But these he *knows* and cannot *honestly* deny. Consequently, it must be supposed that he does not *really* wish to deny them at all, however to the contrary appearances may be. It must be supposed that the view is of such a nature that the facts simply *do not count against it.*

No known facts count against it, and furthermore, it is easy to see that no *imaginable* or *describable* facts could do so either. Suppose we say: 'This is all very strange. You do not deny the existence of various events which Moore calls "temporal facts"; nevertheless you insist that time is unreal. What, to help clear up the mystery, would you describe, over and above such things, which, if there were anything of that kind answering to the description, would make you give up the view? Talking, walking, having tea, and the like are not, it would appear from your view, really temporal. Perhaps we have all been labouring under an illusion about such things; tell us what the real thing is like'. *This he cannot do.* He cannot describe anything, over and above the phenomena he rejects as being temporal, which he would say was

---

[1] Note Bradley's remark: 'It is usual to consider time under a spatial form. It is taken as a stream, and past and future are regarded as parts of it . . .' *Appearance and Reality,* p. 39.

the real thing, really temporal. Unlike the bored seeker for excitement who complains that nothing ever happens, he cannot say what it would be like for anything to happen. Nothing in actual experience, in recollection, in present experience, or in fulfilled expectation, is acceptable as disestablishing his view, and neither is anything which could be described, regardless of whether it exists or not. Unlike 'Centaurs are unreal', 'There are no temporal facts' is such that nothing which we can picture to ourselves would falsify it. It is plain from this that the philosopher who asserts 'Time is unreal' is not using it to express a proposition which could imaginably be false, i.e., *an empirical proposition*. Similar considerations hold for the other views. Consequently, if Moore's refutations are looked on as demonstrations in which empirical facts are brought to bear against the views, it must be conceded that his 'refutations' are not refutations.

Once it becomes clear that in holding views like (1)–(5) philosophers are not asserting empirical propositions, the natural thing is to think that they are asserting necessary ones. As a matter of fact, philosophers who have held such views have themselves frequently thought this. Russell has said with regard to common beliefs that they are 'cocksure, vague, and self-contradictory'.[1] And Bradley has said: 'Time, like space, has most evidently proved not to be real, but to be a self-contradictory appearance'.[2] It may be gathered from this that Bradley supposes himself, by his views with regard to time and space, to be implying not merely that there are no temporal and spatial facts but that it is logically impossible for there to be any. He thinks himself to be holding views from which it follows that ordinary spatial and temporal propositions, e.g., the propositions to the effect that half my sheet of paper is covered with writing and that it has taken me twenty minutes to accomplish this, are not merely false but are self-contradictory. And the statement 'Time is unreal' is to be taken on this supposition as expressing a *necessary* proposition, namely, 'Time is self-contradictory' or, to translate it 'into the concrete', 'It is logically impossible for there to be temporal events'. This interpretation also requires that we revise our idea of the nature of the disputes between Moore and other philosophers. His refutations, just as the philosophical

[1] *Philosophy*, p. 3.
[2] *Appearance and Reality*, p. 43.

views, have to be considered as different from what the language in which they are expressed naturally leads one to think they are, viz., demonstrations in which views are countered with empirical facts. What they come to, as necessitated by the supposition that the philosophical views in dispute are necessary ones, can easily be seen by bringing out a further fact about those views.

'Time is unreal', when the intention is to use it as the expression of a necessary proposition, presumably means the same as 'It is logically impossible for there to be any temporal facts'. In place of the latter form of expression it is more usual to use the words 'There *cannot* be any temporal facts'. Compare now 'There cannot be any temporal facts' with 'Water cannot flow uphill'. It is a simple matter to imagine or to picture to oneself water flowing uphill; we know what it would be like for there to be a state of affairs which would make false the proposition that water cannot flow uphill. In other words, part of understanding 'Water cannot flow uphill' consists in knowing what it would be like for water to flow uphill. And in general, in the case of every sentence of the form 'x cannot . . .' which expresses an empirical proposition, understanding the sentence consists in part in knowing what it would be like for a situation described by 'x *does* . . .' to obtain. Thus, 'Water flows uphill' describes something which the original sentence says cannot obtain. However, with regard to no sentence which expresses a necessary proposition is this ever the case. On the contrary, understanding a sentence of the form 'x cannot . . .', in which 'cannot' has the meaning of *logical* impossibility, is *inconsistent* with knowing what it would be like for there to be states of affairs described by 'x does . . .' This can be seen by noticing with regard to 'There cannot be any temporal facts' that, if understanding it entailed knowing what it would be like for there to be anything described by 'There are temporal facts', or if 'temporal fact' described anything which 'There cannot be any temporal facts' says cannot exist, it would not express a necessary proposition. For situations could then be imagined which would render the proposition expressed by it false. Only by preventing 'temporal fact' from having a descriptive use, by preventing any phenomenon, actual or imaginable, from being *called* a temporal fact, does 'There cannot be any temporal facts' become an expression for a necessary proposition. By using sentences to express necessary propositions we prevent certain expressions from having a use: ' "There cannot be any temporal facts" expresses a necessary proposition' means the same as ' "Temporal fact" has no use'. It is clear then, that the *information* conveyed by sentences expressing necessary propositions is *verbal*. Now I do not wish here to suggest that necessary propositions are verbal; I do not wish to be understood as holding any view whatever with regard to their nature. For it seems to me that the question, 'Are necessary propositions verbal?' *has no answer*; and the thing that has made some philosophers *give* it an answer in the affirmative is that they have noticed an important similarity between sentences for necessary propositions and those for linguistic ones, viz., that the information both sorts of sentences convey is verbal. This feature of similarity is not, however, sufficient for asserting *truly* that necessary propositions are verbal. And I do not wish to be understood as claiming to assert this; although what I have suggested might be said to be self-contradictory on the grounds that the proposition expressed by a sentence which conveys verbal information must itself be verbal. The information conveyed by sentences expressing necessary propositions is verbal, and as the word 'verbal' is at present used in the English language it is not *true* to say that necessary propositions are verbal.

If expressions for the philosophical theories, 'Physical objects exist only while being perceived', 'Material bodies are unreal', 'Time is unreal', etc., are viewed as being such that the information derived from understanding them is verbal, or, more specifically, is about the use of an expression, the disputes between Moore and other philosophers must be interpreted in this light. The philosopher who asserts that time is unreal, or that there cannot be any temporal facts, informs us that expressions using verbs with tense have no use: that such sentences as 'Moore lectured for an hour on perception this afternoon', 'Moore is now having tea', 'To-morrow he will lecture on definite descriptions', express self-contradictory propositions, and consequently describe nothing actual or imaginable and are devoid of sense. Moore's refutations, in which philosophical theories seem to be countered with empirical facts, must then be interpreted to be attempts at showing the views wrong by showing that ordinary propositions expressed by sentences involving verbs with tense are not self-contradictory. Now the *only* way in which it can be demonstrated that such propositions are not self-contradictory is to show that the sentences which express them are used in ordinary discourse to describe various situations, actual or imaginable. Hence, when in refutation of 'Time is unreal' Moore points out that Zeno held the view more than 2,000 years before Bradley did, he may be construed as arguing: 'The sentence "Zeno held the view that time is unreal more than 2,000 years before Bradley held it" describes what happened or what can be imagined to have happened; therefore the proposition it expresses is not self-contradictory; therefore the theory from which it follows that the sentence does express a self-contradictory proposition is false'. The disputes between Moore and other philosophers, on the supposition that philosophical statements express necessary propositions, are to be reckoned as disagreements in which the points at issue are verbal, i.e., points as to whether ordinary expressions of various sorts have a use. It is highly doubtful that Moore would agree that this is what the disputes come to, although he at least seemed to hint at this when he said: '. . . I have assumed that there is some meaning which is *the* ordinary or popular meaning of such expressions as "The earth has existed for many years past". And this, I am afraid, is an assumption which some philosophers are capable of disputing'.[1] This is, however, what the disputes do seem to me to come to, *if* it is supposed that the philosophical statements express necessary propositions.

Moore's paradox may now be paraphrased to read as follows: philosophers '. . . have been able to hold sincerely, as part of their philosophical creed, views according to which expressions of various sorts, which they *know* are used in ordinary discourse to describe real or imaginary states of affairs, have no use or sense'. To formulate it in terms of the concrete example, 'Time is unreal', Moore is to be understood as saying that philosophers who hold this view know that expressions involving verbs with tense have descriptive use in ordinary language. Also, on the supposition that philosophical statements express necessary propositions, so that the points at issue in the disputes are verbal, views (1)–(5) are to be taken as constituting in effect an attack on the *language* of Common Sense: as views according to which no sentences of very

[1]'A Defence of Common Sense', p. 198.

15

large classes of sentences employed in ordinary discourse ever describe anything at all, that they make no sense. Moore's defence of Common Sense is to be construed as a defence of the *language* of Common Sense; and the refutations, which by the way in which they are expressed give the impression that he brings empirical facts to bear against the views, are to be considered as linguistic in intent. 'A railroad train *has* wheels while it is going and no one sees them' translates into '*It makes sense* to say "A railroad train has wheels while it is going and no one sees them".' 'Here is a hand' translates into ' "Here is a hand" does not express a self-contradictory proposition, it does have a descriptive use in the language, it is not a senseless expression'. This, now, may seem to be a satisfactory way of looking at the matter. Again, however, as on the first interpretation of the disputes between Moore and other philosophers, difficulties emerge.

It is difficult, in the first place, to see why Moore should think it necessary or at all important to defend Common Sense against attacks on its language by philosophers, who in ordinary life find it quite satisfactory for their communicative needs. There clearly is no actual need to defend Common Sense against such attacks. They are *just* academic, and have had no influence whatever on ordinary language. Changes have of course occurred in it, but they have not been brought about by any philosophical attacks. Zeno, for instance, stated the view that motion is impossible, the verbal point of which is that expressions using verbs denoting an action are senseless; but Common Sense still uses such expressions, and no doubt will continue to use them regardless of what philosophers say. Even philosophers continue to use them, despite their views. It is not easy to see what would ever make anyone hold views like (1)–(5); but neither is it easy to see why anyone should show any concern at all to refute them. And again, it seems to me, if Moore is right in asserting as part of his paradox that philosophers *know* that ordinary expressions using verbs with tense, verbs denoting an action, nouns which are general names for material objects, etc., are used in ordinary life to describe various matters, then his 'refutations' are not refutations. His refutations show views which are in conflict with the language of Common Sense to be false; but since philosophers continue to maintain *their* views in spite of such refutations and in spite of knowing what they do about ordinary language, it must be the case that his refutations are not refutations of *their* views. Their views are still to be construed differently.

Moore is entirely right in saying that philosophers know the facts about the language of Common Sense to which his demonstrations call attention. Again, if the test of behaviour is applied to them, this becomes plain. A good test for ascertaining whether a person knows that expressions of various sorts make sense is to observe how he uses them and how he responds to other people's use of them. It is of course a fact that philosophers use and respond to the use of ordinary expressions in the same way in which people who do know their use commonly respond. Philosophers know how to ask for the time of day, the distance to a place to which they wish to walk, whether there are films inside the camera, etc.; and by their behaviour they show that they understand other people's use of such expressions. There is no doubt whatever that in everyday life they use and understand the language of ordinary people. And even though on the foregoing interpretation their *views* may make them appear to be like foreigners who are ignorant of the language they hear but who believe that it makes no sense because it makes no sense to them, all evidence points to the contrary. Even in their academic talk they betray their knowledge of the language. This recalls Moore's remark: '. . . all philosophers who have held such views have repeatedly, even in their philosophical works, expressed other views inconsistent with them; i.e., no philosopher has ever been able to hold such views consistently'.[1] This may now be taken as stating that philosophers who have held views, the verbal points of which are that ordinary expressions of various kinds have no use, have repeatedly, even in their philosophical works, made statements using such expressions. Consider, for example, Bradley's remark: 'Time, like space, has most evidently proved not to be real, but to be a self-contradictory appearance. I will, in the next chapter, reinforce and repeat this conclusion by some remarks upon change'.[2]

Again it looks as if holding such views is nothing but a deception. The natural feeling in connexion with Bradley's remark is

---

[1] 'A Defence of Common Sense', p. 202.
[2] *Appearance and Reality*, p. 43.

that by inadvertence he has given the game away and that a more careful philosopher would not have done so. But Moore is right when he states, as part of his paradox, that philosophers hold such views sincerely. I should say that the lack of caution shows that it is not a deception: these philosophers have nothing to hide, otherwise they would be more circumspect. And it shows more than this. It reveals that what they know about the language does not count against *their* views, against what they really mean to say. If what they knew did falsify their views, Moore's 'refutations' would refute them. But then the disputes between him and other philosophers would again be incomprehensible: they remain unresolved. Since philosophers understand the language and know how to use it, and since Moore's demonstrations only call attention to what they already know, they must see that his refutations do establish the falsity of views according to which great parts of language in everyday use make no sense. The fact that they see this and do not give up their views would be entirely unintelligible if facts of the sort he adduces were incompatible with their views. Undoubtedly it would not disturb Bradley in the least to have it pointed out to him that in conjunction with his theory about time he says: 'I will, in the next chapter, reinforce and repeat this conclusion by some remarks on change.' It should; if what he says is inconsistent with his view he should give it up. But, since what he himself has said does not make him relinquish the theory, it can only be supposed that *his* theory does not conflict with the language he uses. What philosophers know cannot be used to disestablish their theories; and since Moore's demonstrations call attention to what they already know, it must be admitted that his 'refutations', viewed as arguments employing facts to the effect that expressions in ordinary use make sense, are not refutations of their views. If this is so, it will be plain that the philosophical views *have no refutations*. If no considerations, either of the sort which disestablish empirical theories or of the sort which disestablish *a priori* ones, are *relevant* to them, then they are neither empirical nor *a priori*. It makes no sense to speak of refuting them, nor, for that matter, of proving them. This is important, because it leads to seeing what the views really are.

Philosophers do of course speak of proving their theories, and actually produce arguments for them. This is what makes philosophical theories impressive, despite their looking like 'moonshine'. Arguments for views like (1)–(5) are of course also arguments against Common Sense, and Moore has challenged them. He has said: 'I think we may safely challenge any philosopher to bring forward any argument . . . which does not at some point, rest upon some premiss which is, beyond comparison, less certain than is the proposition which it is designed to attack.'[1] To be sure, if an argument attacks *known* fact it may safely be challenged; and if Moore's demonstrations establish the falsity of the views they also establish the incorrectness of arguments of which the views are consequences. It is important, however, to notice what a philosopher *does* when faced with facts of the sort to which Moore's demonstrations refer. When in ordinary life, as well as in scientific investigation, a person is faced with facts of a sort with which his argument conflicts, he looks for a mistake in his reasoning. Even when he fails to discover what is wrong with it, he admits that it is wrong. This is the normal reaction: to give it up, to look for the mistake. This the philosopher does not do. When faced with a fact which apparently disestablishes his view he brings forward an argument. *He counters facts with arguments.* If, for instance, Bradley's attention were called to the fact that he concludes his chapter on 'Space and Time' with the words 'I will, in the next chapter, reinforce and repeat this conclusion by some remarks on change', he undoubtedly would say that his argument has not been understood and ask that it be looked at again with more care.

What are we to understand from his behaviour? Is it that he wishes to maintain and to have us see that his argument is correct? This could hardly be the case; he cannot both know the facts and urge that it is nevertheless a correct argument against them. His behaviour must be interpreted differently. It is plain that he wants us to look at the argument rather than at the facts, as if the facts were somehow beside the point. This shows that his concern is not to have us see that his argument is not mistaken, but *something else*. When he complains that his argument has not been understood, he means that *the nature* of his argument has not been understood. His argument is not designed to establish the truth of any view, empirical or *a priori*. It is meant to back *a verbal recommendation*. His 'views' are really proposals with regard to the use

[1] *Philosophical Studies,* 'Some Judgments of Perception', p. 228.

of ordinary expressions; this is the explanation of the problem as to what has made it *possible* for philosophers to '. . . have been able to hold sincerely, as part of their philosophical creed, views inconsistent with what they themselves *knew* to be true'. And the thing which prevents its being seen that his 'views' are not inconsistent with known fact and that his 'proofs' are only reasons for making verbal recommendations is the manner in which he expresses himself. He uses the language of assertion rather than the language of proposal. Instead of saying 'Let us not use the word "time" (or the word "now"), let us delete it from the language', he says 'Time is unreal', and so creates the impression that he is framing theories, *a priori* or empirical. Instead of saying 'Let us not use "know" in sentences referring to other people', he says 'No one can know that other people exist'. Instead of saying 'Let us not use "not perceived" in sentences referring to physical objects', he says 'Physical objects cannot exist unperceived'. This creates the illusion that they are 'theories', and gives rise to the attendant puzzling stalemates. He does the same with his 'proofs' and so furthers the illusion that he is concerned to establish the truth of theories. An examination of a well-known philosophical proof, for the 'view' that time is unreal, will help make this clear.

It has been argued:—

The question at once before us will be as to the 'now's' temporal contents. First, let us ask if they exist. Is the 'now' simple and indivisible? We can at once reply in the negative. For time implies before and after, and by consequence diversity; and hence the simple is not time. We are compelled then, so far, to take the present as comprehending diverse aspects. How many aspects it contains is an interesting question. According to one opinion, in the 'now' we can observe both past and future . . . All that we require is the admission of some process within the 'now'. For any process admitted destroys the 'now' from within.[1]

In other words, with regard to the question, 'How much time does now consist of?' it is only possible to say either that now consists of zero time or of some unit of time, however small. Neither of these alternatives, however, is possible. If it consists of zero time, then 'as a solid part of time, the "now" does not exist'.[1] And if it

[1] *Appearance and Reality,* pp .40-1.

consists of some time interval, has duration, then it contains 'an after and before',[1] which is self-contradictory. This looks like the 'proof' of a view with regard to the nature of time; the language in which it is expressed tempts us to imagine that what it shows is that 'now' has a self-contradictory meaning and that sentences using 'now', or verbs in the present tense, say what is self-contradictory. What it really is and what philosophers wish to accomplish with it is not, however, difficult to see. 'Now cannot consist of some stretch of time', in which 'cannot' expresses logical impossibility, conveys the same information as 'It makes no sense to say that now consists of $\frac{p}{q}$ seconds'. What it shows is that the word 'now' is not used as the name of a time interval, like 'hour', 'second', etc. On the other hand, 'Now cannot consist of zero time' conveys the same information as 'It makes no sense to say that now consists of zero time', and tells us that 'now' is not used as a synonym for it. These two things can also be seen by considering the question 'How much time does "now" contain?' The fact that it is formulated shows that the use of 'now' is in *some* respects like the use, e.g., of 'minute': compare with 'How much time is there in a minute?' But unlike the latter question it has no answer; or, if there is an inclination to make up an answer, one might say it consists of no *definite* time. This shows that the use of 'now' differs radically from the use of 'minute', 'second', 'half a second', etc.

These two facts about the word result in conflicting tendencies; they lead us, so to speak, in opposite directions. Consider, for example, the statement 'Now is the time for the equinoctial storms'. In it 'now' has a use which bears *some* resemblance to the use of 'month' in 'During this month we may expect equinoctial storms': it does not mean 'zero time'. This makes us tend to exaggerate the similarity and to speak of 'now' as if it were the name of a unit of time. But noticing that it is *not* leads to the opposite extreme; it tends to make us exaggerate the difference to the point where we wish to deprive 'now' of a use having any such resemblance. This produces a feeling of uneasiness about the word which is based on a desire to make irregular words behave in strict ways. And what the philosopher wants is *to get rid of the*

---

[1] *Appearance and Reality,* p. 41.

word and so rid himself of his uneasiness. By his argument he shows us what a queer irregular word it is, and tempts us to acquiesce in his recommendation, which he misleadingly expresses in the words, 'The "now" is self-contradictory', 'Time is unreal'. What he really means is this: ' "Now" is not the name of a unit of time, nor does it mean no time; let us stop using it'. Moore of course knows these facts and apparently they produce in him no desire to give up the word. In general, with regard to views like (1)–(5), his defence of Common Sense is a defence against *changing* the language of Common Sense; and his refutations are simply counter-proposals, to be understood as recommendations not to follow academic wishes to alter it.

II

THE NATURE OF METAPHYSICS

I. INTRODUCTION

METAPHYSICS presents us with an intellectual phenomenon that is both remarkable and mystifying. It is without doubt one of the highest of man's cultural achievements, combining in itself both grandeur of conception and subtlety of thought. But what it is, its nature, remains unknown to us. It looks to be the deepest of the sciences, in which the attempt is made to arrive at an understanding of the ultimate constitution of the world, its basic material and structure, and of the nature and limits of our knowledge. Further, metaphysics has a scope, by comparison with which the ordinary sciences, with their laboratory techniques, appear to comprehend only the surface mechanics of the material universe, while, moreover, resting on tremendous assumptions that are the proper province of metaphysics, e.g., that nature is uniform.

But although metaphysics looks like science, it differs from science in an important respect, a respect which is overlooked by philosophers but which is a source of profound disturbance to intelligent outsiders. No one, except a person who must for some reason blind himself to the facts, can fail to contrast the special sciences, with their imposing edifices of solid results, and metaphysics, with its chronic condition of endless and unresolved debates. Theories which are accepted as undeniably true by many philosophers are rejected as certainly false by others. And what is perhaps even more perplexing, demonstrations which, according to the considered opinion of some philosophers, are absolutely conclusive are, according to the considered opinion of other and equally able philosophers, inconclusive or mistaken. This is a state of affairs which is an enigma to our understanding. How is it to be explained?

Is the source of the condition to be discovered in the complexity and difficulty of the problems dealt with? Or is it to be found in the incompetence of philosophers? Neither of these alternatives is an impressive possibility, and the evidence against them need not detain us. There remains another possible explanation which, however unacceptable it may be to us emotionally, has to be faced and examined. This is that the irresolvability of the disagreements flows from the very nature of the problems, which is to say that the problems are *intrinsically* insoluble, in the sense that no *new fact* will finally establish one answer and lead to the discarding of other possible answers as false. This is an explanation which places a hardship on us, for it requires that we change our way of thinking about metaphysical problems. The difficulty of doing this can be put into its proper perspective if we imagine ourselves in the position of a person living in the sixteenth century who is told that the earth revolves around the sun, or, to use a more homely example, if we imagine ourselves trying to look at our wonderful children through the eyes of our annoyed guests. However that may be, the last explanation is one which can no longer be ruled out of court; for it must be realized that the condition of metaphysics is chronic and pervasive. Until the permanence of the disagreements has been satisfactorily explained a metaphysical theory remains an intellectual creation which we do not understand, or perhaps it would be better to describe it as a linguistic symptom for which there exists no diagnosis.

The traditional idea of metaphysics is that its theories are perfectly well understood and that the debates about them are debates over whether they are true or false. This idea is so entirely natural that it is difficult to think that it could be subject to question. Descartes' dissatisfaction with the intellectual anarchy he found everywhere in philosophy was based on the unquestioned acceptance of this idea, and he conceived his task to be one of devising a reliable method for determining the truth-values of theories. This was also the problem of the empiricists, from Locke on. But metaphysics, and in fact the whole field of technical philosophy, still remains in dispute. If we take the long history of philosophy into consideration, it becomes not altogether unreasonable to question whether there is a theoretical procedure for ending the disagreements by 'solving' the problems. It is worth calling attention to William James' observation, which he himself did not elaborate, that 'philosophical theories are not refuted; they are only outmoded'.

There is reason, indeed, for suspecting that the disputes are, *by their very nature,* not resolvable by scientific means of any sort, *a priori* or empirical, and that the real method, whatever that may be, which is employed for accepting or rejecting theories is effectively concealed behind a deceptive façade of demonstrations and refutations. It may well be the case that the proofs and refutations are not what we take them to be, that the theories, unlike those of the natural sciences and mathematics, are not open to proof or disproof, and that the disputes cannot be resolved, although it may be possible for insight into their nature to *dissolve* them. It may quite well be that *understanding,* not solving, is the real intellectual problem. In fact, I shall argue that metaphysical problems *have no solutions,* though this does not mean that we cannot understand them. Only because we *fail* to understand them do we *seek* for solutions, and to understand them is to rid ourselves of the feeling that there *must be* solutions.

This is a possibility which needs now to be investigated. To question the assumption that philosophers are engaged in the task of trying to discover the truth-values of metaphysical views, which brings into question the idea that the views are understood, is to initiate a new Copernican revolution. But there can no longer be any hesitation about investigating this assumption. The curious fact that there are no firmly established results in metaphysics needs to be explained; and any path which gives any promise whatever of leading to an explanation is to be followed, however emotionally disturbing it may be to do this. It must, of course, be admitted that we take the risk of following an intellectual will-o'-the-wisp.

It will be my purpose in these pages to pursue the consequences of supposing that metaphysical theories have no truth-values and that the controversies about them are not debates over whether they are true or false. I shall try to show that the sentences used to express metaphysical theories are not understood, not because they lack intelligibility, but because we simply are not cognizant of what the words which express the theories and their fortifying or refuting arguments come to. We are not consciously aware of what we are doing with language when we imagine ourselves to be expressing and demonstrating or refuting profound and important views about the limits of human knowledge, the nature of space, or the will. We do not understand our own linguistic creations. Like a dream, a metaphysical theory is a production of the unconscious and has both sense and motivation. We enjoy it or are repelled by it, it gives us pleasure or pain, a feeling of security or one of danger; but its meaning is hidden from us. Just as in our sleep we dream with images, so many of us in our waking intellectual life dream with words. A metaphysical theory, I shall try to show, is a verbal dream, the linguistic substructure of which has to be uncovered before we can see what it comes to and how it produces its effect. The main problem will be to expose to clear view the linguistic machinery which is used to create the illusion that metaphysics gives us views about pervasive and fundamental phenomena and that the arguments for or against these views are demonstrations of their truth or falsity. But it is necessary first to see that none of the explanations of the nature of metaphysics so far advanced, explicitly or by implication, is correct. And above all it is important to see that none of them gives a satisfactory account of the disconcerting fact that metaphysical differences of opinion never get resolved, though interest in various problems may pass out of fashion.

Four important hypotheses, classical and contemporary, have been either assumed or explicitly proposed and argued for as answers to the question, 'What is the nature of metaphysical theories?' According to one hypothesis they are empirical propositions about the world, about its fundamental aspects and ultimate nature, and are to be confirmed or discarded by experience. Another describes them as being *a priori* propositions about reality, i.e., as being propositions about reality which are arrived at or refuted *a priori,* without the help of any sort of experimentation or observation. A third hypothesis construes them to be disguised linguistic claims about the proper or correct or established usage of expressions. And still a fourth has it that metaphysical statements are meaningless strings of words, that they are sentences which conform to the rules of grammar but are lacking in literal intelligibility, even though they may arouse strong emotional reactions in people.

These hypotheses, it seems to me, have been in part the result of the fact that different philosophers have been impressed by and have concentrated their attention mainly on different aspects of metaphysics or on particular classes of views. If a philosopher is especially impressed by the appearance metaphysics has of being about phenomena, their existence or nature, he will be likely to think that the theories are open to empirical testing of some sort. If, instead, he is impressed by the demonstrations that are adduced, he will tend to think that the views are *a priori* descriptions of reality. And if he has insight into the nature of both *a priori* and empirical propositions and concentrates his attention mainly on theories which, at least in appearance, go against the beliefs of common sense, he will hold that they are concealed linguistic statements about proper usage. Or if he concentrates mainly on theories which refer to the supersensible, he will hold them to be nonsensical counterfeits which philosophers have, somehow, been duped into taking for the real thing.

Consider the following selection of views:—

Everything flows.

Motion is impossible.

Physical things depend for their existence on being perceived.

There are no material things.

There are two distinct kinds of substances, minds and bodies, and they interact.

Every event must have a cause.

It is possible for one person to know that another person exists.

There are such entities as universals.

In addition to a person's introspectible states and processes there is a self which is their subject.

A thing is constituted by an unknowable substratum in which attributes inhere.

Ultimate reality is will.

A transcendent, absolutely perfect Being exists.

It can be seen that three distinct groups of propositions can be formed from this list. There are those propositions which, like 'Everything flows' and 'There are no material things', seem to go against the most fundamental beliefs of common sense. These strike practical-minded people with a well-developed sense of reality as being bizarre and shocking, to be dismissd as intellectual chimeras; but they hold great fascination for people with mystical tendencies, who, moreover, may be subtle reasoners. The list contains other propositions which seem consistent with, or even to fortify, the beliefs of common sense. Thus, the view that there are two distinct kinds of substances, minds and bodies, which can produce changes in each other, agrees with the most common conception we have of ourselves. And the statement 'It is possible for one person to know that another person exists', when maintained by a philosopher, fortifies a belief against the attacks of many metaphysicians, a belief we should all say we had, if asked. Then there are those propositions which state the existence of transcendent objects, objects which lie beyond the limits of ordinary, everyday sense-experience. A philosopher who maintains that there are suprasensible universals, entities which he can only apprehend with his mind's eye, gives one the idea that he is acquainted with objects which would not be accessible to him were he limited to his five senses. And a philosopher who claims that in addition to the various experienced qualities of a thing, such as a pebble, there is an unknowable substratum in which the qualities inhere, gives the impression of having discovered evidence for the existence of an object which he is prevented from examining, from knowing as it is 'in itself', by some sort of insurmountable barrier. The important proposition that a transcendent, absolutely perfect Being exists belongs to this last group.

The propositions of all three groups have the look of being about the world; they represent the conclusions of attempts 'to know reality as against mere appearance'. Whether in fact they are about the world, they undeniably have the appearance of making factual claims. That the sentence 'Motion is impossible', for example, has empirical descriptive sense seems entirely clear; and though the proposition it expresses may strike many readers as odd and certainly false, it must strike them as even more odd that anyone should wish to assert that the literal meaning of the sentence actually is unknown. What else could the sentence be saying except the startling thing that objects are incapable of moving, that rivers do not flow and that my pen, which appears now to be moving, is really stationary? It may be absurd to say that motion does not exist; but it would seem even more absurd to maintain that the sentence does not deny that rivers flow and that birds fly, and to maintain, moreover, that we have no idea of what it does state. It is the same with the other statements in the list. What could the sentence 'It is possible for one person to know that another person exists' be saying except something re-assuring about human knowledge? And what could the statement 'In addition to the gross things of sense, there are suprasensible universals' be saying except that objects exist which cannot be seen or felt but require a higher faculty than any used in sense-experience? What the statements of the list are about, regardless of whether we agree with them or not, seems undeniably plain, at least on the surface. And unquestionably, a great part of the fas-cination they have for most people lies in their being believed to be about the world, sensible or supra-sensible.

II. METAPHYSICAL THEORIES AS EMPIRICAL

It is natural, if we believe metaphysical statements to be about phenomena, to take them to be expressing empirical propositions, dependent for their truth or falsity on what reality is like and testable by some sort of examination of the world. What makes people immediately reject an assertion like 'Motion is impossible' is the evidence of their senses; the claim it appears to make about the world their *experience* of the world shows to be false. They react to the putative claim in the way they would normally react to the suggestion that they were completely paralysed and could move no part of their bodies, i.e., by moving their hands or getting up and walking about, as Diogenes did in refutation of Zeno. The language Hume, for example, uses to describe how he came to reject the notion of the self as a 'simple and continued' spiritual substance makes it evident that he imagined himself to be resorting to an empirical process of testing the notion, a process of introspecting, which he allowed may lead to different findings by different people. He wrote:—

For my part, when I enter most intimately into what I call *myself,* I always stumble on some particular perception or other, of heat or cold, light or shade, love or hate, pain or pleasure. I never catch *myself* at any time without a perception, and never can observe anything but the perception . . . If anyone upon serious and unprejudiced reflection, thinks he has a different notion of *himself,* I confess I can reason no longer with him. All I can allow him is, that he may be in the right as well as I, and that we are essentially different in this particular. He may, perhaps, perceive something simple and continued, which he calls *himself;* though I am certain there is no such principle in me.[1]

Whether Hume in fact had recourse to an empirical process of self-examination in order to test the notion of the self is open to question, but his language makes it certain that he imagined himself to be describing such a process.

The idea that metaphysical theories are testable empirically is deeply rooted in our minds, and its existence can be detected in the minds of philosophers who explicitly reject this notion and effectively conceal it from themselves behind the rationalization of 'philosophical analysis'. A question like 'Is there such a thing as the *self* which has wishes, thoughts, feelings, volitions, and a variety of perceptions?' too easily and without sufficient insight gets converted into the question 'What is the analysis of the concept of the self?' which in turn gets too easily converted into the question 'Are sentences which use the word "self" translatable into sentences which mean the same but do not use the word or any synonym of it?' Intellectual inventiveness does not always keep pace with intellectual insight; to the contrary, it is frequently designed to prevent insight. The child sees that the emperor is naked, but philosophers instead argue over whether a man who wears an invisible robe is dressed.

Professor G. E. Moore, perhaps the most outstanding philosophical analyst, has been led to maintain that metaphysical theories are not empirical; but in his case, too, we are compelled to think that, despite his denial, he has the idea that they are open to testing by observation. The style of language he uses to express his refutations of theories which seem to go against common-sense

[1] *Treatise of Human Nature,* Book I, Part IV, Section 6.

beliefs makes it obvious to anyone but a philosophical barrister defending metaphysics that Moore conceives his refutations to be empirical. As a refuting instance of such a view as that everything flows he would refer to the chair he was sitting on or to the clock on his mantelpiece and say, 'My chair does not flow and neither does my clock; it would be absurd to suggest that they do. Therefore, the proposition that everything flows is false'.

Moore has protected himself against the possible charge that his method of refuting a view is appropriate to empirical, not to *a priori,* propositions, and thus against the charge that he thinks the theories empirical. He has maintained that the facts to which he calls attention are refutations of *consequences* of the theories and not directly of the theories themselves. The theories are shown to be false by *modus tollens.* In other words, Moore conceives himself to be disestablishing on empirical grounds only what have been called 'translations into the concrete' of such views as 'Motion is impossible', 'Everything flows', 'Material things do not exist', and then *deducing* the falsity of the views from the falsity of their consequences, e.g., deducing the falsity of 'Everything flows' from its empirically falsified consequence 'The clock on the mantelpiece flows'.

But this kind of defence won't do. It rests on the assumption that a non-empirical view can have deductive consequences which are empirical, open to testing by observation or an experiment; and this assumption contains a simple and obvious mistake. Any proposition p which entails some other proposition q will have to be such that its falsity is determined by the falsity of $q,$ so that if the falsity of q is empirically determinable the falsity of p will be determinable in the same way. A proposition cannot both be *a priori,* such that the truth-value it has is its only possible truth-value, and have empirical consequences the truth-values of which could possibly be other than they are; for if it could both be *a priori* and have empirical consequences it would follow that the truth-value it of necessity has is not its only possible truth-value. A proposition cannot be non-empirical and at the same time be logically dependent for its truth-value on the truth-value of an empirical proposition. It is plain that if its truth-value is contingent on the truth-value of an empirical proposition, it must itself be empirical. The mistake contained in the assumption is so transparent that it is difficult to see how it could have come to be overlooked. It is hard to rid oneself of the feeling that the failure to see it is caused by the unconscious wish not to see it, in order to cover up an opinion which insight has made inadmissible but which is still held. It is by no means rare for a person to have incompatible opinions, one conscious and the other unconscious; and one reliable way of discovering an unconscious opinion, which may be concealed by a contrary consciously expressed belief, is to notice the form of expression, the style of language, used. In Moore's case, the language he uses makes it plain that he imagines metaphysical theories to be empirical,[1] like those of the natural sciences, regardless of what he may have declared them to be.

This conception of the nature of metaphysical theories is not to be dismissed easily. More than a superficial insight into its inadequacy is necessary before it can be genuinely relinquished. Otherwise it remains, and, like a wish behind a neurotic symptom which has been removed by an analysis that failed to expose the unacceptable wish itself to the patient, it tends to become less accessible to our scrutiny. One thing that has to be seen first is that on this conception there is no way of explaining the irresolvability of metaphysical disputes.

Take, for example, the view that no physical thing exists when not perceived. The picture this gives us is that of a mad-hatter world in which the existence of things is in some miraculous way synchronized with our perceptions. Things pop out of existence and back in again according to whether we gaze at them or not. The words 'Nothing exists unless it is perceived' seem to express an astonishing fact about the behaviour of things, which may for all we know be the case. After all, science tells us many astonishing things, too. Empirical tests of some sort should show whether physical objects are dependent for their existence on our perceptions, providing, of course, that the proposition is empirical and that the picture the philosophical sentence brings to our minds is appropriate to what the sentence actually describes. But this turns out not to be the case.

[1]See especially his 'A Defence of Common Sense', *Comtemporary British Philosophy*, Vol. II, and 'The Concept of Reality', *Philosophical Studies*. See also his *Some Main Problems of Philosophy*, where the task of philosophy is said to be 'no less than this; namely: To give a general description of the *whole* of the Universe . . .' (p. 1).

If we look on the view as factual and the disagreement over it as one with regard to the facts, we have no explanation of why the dispute does not get resolved and why the theory does not get established or refuted. We shall discover to our bewilderment, if we take the view seriously and apply tests to it, that what the tests show will not in the slightest degree influence a philosopher who holds that physical things exist only when perceived. No evidence, however strong or conclusive it may seem to us, is conceded as in any way discrediting the view. If we call attention to the fact that there is a mirror image of the table behind us, which would be a miracle if there were no table of which the image was a reflection, we shall find that this is disregarded or that it is turned away with the answer that seeing things in a mirror is a way of perceiving them. If we try the further experiment of photographing the table behind our backs, we shall discover that the photograph, which, in a case of genuine doubt, would be taken as conclusive evidence for the continued existence of the table, is also discounted. And if, in addition to the evidence of mirrors and cameras, we point out that the heavy chandelier remains suspended while the ceiling from which it is suspended and the chain which holds it are not being looked at, we shall make no advance in moving a philosopher who holds the view. It becomes entirely clear now that no evidence will have the slightest influence on settling the question as to whether unperceived things exist or not. And this is a complete mystery, if the view and the dispute about it are empirical.

Or consider the theory that there are no material things. Again, the attempt to investigate it by recourse to observation of matter of fact leads to the same inexplicable situation. Those of us who are convinced that there are such things as doors and mountains might think that we could check our belief, which this theory appears to challenge, by looking more carefully than is our wont, feeling with greater care, and so on. Suppose we do this, satisfy ourselves that there really are doors and mountains, and now try to convince the metaphysician that his view is mistaken. As we might expect, the metaphysician remains unmoved. His behaviour does not come as a surprise to us, but at the same time it is incomprehensible. Suppose, as Moore has suggested,[1] we try to convince him by holding up a hand before his eyes and saying, 'Here

[1]'Proof of an External World', *Proc. British Academy,* Vol. XXV (1939).

is a hand, therefore, there is at least one material thing'. This will not make him give up his view, not even if we let him pinch our hand and take a cigarette from it. His behaviour is not unexpected, because quite obviously he is already familiar with hands and the like. Holding up a hand before his eyes presents him with *no new evidence,* the lack of which might be considered a reason for his holding his view. He has his belief while in full possession of such evidence. A surprising thing, if one stops to think about it, is that we should even dream of resorting to such a procedure, as if the intent were to direct the metaphysician's attention to something he might have overlooked. How could we ever get ourselves into the frame of mind of supposing that he was aware of *us* but that he needed to be made aware of the existence of our *hands* in order to see that his theory is false? Quite clearly we do not understand what we are doing, nor do we understand how he can continue to hold his view or how he could ever have come to hold it. If his theory concerns the existence of hands, doors, chairs, and the like, then his maintaining that there are no such things is incomprehensible to us, *but neither do we know how to show him that he is wrong.*

In a non-philosophical case of two people disagreeing over whether there is a table in the room, they settle their difference of opinion by going into the room and looking. If, for some reason, one of them is still sceptical as to whether what he sees is really a table, he goes up to it, feels it, pushes it, and puts things on it. In this way he assures himself that there is a table in the room and brings the disagreement to an end. But this does not happen in the philosophical case. Instead of accepting the evidence of his senses, the metaphysician calls to his aid the philosophical distinction between appearance and reality, behind which he makes his position secure. He will grant that there do appear to be material things; but he will insist that the appearance is delusive, 'mere appearance'. Or he may weaken his position and assert that we can never know that the appearances of books and tables and pavements are not delusive. He holds his view with impregnable safety by successfully stalemating his adversaries, who now find that all their evidence is ruled out of court. In an ordinary dispute between people over whether there is, say, a lake in the distance or whether what they see is a desert mirage, it is possible for them to satisfy themselves who is in the right and who is in the wrong by the simple expedient of going up to the place where the lake appears to be. But the philosophical proposition that what we take to be the world of material things is only an illusion of the senses cannot successfully be challenged by looking, feeling, etc., however carefully done. It is to be noticed, also, that a person who maintains the proposition is in no position to produce any experiential evidence which carries conviction to anyone who rejects the proposition. Looking and feeling and the use of our other senses do not, for some reason that cannot yet be fathomed, settle the matter either way.

It turns out, as can easily be seen, that anyone who is convinced that there really are material things and, supposedly, bases his conviction on sense-observation, finds himself in exactly the same position with respect to his own evidence as the metaphysician is with respect to it. He is a brother metaphysician who, if he looks at the situation objectively, will see that he holds his own view with as little reasonableness as he is inclined to impute to his colleague, and also with as much assurance. For he can adduce no better experiential evidence with which to convince himself of his own belief than he is able to adduce against the metaphysical proposition of his adversary; and since the evidence fails to make his opponent give up his position, he cannot use it to convince himself of his own position. Or if he reckons the evidence of his senses as good evidence for the proposition that there really is a world of material things and its existence is not just an illusion, then he cannot understand his opponent's indifference to it. And on the present hypothesis there is no understanding this. In ordinary affairs we know well enough how to evaluate evidence, but we are at a total loss as to how to evaluate the evidence brought against the metaphysical proposition that there are no material things. This should make us suspect that perhaps the proposition is not what it gives the appearance of being.

The statement 'There are no material things' seems to make the same sort of claim that the statement 'There are no pink elephants' makes, but we may begin to suspect that this is not the case. Once this suspicion is aroused we see that we should be equally curious as to what the more sober assertions of philosophical common sense, e.g., that material things exist, that not all things flow, that motion exists, actually are about, what they really say. Further investigation is necessary before we can hope for insight. But first the other hypotheses regarding the nature of metaphysical theories have to be considered.

III. METAPHYSICAL THEORIES AS *A PRIORI*

One of these hypotheses, which has the merit of giving us a possible explanation of why it is that no sort of empirical evidence has the slightest tendency to settle metaphysical differences of opinion, tells us, in effect, that the disagreements are not the kind that can be resolved by recourse to an examination of matter of fact. This is the hypothesis that metaphysical views are *a priori*. Of course, if the views are not empirical and are demonstrable or refutable by pure reason or by an analysis of concepts, we can understand why no evidence of the senses can count either for or against them. Looking is not an appropriate or a relevant way of determining the truth-value of the propositions 'Yellow tulips are not mauve' and '$2+3=5$'. Similarly, if the propositions 'There are no material things', 'Nothing exists unperceived', 'Everything flows' are *a priori,* the claims they make are not open to testing by observation or an experiment. And the fact that many of us imagine that an examination of phenomena is relevant to the ascertaining of whether they are true or false might be explained as being due to our wrongly taking them to be factual statements about reality, which they do look to be.

Philosophers who are especially aware of the way in which metaphysical theories are actually argued for and against are likely to think them *a priori*. They notice, for one thing, that a view like Zeno's about the impossibility of motion is not an inference from a subtler examination of objects which are normally taken to be in motion, e.g., birds on the wing and horses at a gallop. It would be absurd to say, 'Careful observation shows that motion does not exist' or 'Experimentation has established that things do not exist unperceived'. Instead of calling our attention to features of the behaviour or condition of bodies which would make us see that they are really at rest and their motion only apparent, Zeno gives us a logical chain of reasoning designed to prove the *self-contradictoriness* of motion. He supports his conclusion by a logical demonstration, by an analysis of the concept motion. And philosophers who are aware of the fact that this is the method used in metaphysics, the method of logical analysis which makes no use of observation or experimentation, will construe the theories as *a priori*. Thus, Bertrand Russell has said that the essence of philosophy is logic.[1] And Professor C. D. Broad has said:—

> It should now be clear why the method of Philosophy is so different from that of the natural sciences. Experiments are not made, because they would be utterly useless. If you want to find out how one substance behaves in the presence of another you naturally put the two together, vary the conditions, and note the results. But no experiment will clear up your ideas as to the meaning of *cause* in general or of *substance* in general . . . The method of Philosophy resembles that of pure mathematics, at least in the respect that neither has any use for experiment.[2]

What Professor Broad writes is unquestionably correct. It is hardly necessary to call attention to the fact that there are no metaphysical laboratories, a fact which has won for metaphysics the title 'armchair science'. Scientists devise ingenious experiments to show that the velocity of freely falling bodies increases at a regular and definite rate, while Zeno proves by a sort of mental penetration into the concept of motion that no bodies actually fall.

Consider one of Zeno's arguments against the existence of motion, to the following effect: A moving body must go half of a given distance before it can traverse the whole distance, and the same for each half of half the distance, *ad infinitum*; hence, since it is impossible to complete traversing an infinite number of distances, however small they become, motion is impossible. The premises from which the non-existence of motion is deduced are non-empirical. The 'must' of the first premise denotes a logical necessity, and the 'impossible' of the second premise denotes a logical impossibility. It is logic, *not experience,* which tells us that in order for a body to go from one place to any other place it must complete traversing an infinite number of distances. And it is

[1] *Our Knowledge of the External World,* Lecture II.
[2] *Scientific Thought,* p. 19.

logic which tells us that it is impossible to complete traversing a non-terminating number of distances, i.e., that 'finished a non-ending series of changes of position' is self-contradictory. The conclusion that motion does not exist, which purports to state a fact about the world, is thus quite naturally taken by some philosophers to make an *a priori* claim about the phenomenon of motion, namely, that its existence is ruled out by logic and that what we suppose to be the real thing can be no more than appearance. In general with regard to the theories of metaphysics, philosophers who concentrate their attention on the method of proof and refutation are led to the hypothesis that they are '*a priori* theories about the nature and structure of reality'. That is to say, the theories are taken to be about the world, which the nature of their proofs show to be *a priori*; consequently, according to the hypothesis, they are *a priori* descriptions of phenomena. Notice how Russell describes F. H. Bradley's book, *Appearance and Reality*:

> The first part examines and condemns almost all that makes up our everyday world: things and qualities, relations, space and time, change, causation, activity, the self. All these, though in some sense facts which qualify reality, are not real as they appear. What is real is one single, indivisible, timeless whole, called the Absolute, which is in some sense spiritual, but does not consist of souls, or of thought and will as we know them. And all this is established by abstract logical reasoning professing to find self-contradictions in the categories condemned as mere appearance, and to leave no tenable alternative to the kind of Absolute which is finally affirmed to be real.[1]

It is easy to see why, if this account is correct, disputes over such propositions as 'Material things do not exist', 'Everything flows', 'The world is really composed of spirits', 'There are such entities as universals' are not to be resolved by any sort of examination of phenomena. For if wrong metaphysical theories are self-contradictory and true ones are logically necessary, then not only is experimentation useless, as Broad says, but it could not even be relevant. There could be no sort of connexion between any conceivable observation and 'Everything flows' or 'Motion is impossible', just as there could be no experiments or observations

[1] *Our Knowledge of the External World*, p. 6.

that would establish that the sum of the interior angles of a Euclidean triangle equals 180° or that would show the self-contradictoriness of the proposition that a thing is not at the place where it is.

But although on the present hypothesis we can explain why the disputes are not empirically resolvable, we nevertheless are not in a position to explain why they do not get settled and why theories do not finally get established. The arguments, whatever their nature may be, which win the conviction of some philosophers fail to win the conviction of other equally competent philosophers, or are thought to be erroneous by them. The demonstrations are by no means as complicated as those in mathematics, nor are they more subtle. But in mathematics, which, to be sure, does not lack controversies, there is a great accumulation of solid, unquestioned proof, whereas precisely the opposite is the case in philosophy. There is the quip that mathematicians are happy only when they agree, and philosophers only when they disagree. There is point in this. It may very well be that people, in part, are drawn to philosophy for such a temperamental reason. But it must be the subject and the nature of the arguments that *permit* of endless debate. And for this the present hypothesis gives us no explanation. It is worth observing that when mathematicians, who admittedly are experts in *a priori* reasoning, take metaphysical positions, for example, the position that numbers are abstract entities of which the numerals are names, or the position that there are only the numerals, they are no better off than are philosophers who argue over whether universals exist. We may well think that there is something in the very nature of philosophical arguments, something we have not grasped, which makes possible the astonishing divisions of opinion with regard to the proofs, divisions which persist through centuries with no prospect of solution.

Take, for example, the contention that general words stand for abstract entities. It has been argued that the belief that general words like 'horse' and 'blue' name suprasensible objects, objects which we apprehend in knowing the meanings of the words, is based on the mistake of thinking that because a word has a meaning there must be something which it means. Now, is it a mistake to suppose that the fact that a word has a meaning implies that there is something which it means? Some philosophers think that supposing this is a mistake, others not. If it is a mistake, having their attention directed to it should, after some deliberation, be sufficient to make philosophers see that it is a mistake and give up their view, or at least suspend judgement about it. And if it is not a mistake to suppose this, that is, if the fact that the word 'horse', e.g., has a meaning *does* imply that there is something which 'horse' means and, therefore, that in addition to the actual animals the word denotes there is a more subtle object for which it stands, philosophers who claim it is a mistake could, it is to be expected, be made to see that the implication does hold. Instead we see an unbreakable intellectual deadlock. And this we do not understand. On the second hypothesis we seem to be able to clear up the mystery as to why no empirical evidence in the least contributes toward settling a metaphysical controversy. But we are then faced with a comparable mystery, this time with regard to the non-empirical demonstrations.

The idea that the theories of metaphysics make *a priori* claims about the structure and composition of the world, claims about what is necessarily real and what is only appearance, contains further difficulties which stand in need of explanation. Before these can usefully be brought out and examined, however, it is necessary to state some elementary facts about *a priori* propositions. In the sense in which *a priori* propositions can be said to have truth-values, it can easily be seen that they are true or false independently of what the world is like. An examination of states of affairs is relevant to the establishment of an empirical statement because the truth-value of the statement depends upon what reality is like. An *a priori* proposition differs from an empirical one in this respect: its truth-value is determined by the existence of no state of affairs. That is why, if the second hypothesis is correct, we can explain the fact that no amount of experiential evidence can ever settle a metaphysical controversy. A true *a priori* proposition is true by logical necessity, not because of what state of affairs happens to obtain; and a false one is false in the same way, by logical necessity. No theoretically possible state of affairs could make the one false or the other true. An *a priori* proposition, if true, is true regardless of what the world happens to be like, and, if false, it is false no matter what the world is like. Consequently, it can say nothing about what the world is like; it can give us no information about the existence or non-existence of anything or about the nature of anything. It states nothing whatever about reality. Whatever it is that we do know in knowing an *a priori* proposition, it is clear that in knowing it we know no fact about the world.

To illustrate, consider the statement: 'Nothing can remain the same distance from something from which it is moving away'. This utterance may seem to many people to state an inflexible fact about the spatial relation between two bodies when one is moving away from the other. But this is a mistake. In knowing the *a priori* true proposition that nothing can remain the same distance from something from which it is moving away we know nothing about what cannot happen in the world. For we cannot imagine what it would be like for, say, a train to be moving away from the station and at the same time remaining the same distance from it. We cannot imagine what it is that cannot happen, not because our imagination cannot as a matter of fact picture this to us, but because the expression 'moves away from *x* while, nevertheless, remaining the same distance from *x*' describes no occurrence in any conceivable universe. It is the use we make of our own language, not the limitations of human imagination, which prevents this from being pictured or from happening. The sentence 'Space is of such a nature that a thing cannot remain the same distance from something from which it is moving away' does not state what cannot take place because of the way space is constituted. It would do this only if the sentence 'Space is of such a nature that, peculiarly enough, a thing remains the same distance from another thing in the process of moving away from it' described what could, theoretically, take place in any universe. But the sentence describes nothing of the sort. Hence, whatever it is that we know in knowing that a train cannot be moving away from the station during the time it remains the same distance from it, we do not know an inflexible fact about motion and space. To take one further example, knowing the *a priori* truth that no two angles of a triangle are equal the sides of which are all unequal is not the same as nor does it imply knowing a fact about physical triangles. On the other hand, if it were known to be the case that no triangles of wood, metal, or any other material were scalene, we should know a fact about the triangles in our world. But 'No two angles of a triangle are equal the sides of which are all unequal' states no fact about physical triangles, because the sentence 'There are triangles two angles of which are equal though their sides are all unequal' states the existence of no conceivable triangle. Hence, in knowing the *a priori* fact about triangles we know no fact of nature.

Now if, as the second hypothesis maintains, the propositions of metaphysics are either true or false by logical necessitation, then they cannot be about reality, about the existence or nature of any phenomenon or about what must or cannot happen. A proposition cannot be non-empirical and at the same time give us information (or misinformation) about what the world is or is not like. Hence, if the proposition 'Motion does not exist' is *a priori,* it can state nothing about the phenomenon of bodies in motion. It does not declare that bodies do not actually move, nor does it deny that eagles soar and that rain falls. The metaphysical theory that every change must have a cause, i.e., the non-ordinary proposition that is supported by the argument 'A thing or any perfection (i.e., quality) of a thing actually existing cannot have, as a cause of its existence, nothing or a thing which does not exist',[1] can make no claim with regard to occurrences in the world. And it will have to be the same with the other theories. If the proposition 'There are no material things' is *a priori,* it cannot deny the existence of hands and pavements and the many other objects to which the expression 'material thing' is applied. The proposition 'Nothing exists unperceived' cannot claim that books and chairs cease to exist when no one perceives them. The proposition 'Everything flows' cannot tell us the astonishing thing that, despite what our senses show us, granite really behaves like butter in the summer sun. And the proposition 'There are supra-sensible entities which can be apprehended only by the mind' cannot declare the existence of objects of any sort. There cannot be *a priori* descriptions of natural phenomena.

It must be obvious that an important determinant of our fascination with these propositions is that we take them to be deep theories about aspects of reality, theories which in some cases arouse our resistance and in others not. But if, as is plain, *a priori* statements cannot be about reality, it is not easy to understand

[1] Descartes' third 'common notion'.

how a metaphysician who satisfies himself that he has demonstrated both the self-contradictoriness of motion and its existence in appearance only, could possibly come to think he has shown something important about a familiar phenomenon. The real puzzle is how he could believe both that he has shown motion is self-contradictory and that he has reduced it to a shadow. For if, as he maintains, motion is impossible because its existence would imply a self-contradictory state of affairs, then the *illusion* of bodies being in motion is also logically impossible, for the same reason. The proposition 'Motion is logically impossible' implies the proposition 'The illusion of motion is logically impossible'; '*Motion* is a self-contradictory concept' implies '*The appearance of motion* is a self-contradictory concept'. If the reality of anything is precluded by the fact that it implies a self-contradiction, the existence of an appearance of that thing is ruled out by the same fact. There can be no appearance of what is logically impossible, else we should be able to imagine the logically impossible. We should be able to imagine red things that are without colour and trains moving away from stations from which they continue to remain the same distance. To put the matter in another way, if the illusion of bodies being in motion is allowed, the conceivability, if not the physical possibility, of their really being in a state of motion must also be allowed, which it could not be if motion were logically impossible. If the concept *being in motion* could have no exemplifications because it is self-contradictory, the concept *appearing to be in motion* would also be self-contradictory and could have no exemplifications. The phrase 'looks to be red all over and at the same time and in the same respect also green' has no application whatever, because the phrase 'is red all over and also green' has been given no descriptive sense. If the former phrase had an application, the latter would have an imaginable application, and it would then be theoretically possible for there to be something which was red all over and also green. Similarly, a person who, in effect, maintains that the expression 'is in motion' (or its equivalent in any other language) has no application to anything whatever, actual or conceivable, that it has no literal sense, will also have to maintain that the expression 'appears to be moving' has no application to any appearance.

It is difficult to understand how anyone could fail to see this.

No one would dream of saying, e.g., that a building looks to be taller than it looks to be; but in metaphysics it is not at all uncommon for people to say comparable things, for instance, that though time is self-contradictory there *seem* to be occurrences and that one occurrence seems to precede or follow another occurrence. This requires an explanation, and it may quite well be the case that something else, which we do not understand, is being done by metaphysicians than what on the surface they give the plain, unambiguous impression of doing. At any rate, the description of the theories which makes them out to be *a priori* propositions about the structure and substance of reality has to be given up. If the theories are about phenomena they cannot be *a priori,* nor have *a priori* demonstrations; but then there is no explaining why empirical evidence counts neither for nor against them. And if they are *a priori,* they cannot be about the world; and we have no insight into what makes possible the chronic variety of attitudes toward their demonstrations nor insight into the nature of the *metaphysical* distinction between appearance and reality, which certainly does not correspond to the ordinary distinction. It seems reasonable to conclude that we do not know how to construe the sentence 'Motion does not exist', nor the sentences for the other theories.

IV. METAPHYSICAL THEORIES AS VERBAL

The notion that metaphysical views are *a priori* true or false descriptions of reality leads to a further hypothesis. This hypothesis is that they are propositions which, in a concealed form, make factual claims with regard to established linguistic usage. A philosopher who is well aware of the fact that examination of phenomena plays no actual rôle in establishing or disestablishing a metaphysical view and, furthermore, has a good grasp of the nature of logically necessary propositions is likely to arrive at this hypothesis. Especially is this so if he concentrates mainly on views like 'Material things do not exist' and 'No one can know that anyone else exists', i.e., if he concentrates on views which seem to go against beliefs which for common sense are most solid and assured. According to this third interpretation, a philosopher who declares that space is self-contradictory and therefore unreal is in effect maintaining that the word 'space' has no literal use and that phrases using space-indicating words, that is, phrases like 'taller than' and 'next to', are senseless and have no application.

It has already been seen that an *a priori* proposition is non-informative about the existence, nature, or behaviour of phenomena, actual or theoretically imaginable. A proposition that is true or false by logic can say nothing about the world: the statement 'A buttercup cannot be yellow all over and also blue' says nothing about what colour a buttercup cannot be. When Spinoza denied, as an absurdity, that God could bring it about that no effect follow from a given cause, it is quite clear he did not wish to maintain that there was something which, because of the physical impossibility of accomplishing it, God could not bring about. The impossibility which prevents there being an effectless cause is altogether different from a physical impossibility, the impossibility, say, of a gas failing to expand when heated. One is an impossibility of nature, the opposite of which is conceivable, however much it may strain our imagination. The other is an impossibility of logic, the opposite of which is inconceivable, no matter how much we strain our imagination.

It is natural to think of a logical impossibility as being the limiting case of a series of increasingly inflexible physical impossibilities. It is natural, for example, to think that the logical impossibility of a thing being in two different places at one time is like each of the series of impossibilities of getting from New York in an hour, in a minute, in a second, in a thousandth of a second, in a millionth of a second, etc., and differs from each of these increasingly impossible impossibilities *only in degree,* in the way in which each differs from its predecessor. But this is a mistake. A logical impossibility is not *the most impossible* of a series of increasingly impossible states of affairs. It is not the last member of the series, any more than $\frac{a}{0}$ is the last member of the series $\dfrac{a}{2^n}$.

We can conceive *any* physically impossible state of affairs, however miraculous its existence would be. We can, e.g., conceive ourselves being transported from New York to London in the wink of an eye, but we cannot imagine the occurrence of anything that is logically impossible. This is because an expression for a logical impossibility is not used to describe anything; it has no descriptive function in any verbal context. It is an expression which has not been given a descriptive use in our language; otherwise, we could imagine what it described. The phrases 'being in two places at once', 'cause not followed by an effect', do not refer to occurrences which most certainly do not take place and would count as miracles if they did. They are phrases which describe nothing at all.

To put the matter somewhat differently, the idea that a logical impossibility describes what the world cannot be like implies the idea that it describes to us what a different 'possible universe' would be like. But then we should have to say that the truth-value of an *a priori* proposition was contingent on the existence or non-existence of a material state of affairs, which would imply that an *a priori* proposition was not *a priori*. As Spinoza seems to have realized, the absurdity of saying that God can bring it about that from a given cause no effect should follow is an absurdity of language, not of physics. It is a metaphysical joke to say, 'God can . . .', because the form of language used suggests the idea of there being something which God could do, whereas the words 'brings it about that the cause of an occurrence is not a cause of anything' describe nothing which might test God's abilities.

It should now be clear that if those philosophers who profess to show that the concepts, of space, time, motion, knowledge of other minds, etc., contain contradictions, actually mean to assert the unreality of space, time, and other familiar phenomena to be logically necessary, their words will have to be interpreted as stating that 'space', 'time', 'motion', and so on, have no application, no literal use in our language. The sentences, 'Motion is impossible', 'Everything flows', 'Time is unreal', which have the air of being about space, time, and the behaviour of things, will have to be construed as conveying linguistic information, to the effect that such expressions as 'is moving from x to y', 'The clock is of solid metal and does not flow', 'Jones begged pardon after having stepped on Smith's toe' are senseless and carry no literal meaning to anyone who understands the English language. The words 'time' and 'motion', and phrases in which they occur, are parts, of course, of the language we use in everyday life. But a meta-physician who insists that time and space are 'self-contradictory appearances' would seem to be trying to inform us that we have been mistaken about these words, that words we have always supposed were used in sentences to convey factual information have, as a matter of linguistic fact, no such informative use. We are all mistaken in thinking that we are using the word 'know' with literal significance when we make an assertion such as 'I know that Jones disapproves of drinking'. For, as the argument goes, since an infinite number of sense-observations would have to be made before we could *properly* and *correctly* be said to know anything of this sort, and since to complete an infinite number of sense-observations is logically impossible, we are wrong in thinking the word has the use it seems to have in ordinary conversation. Our mistake is linguistic, not material.

It must be granted that the hypothesis which interprets metaphysical theories as making, in an indirect mode of speech, factual assertions about linguistic usage throws considerable light on the nature of the theories. Among other things, it throws light on what a common-sense philosopher, who opposes the more extravagant metaphysical views about motion, space, material things, etc., does when he calls attention to facts which not even the metaphysician denies in the ordinary conduct of his life, either in speech or behaviour. Moore's 'refutation' of the view that there are no material things, which consists in his holding up his hand in plain view and saying, 'Here is a hand, therefore, there is at least one material thing', is now to be understood as his pointing out that the word 'hand', and therefore the term 'material thing' also, has an application, something it would, of course, be just captious to deny. He 'refutes' the implicit verbal assertion of the seemingly *a priori* proposition about material things by holding up samples of the sort of things to which the term 'material thing' applies and declaring that the term applies to them. In other words, he 'corrects' the erroneous notions many metaphysicians seem to have about expressions in common use. One gets the impression that Moore explains the use of the word 'hand' in the way we teach its meaning to a child or reteach it to a person who has suffered a lapse of memory. And if, according to the hypothesis under consideration, the metaphysician does imply that words like 'time', 'motion', and 'material thing' are meaningless, Moore's procedure is appropriate and his refutations are conclusive. For these words have well-established senses which everyone knows.

Now, in the usual case of a person being mistaken about a word, there is no special difficulty in showing him that he is wrong and what the right usage is. If he has a wrong idea about the word 'radar' or thinks that 'erse' is a nonsense-word like 'brillig', we experience no particular difficulty about showing him his error and getting him to accept the facts about the words. He accepts the correction, if not on our own authority, then on being shown how other people use it, or on being referred to a dictionary. But if we expect the same success with a metaphysician, we shall be nonplussed to meet with flat failure. In the practice of philosophy we are, of course, not a bit surprised to find that facing a metaphysician with linguistic usage does not have the effect of making him relinquish his views. This is a strange fact about our professional psychology which requires explanation. But the third hypothesis throws no light on it. Nor does it help us see the reason why the metaphysician remains unmoved by the refutations, which in non-philosophical connexions he would accept. It fails to give us a satisfactory answer to the crucial question why metaphysical disputes do not get resolved.

Two things in particular remain a puzzle. One is that a metaphysician, who *knows* established, proper usage as well as anyone, remains adamant in the face both of what he himself knows and of what is pointed out to him. The other is that he is able to maintain, whether outrightly or indirectly by implication, that actual usage is improper or unintelligible and that ordinary people hardly know what they are talking about when they use such words as 'cause' and 'substance'.[1] For the standard of intelligible usage of everyday language is ordinary usage, the use given to expressions by people who, in a non-esoteric sense of the word 'know', know the language. No one would dream of saying that there exist a celestial dictionary and a grammar book which, if only they could be consulted, would enable us to decide questions of proper usage and syntactical correctness. And yet it is something like this that a person who holds metaphysical 'shockers' would seem to be implying. For, according to the third hypothesis, he tells us that anyone who uses certain expressions *in the*

[1] C. D. Broad, *Scientific Thought,* Introduction.

usual way uses them wrongly. If this is, indeed, what he means to say, we can perhaps see why showing him ordinary usage does nothing. Showing him what he condemns as general improper practice would hardly be expected to influence him. But then we cannot understand how he can possibly believe that ordinary linguistic practice, to which he is not a stranger, is mistaken; and we do not understand why, if philosophical disputes are over usage, they do not get settled. Like the other two hypotheses, the third one fails to explain in a satisfactory way the nature of metaphysical theories and disputes.

V. METAPHYSICS AS NONSENSE

One further conjecture about metaphysics has to be examined. This is the hypothesis that there are no metaphysical *theories* and that the sentences of metaphysicians are in fact devoid of literal meaning, however strong the impression they create of making perfectly good sense. They carry with them the illusion of expressing theories, and they unquestionably have emotive significance for us, but they lack literal significance. In respect of having sense the sentence, 'There is a world of timeless, suprasensible universals', to which so much intellectual labour has been devoted for hundreds of years, is no different from the sentence, 'Flying numbers are heavier than yellow'. The main difference between the two sentences is that the first appears to make sense and to state something of great importance, while the second is obviously nonsensical. The only explanation given of how it could have happened that so many men of great intelligence, scientists as well as philosophers, could for so long a time have laboured under the illusion that they were talking sense and intelligibly disagreeing with each other over universals, substratum, or the reality of the physical universe, is that *it is quite easy to fall into talking nonsense without being aware of it*. It has to be admitted that this is not outside the range of possibility, but one may be pardoned for being unimpressed by its plausibility.

Philosophers who adopt the positivistic thesis feel strongly the contrast between metaphysics, on the one hand, and mathematics and the natural sciences, on the other, to the disadvantage of metaphysics. These philosophers have become dissatisfied with those pronouncements which refer to the suprasensible, and have framed their criterion of literal significance with the aim of cleaning house, of ridding philosophy of these pronouncements and so making it intellectually more respectable. It is not easy to dismiss the feeling, derived from a reading of the literature of contemporary positivism, that the rejection of metaphysics, though backed by reasons, is primarily emotional, an important part of the emotion being shame. The rejection, one may suspect, constitutes a refined form of book burning. A passage from Hume which positivists are fond of quoting lends this suspicion plausibility. The well-known passage is: 'If we take in our hand any volume; of divinity, or school metaphysics, for instance; let us ask, Does it contain any abstract reasoning concerning quantity or number? No. Does it contain any experimental reasoning concerning matter of fact and existence? No. Commit it then to the flames. For it can contain nothing but sophistry and illusion'.[1] But positivists have not said this in so many words; they have only said that metaphysics is *nonsense*. And they have given reasons for this view which deserve looking into independently of what their motives and our own subjective reactions may be. For logical positivism may very well be right. Metaphysical theories seem, now, to belong neither to logic nor to natural science, and positivism does offer a possible account of the puzzling fact that metaphysical disputes do not get settled and the theories do not get established. The picture conjured up for us of what goes on in a solemn metaphysical discussion is grotesque, to say the least; but it *may*, nevertheless, be a correct picture.

The positivistic principle for exposing philosophical nonsense lays down two criteria, to one or the other of which a sentence in the indicative must answer in order to count as having literal significance. Either an indicative sentence must express an *a priori* proposition, for example, one of logic or mathematics, or, if it fails to do this, it must express an empirical proposition which is testable in sense-experience, practically or theoretically. The second condition is the so-called 'Principle of Verifiability', according to which no non-*a priori* statement has literal meaning

[1] *Enquiry Concerning Human Understanding*, Sec. 12, Pt. 3 (Selby-Bigge edition), p. 165.

unless what it states is open to verification by sense-observation, if not practically because of physical obstacles standing in our way, then in principle. That is, an assertion will make sense to us only if we can put ourselves actually or imaginatively in the situation of establishing or discrediting it. If no conceivable observation could in any way tend to confirm or disconfirm it, the assertion will have to be reckoned senseless. There are, accordingly, two and only two classes of significant declarative sentences: the class of sentences expressing *a priori* propositions and the class of sentences expressing empirical propositions verifiable in sense-experience. If it is determined that a given utterance belongs to neither of these two classes, we can, according to the positivistic principle, be sure that it says nothing at all and is an empty string of words, however much its syntax and the meanings of its separate words suggest that it does have literal meaning.

Thus, the Leibnizian view that material things are really colonies of monads fails to satisfy either of the two conditions laid down. The sentence 'Material things are composed of colonies of rudimentary minds' does not, like 'If I have fourteen pennies, then I have nine more than five pennies' and 'A father must have children', express an *a priori* proposition. For its denial is not self-contradictory: 'A chair is not a collection of monads' is not a self-contradiction. But neither does it express an empirical theory which could even in conception be confirmed or disconfirmed by experience. The claim it appears to make with regard to the nature of things lies wholly outside the theoretical limits of investigation by sense-observation. No amount of looking at a chair, however subtle and super-microscopically sharp our eyes might be imagined to be, and no sort of experiment, however advanced its technique, could render it probable or improbable in the slightest degree that a chair is made up of minds. Hence, the statement will have to be counted amongst those which are senseless combinations of words and as having no more intelligibility than 'Yellow multiplied by lavendar is elation'. In general, no sentence which purports to give information about the nature or existence of a phenomenon is literally meaningful if the 'reality' it refers to lies wholly outside the limits of possible sense-experience. An application of the positivistic principle to the theories that there are supra-sensible objects which can be contemplated only in thought and that a thing is constituted by an unknowable substratum in which attributes inhere gives the same result: the supposed theories are non-existent, and instead we have senseless expressions, which produce the illusion of making sense and of stating theories which are defended by many philosophers and attacked by others.

The positivistic hypothesis about metaphysics does have the merit of giving us a possible explanation of the fact that disputes never get conclusively settled in favour of one or other competing theories. It cannot, however, be granted that any plausibility whatever attaches to the explanation. Precisely the opposite is the case. Indeed, we may wonder how anyone could bring himself to believe that since it is easy to fall into talking nonsense, it is reasonable to think that philosophers could, for so many centuries, have devoted their intellectual abilities to the concoction of nonsense, and, moreover, could have retained their interest in the *same* nonsense. If we could disengage our emotions and think dispassionately on the matter it should be quite impossible to believe that the Platonic 'nonsense' about universals, which has been and still is the subject of an extended and *reasoned* controversy, could have occupied the attention of intellectuals for so long a time simply because it is easy to fall into talking nonsense. Whatever the facts about metaphysics may be, there can be hardly any doubt that the belief in the positivistic hypothesis has its main source in the wish to disparage metaphysics.

Psychologically speaking, metaphysics is an unconscious intellectual substitute for religion for many thinkers. But 'radiation of affect'[1] frequently catches up with substitutes for former objects of scorn; and it heaps on them its old scorn, but this time in a disguised form. The psychological drama of need and rejection repeats itself. A curious thing in this connexion may be noted. This is that some positivists, after first having condemned the Platonic theory of suprasensible universals, are coming back to one or other of its classical forms, and now accept as perfectly intelligible what for years they had *seen* to be nonsense. Sometimes the acceptance is followed by a new rejection. There is the temptation to treat this sort of metaphysical backsliding frivolously, but that won't do. We have to try to understand what it is

[1] Phrase taken from Dr. Ernest Jones.

about metaphysics that makes this sort of situation possible. The change of mind is not to be confused with an ordinary case of a person first thinking that a long sentence with a complicated grammar, or one with unknown words or with known words put together in queer ways, is meaningless and then after careful study with the help of a dictionary and grammar coming to see that it does make sense. In the metaphysical case, the reconsideration brings no new linguistic facts to light. The philosopher knows no more about the sentence after his change of mind than he did before. He knew all along everything necessary in order to know whether it is intelligible or not.

Consider, now, the criterion of verification itself, to the effect that no synthetic, or non-*a priori*, sentence has literal import if what it says, the proposition it expresses, is in principle not verifiable in sense-experience. It is on the authority of this principle that statements referring to 'suprasensible realities' are rejected as senseless.

One thing is to be noticed immediately about the principle; this is that the rule for casting out metaphysical sentences is *nothing more* than the contention that they are senseless. Any positivist who thinks that the principle *shows* the literal senselessness of statements referring to what lies beyond the limits of sense-experience thinks mistakenly. The phrases, 'synthetic sentence expressing a proposition not verifiable in sense-experience' and 'sentence referring to a suprasensible reality' mean exactly the same thing. Hence, anyone who thinks that the principle shows the senselessness of metaphysics maintains, in effect, that a synthetic sentence which expresses a proposition not verifiable in sense-experience is devoid of sense *because* it expresses a proposition not verifiable in sense-experience; he makes the empty claim that a sentence referring to a suprasensible reality is senseless *because* it refers to a suprasensible reality. But plainly one does not *show* that a sentence denoting an unverifiable proposition is senseless by giving as the reason that the proposition it denotes is unverifiable. It can be seen that the criterion of the positivists consists merely in declaring, against what others declare, that metaphysical sentences are unintelligible. The criterion *is* their contention. To an outsider, they give no better evidence for his honouring their check than does the philosopher whose metaphysical check they maintain is not backed by money in the bank. It is hardly to be expected that the criterion will move a philosopher who, like Bertrand Russell, both proves to his satisfaction the existence of supra-sensible universals and, furthermore, claims acquaintance with them.[1]

Another thing has to be seen. As it is formulated, the principle suggests the idea that statements are retained or cast out by a process of inspecting their meanings, by examining the propositions they state: those sentences being retained which express propositions that are testable by looking, feeling, and the like, and those being cast out which express propositions shown by examination not to be so testable. The only possible conclusion to draw is that metaphysical sentences are rejected because of the *kind* of propositions they stand for. To illustrate, in applying the rule to the sentence, 'A material thing is constituted by an unknowable substratum in which experienceable attributes inhere', we inspect the proposition it expresses, see that it is not of a kind that is open to sense-testing, and conclude that the sentence is really a senseless jingle of words. The rule can only be applied to sentences which express propositions; at most it is a special, not a general, formula for ascertaining whether a sentence has literal meaning. Thus, the words ''Twas brillig and the slithy toves did gyre and gimble in the wabe' are not open to investigation by the rule, because they fail to denote any sort of proposition, verifiable or unverifiable, by reference to which their intelligibility might be tested. But as a special rule, its application to metaphysical utterances leads of necessity to false inferences about them. For the meaning of a sentence and the proposition it expresses are the same thing. An indicative sentence cannot express a proposition and not have a meaning or have a meaning and not express a proposition. And since on its own condition, the applicability of the criterion to a metaphysical assertion S implies that S expresses a proposition, which is to say, has a meaning, while its application compels us to infer that S has none, it requires us to assert what it compels us to deny. Application of the rule to metaphysical sentences can only lead to false inferences with regard to the question as to whether they make sense.

In order to avoid this difficulty, we might try to reformulate

[1]*Problems of Philosophy*, Chapter IX.

the criterion in the following way: A sentence which professes to denote an empirical proposition, and is such that if it does not denote an empirical proposition, it denotes no proposition whatever, is literally significant only if it expresses a proposition open to verification in sense-experience. This revised version, it is clear, implies that an empirical proposition is the same as one that is verifiable in sense-experience, i.e., the terms 'empirical' and 'verifiable by sense-observation' are to be taken as synonyms. But it can be seen that although the reformulation avoids the former consequence that the application of the verification principle to metaphysical sentences entails our making false inferences about their literal meaningfulness, it achieves this at the cost of becoming a *useless* principle, one which certainly cannot be used to eliminate metaphysics. For now it amounts to the empty tautology that a sentence which purports to denote a proposition open to verification in sense-experience, and fails to express any proposition if it does not, is literally significant only if it denotes a proposition open to verification in sense-experience. In other words, a sentence which either denotes a verifiable proposition or is meaningless is literally significant only if it denotes a verifiable proposition.

If we try to reformulate the principle again in such a way that it does eliminate metaphysics, then we cannot avoid begging the question. The further formulation would read: A non-*a priori* declarative sentence will be literally significant only if it expresses a proposition capable of being verified in sense-experience. This is free from the first difficulty of requiring metaphysical sentences to have meaning while implying that they have none, and it has the consequence of ruling metaphysics out. Thus, e.g., if we adopt the criterion as now stated, the sentences, 'Numerals denote numbers which are abstract objects apprehended only in thought' and 'A material thing is composed of an unexperienceable substratum in which attributes inhere', must be condemned as nonsensical by the fact that neither denotes either an *a priori* proposition or one that is verifiable in sense-experience. But this result is obtained at the cost of committing a *petitio principii*. The criterion eliminates metaphysics by fiat, by being tailored with an eye to what it will eliminate, and it can carry no conviction to a philosopher who does metaphysics under the impression that it is perfectly intelligible. We can imagine a traditional philosopher arguing against the criterion in the following way:—

The principle of verifiability does not *show* that metaphysics is nonsense, for it assumes the very thing positivists claim to demonstrate by the use of it. No sentence which refers to a 'reality transcending the limits of all possible sense-experience' can be shown to be devoid of literal sense by the fact that it fails to express a proposition verifiable in sense-experience. If it did denote such a proposition, it would not be referring to a transcendent reality; and if it referred to a transcendent reality, it would not express a proposition capable of being verified in sense-experience. You cannot condemn a statement which refers to one type of reality on the grounds that it fails to answer to the condition of a sentence which refers to an altogether different type of reality. To do this would be like 'demonstrating' that the sentence 'The rose smells sweet' is nonsensical because it does not answer to the requirement (laid down, say, by a person without the sense of smell) that no sentence is to be counted as having meaning unless the phenomenon it refers to is verifiable visually. In fact, we could frame a condition of literal import for non-*a priori* sentences according to which none which failed to refer to a transcendent reality, and was not open to *suprasensible* verification, made sense. And if we did set up such a principle we should be as arbitrary and unreasonable as those who set the requirement of verifiability in *sense*-experience. Our criterion would then be open to the same charge of begging the question as the positivists' is at present.

As was pointed out earlier, it must be granted that the positivistic claim that metaphysics is nonsense gives us a possible answer to the question as to why metaphysical disputes are sterile and never get conclusively resolved. It may be just nonsense to talk about transcendent realities, and such talk may go on interminably. Positivists do not, however, give any explanation of the fact that pointing out in a detailed way to philosophers the nonsensicalness of statements referring to transcendent realities does not make philosophers see that they are senseless. Instead of terminating old disputes, the positivistic hypothesis has merely added a new one, this time the factual-linguistic dispute over whether sentences referring to suprasensible realities are or are not meaningless. The hypothesis throws no light whatever on the problem of what it is that makes it possible for equally able and equally literate people to divide and remain divided over whether sentences referring to suprasensible realities have meaning or lack it, and whether 'suprasensible reality' is a senseless expression or not. In an ordinary case of a difference of opinion as to whether an expression has an intelligible use we know how to go about settling the matter, but in a metaphysical case we are at a loss. The positivistic hypothesis leads to no understanding of how the metaphysical case differs from a normal one.

VI. METAPHYSICAL THEORIES AS LINGUISTIC INNOVATIONS

Four meta-hypotheses about the nature of metaphysics have now been examined and each has been rejected on the ground that it fails to explain the irresolvability of metaphysical disputes. What, then, is the right, or nearly right, explanation of the nature of metaphysical theories and arguments? In pursuing this question it has to be kept constantly in mind that no hypothesis can possibly be the right one if it fails to explain in a satisfactory way the curious permanence of metaphysical differences of opinion.

I shall try to state my own position briefly and in a general form and shall leave it to subsequent applications of the theory to classical problems of philosophy to supplement the outline and fill in some of the detail. I might say that I do not expect my explanation to please anyone; I should be very much surprised if it did. Nor, indeed, do I expect it to be easily accepted by anyone. Nevertheless, I think that it is substantially correct.

It may be asked why, if after having explained the position to others and they do not accept it, I should continue to think it has quite a different status from that of the other four hypotheses. What right do I have to think that it is correct and the others are delusive? In answer to this question, perhaps the best thing that I can say is that the position has 'clicked' for me, that I *see* that it is correct, if not in every detail, then at least in substance. Against this it will undoubtedly be objected that each of the other four hypotheses has seemed right to many philosophers, so that I am really no better off than they are and am only another brother metaphysician. To this I can only say that each of the four hypotheses has attracted philosophers, as several of them once attracted me, because they satisfied unconscious needs, needs which blind one to the recalcitrant fact that these hypotheses fail to explain the chronic condition of philosophical differences of opinion. The hypothesis I am going to formulate meets the intellectual need of facing and explaining this fact, and to put the matter subjectively, has 'clicked' intellectually for me.

What, to be more concrete, do I mean by the term 'clicks'? I mean something like this: you look at a drawing in which there are hidden animals sketched into trees, bushes, the ripples in a brook, the contours of a hill, and so on, and suddenly you *see* them. That is all there is to it. But once you see the drawing in a certain way, you see *what is there*. If I may permit myself a tautology with point, the fact that others do not see shows no more than that they do not see.

In any case, regardless of whether or not the hypothesis I am going to put forward clicks for others, I hope it will be seen that I do seriously try to explain what it is about metaphysical theories that makes their truth-values undecidable and how, specifically, the proofs and refutations *connect up* with the theories. And I hope it will be granted that not only possibility but *some* probability attaches to the hypothesis. This is sufficient to warrant its receiving a hearing that is more than cursory.

Now to the outline of the position. Consider the following sentences:—

'All words are vague.'
'Everything flows.'
'Nothing changes.'
'All desires are selfish.'
'Everything happens by necessity, nothing by chance.'
'No material thing, e.g., a cloud, is formless.'
or
'Every material thing has a form.'

I shall select for specific discussion the sentence 'Nothing changes', or better still the equivalent sentence 'Everything remains unchanged'. It will be readily seen that the considerations brought forward apply equally to the other sentences.

The sentence 'Everything remains (or *really* remains) un-changed' seems to express an *empirical* proposition. To use an expression of Professor John Wisdom's, it has an empirical air about it. It appears to describe, truly or falsely, a feature of things. But this is no more than a verbal illusion. The sentence does not, as a matter of fact, express an empirical proposition or describe a condition of objects. To show this briefly, it has to be made clear that as a philosopher is using the words 'Everything remains the same', they express no proposition which is open to falsification, either in fact or in fancy, no proposition which is upset by actual cases or could be upset by imagined cases. In other words, it has to be made clear that his words are not used to express a theoretically refutable theory about things and therefore are not used to express an empirical proposition.

It will be obvious, since he is as well acquainted with ordinary natural occurrences as anyone, that nothing actual to which we might call attention as being an instance of a thing undergoing change, e.g., a melting cube of ice or a bit of burning paper, will do its expected work. There is nothing which a metaphysician who holds that everything remains unchanged will accept as a refuting instance of his position. Instead of allowing that melting ice and burning paper show that what he maintains, the proposition he expresses with the words 'Everything remains unchanged', is false, he takes refuge in the baffling metaphysical distinction between appearance and reality and *protects* his position in some such way as the following:—

I grant you that things *seem* to change, but their seeming to change is just an illusion of the senses. In reality, behind the appearance of their changing, they remain the same and un-changed.

Now, if we take seriously his distinction between appearance and reality, between appearing to change and really remaining unchanged, and point out the obvious fact that what visually appears to be a state of affairs could, if only as an outside theoretical possibility, actually be a state of affairs, we meet in the metaphysician a peculiar reaction. Suppose we continue our argument in this way.

'If a thing appears to change, then even though its appearing to change is an optical illusion, there *could be* something which really changes in the way in which the thing appears to be changing. Whatever can be represented to us, either visually or to our imagination, *could exist in fact*, and only further experience can show that it does not exist in fact. To put the matter linguistically, if an expression of the form "looks ϕ" or "looks to be ϕ" has a descriptive use, then so must the corresponding expression of the form "is ϕ". It must describe what could exist, even if what it describes is in fact physically impossible. Thus, the fact that the phrase "appears to be flowing uphill" describes a possible appearance of the behaviour of water *implies* that the phrase "is flowing uphill" describes a conceivable if altogether improbable reality. And the fact that the phrase "appears to be standing erect on his own shoulders" describes no possible appearance of a person doing something *implies* that the phrase "is standing erect on his own shoulders" describes nothing whatever. It implies, in other words, that it has no descriptive sense'.

And suppose we continue farther:—

'Now, if changing things did exist, your view would, of course, be false; this much you have to admit. But you deny that things change. Nothing we call your attention to, phenomena like age-ing, melting, freezing, burning into ash, and the like, count with you as cases of *real* change. Well, then, suppose we admit that what we have been taking to be instances of a thing really chang-ing are all illusory. Now describe to us a state of affairs which you would say was one in which a thing really was undergoing change. And don't say that it would be a thing which *actually* behaved in the way in which things now only *appear* to be behaving. For if your distinction between appearing to behave in a certain way and really behaving in that way is a genuine distinction, there will have to be a way of distinguishing between the two; there will have to be a procedure for deciding which is only appearance and which the real thing. Since you dismiss everything that we take to be an instance of a thing *really* changing, tell us what you would count as an instance of a thing really undergoing change, i.e., a state of affairs which, if it existed, would make you give up saying, "Everything really remains unchanged".'

This he cannot do. He cannot describe anything over and above and in addition to such phenomena as coal burning and changing into ash and wax melting. He cannot describe anything which would be an instance of a thing really changing, such that if it existed, his view would be false. It becomes entirely clear, then, that the view he is using the words 'Everything remains unchanged' to express has no possible empirical refutation, actual or theoretical. *His* view, whatever it is, is not open to falsification by any sort of matter of fact. But this is the mark of an *a priori* proposition.

Then does the sentence 'Everything remains unchanged' express an *a priori* proposition? Let us assume it does and ask what must be the case with regard to it. What are the linguistic facts about it?

It is not difficult to see that if the sentence does not express an empirical proposition about things, *it says nothing whatever about things,* it describes no conceivable or imaginable condition of things. For if it described an imaginable condition of things, its denial, namely, the sentence 'Some things change', would also describe an imaginable condition of things. But if 'Some things change' described a possible condition of things, it would describe a state of affairs which would constitute a theoretical falsification of the proposition expressed by the sentence 'Everything remains unchanged'. The proposition would then have to be such that it could, theoretically, be falsified. But this, as has been seen, is not the case. Whatever the proposition is that a metaphysician like Parmenides or Bradley expresses with the sentence, the proposition has no refutation in any conceivable experience, which is to say the word 'change' has no descriptive use. But if the proposition has no refutation in any conceivable experience, then neither does it have a confirmation in any conceivable experience. No imaginable series of sense-observations could ever establish or render it probable in the slightest degree. Hence the proposition is not about reality, about the nature of things, and the phrase 'remains unchanged', like the word 'change' in the sentence 'Some things change', is *not being used descriptively* in the sentence 'Everything remains unchanged'. If the sentence does express an *a priori* proposition, it is *made* to do so by *preventing* the phrase 'remains unchanged' *from having a descriptive use,* i.e., a use to describe a condition of things. And although the sentence does not express this verbal fact, we have to know this fact in order to understand the sentence.

We may say that in order for the sentence 'Everything remains unchanged' to express an *a priori* proposition, the phrase 'remains unchanged' will have to lack application to anything actual or envisageable. And in order to know that the sentence expresses an *a priori* proposition and also to know what the proposition is, a person must know that the phrase 'remains unchanged' has no application to things, to ice and coal and human beings.

But there can be no question whatever that a metaphysician, who utters the sentence 'Everything really remains the same' and does this with the air of having made a discovery which cannot successfully be controverted, *knows perfectly well* that the words 'remains unchanged' describe not only a theoretically possible condition of things but also an actual condition of many things. The words have a descriptive use, and he knows this and also what their use is. Only as a result of being swept into the metaphysical dispute over whether things change or do not change could anyone fail to see this. Only as a result of looking at the sentence through metaphysical spectacles could anyone avoid seeing it.

We can say with complete confidence that the metaphysician knows the ordinary use of 'unchanging thing' as well as of 'changing thing'. We cannot reasonably suppose him to be believing that it makes no descriptive sense to say things like 'This block of granite hasn't changed at all in years, but the bit of wax near the fire has changed its shape and colour in the last few minutes'. But this precisely is what we should have to think if we supposed him to be imagining that, *as they are used ordinarily,* the words 'Everything remains unchanged' express an *a priori* proposition. And everything, all the evidence, goes against our believing this: the fact that he uses the words 'changed' and 'unchanged' in everyday discourse in the same way in which everyone else does, the fact that he does not accept linguistic correction, and so on.

The metaphysician's theory is open neither to empirical refutation nor to linguistic refutation. Whatever it is that he is saying, he is not describing a condition of things. And whatever it is that he is saying, he is not using the words 'changed' and 'unchanged' under the impression that in their ordinary, accepted senses they have no descriptive use. How, then, is he using them? What is he doing with the words 'changed' and 'unchanged'?

I think that light is thrown on what he is doing linguistically, i.e., on what he is doing with ordinary words, if in spite of our being compelled to reject the notion that the metaphysician believes that, as English is ordinarily used, the sentence 'Everything remains unchanged' states an *a priori* proposition, we nevertheless suppose *his* sentence does state an *a priori* proposition. For he is as confident of what he is saying as a person is who says '$2+2=4$'. Now, if he *is* expressing an *a priori* proposition with the sentence, then he is not using the words 'remains unchanged' *in their ordinary senses*. He can *make* the sentence state a non-empirical truth only by *altering* the actual use of 'remains unchanged'. Just as the sentence 'All tulips are flowers' denotes an *a priori* proposition by virtue of the linguistic fact that 'tulip' is so used that whatever it correctly applies to 'flower' also correctly applies to, so if 'Everything remains unchanged' denotes an *a priori* truth, it does so by virtue of the fact that 'remains unchanged' correctly applies, as a matter of usage, to whatever 'material thing' applies to. There is, of course, no such fact about actual English usage. Consequently, if the phrase 'remains unchanged' is made to apply to whatever the word 'material thing' applies to, the use of 'remains unchanged' *has been altered and no longer has its ordinary use.*

I think we are now in a position to understand what has happened and what it is about the metaphysician's position that makes it irrefutable and the controversy over it irresolvable. The metaphysical sentence uses the words 'remains unchanged' *in a new way,* and not because the metaphysician has a mistaken idea about its actual use in common speech. For if his usage were just a mistake, he would be open to correction, and he is not. The altered use of the words is *deliberate,* if not conscious, and is made in face of the linguistic facts about their actual use. That is why calling his attention to the facts does not move him in the least. He does not accept the linguistic facts as counting against what he is saying, i.e., as counting against *his* use of the words, *because they do not count against his use.* We may say that he is being linguistically creative, not wrong.

When some metaphysicians, with complete conviction, maintain that 'Everything is constantly changing' and other metaphysicians, with equal conviction, maintain that 'Nothing changes', there results an unbreakable intellectual stalemate, an undecidable disagreement, the nature of which can be explained satisfactorily in only one way. It is not difficult to see what makes the dispute *intrinsically* irresolvable, i.e., irresolvable in the sense that no *new fact* will settle it one way or the other: all the facts, material or linguistic, that are relevant to the solution of the problem are perfectly well known by the metaphysicians who take part in the dispute. There is no question of a super fact-finder breaking the deadlock. This makes it clear that the disagreement is not factual, not about what is or is not the case. What has happened is that metaphysicians, who divide on the question as to whether things change or not, have decided to alter customary language: some have decided to alter it in one direction and others in the opposite direction. And perhaps their decisions are dictated by concealed psychological motives. Regardless of this, it is easy to see that each side can go its own linguistic way *securely*, because what each side maintains is not open to possible refutation. The positions taken *have no theoretical refutations*. One cannot refute, nor for that matter establish by proof, a language innovation. One can only like it or dislike it. It can attract or repel, become popular, lose its popularity, be forgotten, be revived, be forgotten again and revived again. But it cannot be refuted or established, be *proved* false or *proved* true.

One of the 'proofs' for the view that everything remains unchanged might be looked at briefly. It is the case that in ordinary language there are no sharp criteria, or rules, for the application of the expressions 'has not changed' and 'has changed', just as there are no sharply defined rules for the application of the words 'rich' and 'poor'. By making use of this lack of criteria an eminent logician once 'proved' to me that there is no real difference between being rich and being poor. There are, of course, clear cases of a thing having changed, or of someone being poor, and there are clear cases of a thing not having changed or of someone being rich: a piece of granite and a burning twig, Oliver Twist and Rockefeller. But there are *penumbral* cases with regard to which we are at a loss as to what to say, 'changed' or 'unchanged', 'rich' or 'poor'. And we are at a loss as to what to say, not, as may of course happen, because we are not fully aware of the condition of an object, but because no rules exist for the application or non-application of the word 'changed' to *all* cases which we conceivably might encounter. C. D. Broad's words of warning might well be remembered: '. . . in the absence of clear knowledge of the meanings and relations of the concepts that we use, we are certain sooner or later to apply them wrongly or to meet with exceptional cases where we are puzzled as to how to apply them at all. For instance, we all know pretty well the place of a certain pin which we are looking at. But suppose we go on to ask: "Where is the image of that pin in a certain mirror; and is it in this place (whatever it may be) in precisely the sense in which the pin itself is in *its* place?" We shall find the question a very puzzling one, and there will be no hope of answering it until we have carefully analysed what we mean by *being in a place*'.[1]

According to Broad,[2] terminologically undecidable situations can only be avoided with the help of logical analysis. But this is a mistake and a misplaced faith in the magical efficacy of logic. For no analysis of the *actual* meaning of a word can make the meaning, or the word's use, sharper and more exact than it is. I think that no one is likely to be tempted to argue that the meanings of words have *hidden* sharpness and exactness. The ordinary meaning of a word is not more precise than its ordinary use, and to make its use more exact than its actual, everyday use is to *alter* its meaning.

Now the penumbral, undecidable cases, whether actual or imaginable, *connect by continuity* the opposite clear and decidable cases. And it is this fact that metaphysicians take advantage of. It is this linguistic fact that underlies the 'proofs' for the opposite positions of Heraclitus and Parmenides. If, and perhaps for an unconscious reason, a metaphysician wants to maintain that everything is constantly changing, he points to the fact that there is no sharp, and therefore no *real,* difference between changing and remaining unchanged; and if he is attracted to the phrase 'constantly changes' and is repelled by the expression 'remains unchanged', he can argue that, since some things do constantly change and since there is not a difference *in kind* but only a difference *in degree* between changing and not changing, everything really is changing. What he has done is to strike 'unchanged' out of his philosophical vocabulary; but in doing this, he has deprived 'constantly changing' of its descriptive use. A Parmenidean or a

[1]*Scientific Thought,* p. 16.   [2]*Ibid.,* pp. 17–18.

Bradleian metaphysician uses the same linguistic fact to 'prove' that nothing *really* changes, that change is an illusion, a bare appearance. To generalize, a metaphysician uses a fact about language as a *justification* (his 'proof') for changing the language, not, to be sure, for practical everyday use, but only for contemplation, for the pleasure his revision gives him. In Berkeley's words, he speaks with the vulgar and thinks with the learned.

It needs no great amount of intellectual penetration to see that the meta-hypothesis which tells us that the sentences for metaphysical theories use familiar words in deliberately altered ways connects the theories with their proofs in a way that is intelligible. No other meta-explanation does this. What the metaphysician does is concealed from us at two different levels. At the linguistic level it is concealed by the form of language the metaphysician uses to express himself, i.e., by the ontological idiom, in which familiar words seem to be used descriptively. At a deeper, psychological level our emotional needs blind us to what is being done with language.

A metaphysical theory may be described as a two-layer structure. Uppermost is the *illusion* of a theory about the nature or real existence of a phenomenon, the illusion, that is to say, that a metaphysical sentence states a view of some sort about reality. And this is produced by altering the use of a word or an expression. The changed use is not explicitly and openly declared, and it remains concealed by the mode of speech in which it is formulated. There is still a further and even deeper and less accessible layer in the total structure of a metaphysical 'theory', and I find that it is impossible for me to refrain from hinting here and there at its existence. It will, perhaps, only be cryptic at this point to say that metaphysical sentences express empirical beliefs which are held unconsciously; but if it is not a mistake to think this, then we have an explanation of the deeply rooted feeling that metaphysical sentences are about reality. The 'realities' referred to by them are subjective, the unconscious contents of our minds, not the physical world. We also have at hand an explanation of the position, which remains unshaken by the claim of logical positivism, that metaphysical sentences are not pieces of literal nonsense and, in particular, that expressions which refer to 'suprasensible' realities are perfectly intelligible.

A number of reasons warn me against bringing this further psychological layer into the explanation of the nature of metaphysics, but perhaps the risk should be taken anyway. Sooner or later philosophy will become a subject of more than passing interest to psychoanalysts; this is inevitable. Certainly philosophy is of sufficient importance as an intellectual phenomenon to deserve to have more light thrown on it than it has had up to the present, and by investigators who do not have a vested interest in it. In part philosophy has largely been neglected and its investigation been delayed by the fact that psychoanalysts have the same mistaken idea about what philosophy is that philosophers have; but there is no reason to think that its neglect will continue indefinitely.[1]

VII. THE THREE-LAYER STRUCTURE OF METAPHYSICS

If in our explanation of metaphysics we take into account the psychological substratum from which the primary value of metaphysics derives and which in fact is responsible for our blindness to what we are doing with language, we shall, of course, have to supplement our former statement and say that a metaphysical theory is a three-layer structure. A metaphysical sentence, which causes, at the conscious level of our minds, the erroneous idea that it states the existence or non-existence of a phenomenon or that the phenomenon has or lacks a certain property, is itself a preconscious re-edition of a familiar term and expresses one or more unconsciously held beliefs, the purpose of which is to satisfy a repressed longing or to ward off a repressed fear. When a metaphysician declares and proves that nothing really changes or that an effect cannot have 'more reality' than its cause or that all relations are internal he imagines himself, and is thought by others, to be announcing the discovery of an important fact about things, effects, and relations; whereas what he is actually doing is introducing a linguistic innovation the contemplation of which gives him and others pleasure. We can be sure that he gratifies himself

[1]Some work is being done. See, for example, John Wisdom, *Philosophy and Psychoanalysis,* and J. O. Wisdom, *The Unconscious Origin of Berkeley's Philosophy.*

67

unconsciously with his sentence, that it works in behalf of unconscious needs.

Ludwig Wittgenstein has made the colourful and penetrating observation that 'a philosophical problem arises when language goes on holiday',[1] and there is truth in this. Metaphysics may be justly described as a game played with language; but there is nothing frivolous about the game. It does not consist in cutting verbal capers, though this is what in an unclear way it seems to be to some intelligent outsiders; nor is it, as it perhaps was with Lewis Carroll, merely having a good time at the expense of ordinary language. Metaphysics is linguistic play with a deep purpose, just as a dream may be said to be mental play with a hidden psychic purpose. Thus, the philosophical sentence 'Nothing really changes' constitutes a fantasied, holiday rejection of the word 'change', which because it is not made consciously, creates the illusion of being a startling pronouncement about things—and in doing this it perhaps indulges our wish to be able to do magical things with words, our wish, as one of Freud's patients phrased it, for 'omnipotence of thought'. But more specifically than this, the make-believe rejection of the word 'change' indicates that the word has become charged with special meaning. The rejection must play an important and serious rôle in the drama of our unconscious life.

What the specific meanings are which are unconsciously attached to the term 'change' and what the unconscious beliefs are which the words 'Nothing really changes' express must obviously be a matter of conjecture, unbacked by substantial evidence. No doubt the objection will be raised by philosophers (who have not been a bit chastened by the lack of solid results in their own field) that such conjectures are idle guesses, guesses which, it is to be gathered from the immediate, uncurious, and frequently hostile rejections they receive, grate and are unpleasant. To a neutral observer it would seem that the worst thing that could be said against the conjectures is that they are supported by as little evidence as their rejections are. But this is not at all the way it looks to most philosophers; to them any surmises about the unconscious contents of philosophical statements are far-fetched, even ridiculous, and, it would not go too far to say, *tabu*. But what is *tabu* excites our curiosity, and justifiably so, and it should arouse the

[1] *Philosophical Investigations,* p. 19.

interest of philosophers, too, if their claim to be seekers after truth is sincere.

It is understandable that conjectures about the unconscious significance of philosophical utterances will be received with displeasure, for a number of different reasons; but the charge is by no means true that they are idle, in the sense that they lie beyond the practical possibility of being established or confuted by an existing technique for investigating them. It is now possible to establish them or disestablish them, for there does exist a science of the unconscious. *The unconscious no longer is an unknowable*, a *Ding-an-sich*. And I act on the maxim that it is better to have guessed and missed than never to have guessed at all.[1] I make them with hesitation and uncertainty because they may be wide of the mark, but I make them nevertheless because they throw light on the *kind* of investigation which has to be made if we are to arrive at a comprehensive and concrete picture of the structure of metaphysical theories. They illuminate to some degree the problem as to why metaphysicians alter language for the purpose of contemplation, and not for practical, everyday adoption, and they help us understand the abiding fascination which the statements embodying their alterations have for cultured people.

We can be reasonably sure that a philosopher who unalterably and with complete assurance maintains that change is unreal is, under the guise of making a scientific statement, covertly reassuring himself against certain feared changes and giving expression to the wish that certain things or conditions remain as they are. Fenichel reports that to many people 'the *status quo* is better than anything a change might bring. The *status quo* is a lesser evil.'[2] Undoubtedly, the thought of certain changes, whether actually experienced in one's past or which are in prospect, floods many people with anxiety; and it is hard to think that what is true of many people is not also true of some philosophers. It is hard to think that philosophers are untouched by inner feelings of insecurity which have to be kept in abeyance, and it does not seem wholly unreasonable to read a psychological purpose into the 'proof' that change does not exist. Its function is to ward off anxiety by strengthening an unconscious belief that threatening

[1] With apologies to Tennyson.
[2] Otto Fenichel, *The Psychoanalytic Theory of Neuroses,* First Edition, p. 298.

changes will not happen in our lives, that, for example, our *status quo* will not be upset by political changes, or economic changes, or change of occupation, or the practice of a profession in a new and unfamiliar environment, or the continued practice of a profession to which newcomers bring advanced and difficult techniques—the possibilities are too numerous to be detailed. For some people the word 'change', in addition to its ordinary meaning, which they do not give up in their everyday conversation, has the private meaning of 'catastrophic change'. They make the unconscious equation

change = dreaded change;

and they reassure themselves with the assertion, which is backed by the verbal necromancy of a metaphysical proof, that their *status quo* will not be disturbed by a new situation which, whether justifiably or not, is felt to be menacing. The hidden sense of the philosophical statement,

Nothing really changes,

is

No changes which would create anxiety in me are real.

In the light of this interpretation we can understand both the importance of the philosophical statement to many people as well as the tenacity with which they cling to it against all arguments, even in the face of its being pointed out to them that in ordinary conversation they use the word 'change' as others use it. We can also understand the claim that the statement is about reality. Without seriously misrepresenting what holding the view comes to, we may say that it is a verbal means of protection against frightening possibilities. Philosophers subjectively rewrite language by casting out the word 'change', for doing which they find subtle justification in language itself; and they do this in a mode of speech, i.e., in the ontological idiom, which both conceals from themselves what they are doing with the word 'change' and gives rise to the notion, which with unconscious duplicity they accept, that they are stating a fact about the world of physics. At the same time they express and fortify an unconsciously held belief, and thus counterbalance the invasion of an idea which brings panic in its wake. With their 'proved' statement they protect themselves and others who have made similar associations to the word 'change' with ingenious verbal armour.

The opposite view that change alone is real, the view attributed by Aristotle to Heraclitus, that 'All sensible things are in a state of flux', is open to a similar psychological interpretation. Fenichel states that 'The fear of change may be replaced or accompanied by its opposite, a tendency to change continuously'.[1] The motive behind a person's replacing his fear of change by a drive to change the circumstances of his life constantly and without let-up must, we are compelled to think, be a determination to master his fear. Some people who suffer from the fear of meeting changes in their lives, because of feelings of inadequacy, counteract their anxiety by using the technique of denial by retreat, i.e., of quieting their rising feelings of inadequacy by rejecting new situations and clinging desperately to their *status quo*. Others counteract their anxiety by convincing themselves over and over again, insatiably, that change can do them no harm. They are the Don Juans of change, the wooers who win but without permanent success: they are the knights errant who are driven to find new opponents against whom to test their strength, because they are chronically uneasy about their own abilities to cope with new situations. They use the mechanism of denial in a special way, not by fearfully retreating behind the belief that threatening situations will not overtake them, but by challenging and meeting new situations which they use to convince themselves obsessionally, without completely stilling their anxiety, that they are not inadequate. They 'transform into its opposite' each new situation, but always there remain new situations which have to be coped with, which must be exposed as harmless.

In one of the fragments attributed to him Heraclitus says, 'In change one finds rest'. I think that we can, in part at least, understand his finding rest in unremitting change, if we see in the rest which he finds the reassurance he wants to win from the very thing he dreads. Like the lion tamer who sticks his head into the jaws of his tamed lion, and receives the plaudits of those in his audience who have identified themselves with him, the Metaphysician of Change meets and subdues change in order to show how harmless it is. It is safe to say that philosophers who, on the surface, say that change alone is real have made the unconscious equation

[1] Otto Fenichel, *The Psychoanalytic Theory of Neuroses,* First Edition, p. 298.

$$change = disarmed, \ harmless \ change,$$

which they substitute for the equation,

$$change = dire \ change;$$

and by 'proving' to themselves, and to others as well, that change is real they produce the conviction that it holds no real menace.

It should not come as a surprise to learn that the word 'change' has in the minds of some people become linked with more deeply buried fears than the adult ones of a change of condition in life, i.e., that the adult fears are 'over-determined' and derive a considerable part of their strength from other sources. Probably later situations, which cause anxiety and have in some way to be rejected, stir into activity complexes in ourselves of which we have not the faintest glimmer of awareness. These then contribute their psychic charge, which both intensifies our feeling of disquietude and weakens our reality-testing abilities. Memories of experiences and wishes repressed in early childhood are not destroyed by repression; they are only imprisoned and are constantly trying to find a way of escape. Like the Midgard serpent which was cast into the ocean and grew until it encircled the whole earth, the submerged contents of our minds continue to exist and make contact with, and in fact encircle, our conscious experiences. In many cases they are responsible for the 'formless fears' described by novelists. Two repressed ideas which can with some plausibility be supposed to be unconsciously associated with the word 'change', and which make understandable the dreamlike rejection of the word, may be touched on. These are the ideas of birth and death. It is not unplausible to think that the word has been invested with these ideas, because like the word which is exorcised out of the language by the philosophical statement 'Nothing really changes', these ideas have to be exorcised from our minds: the idea of the traumatic experience which starts our biography in 'this world', and the idea of the event which concludes it.

According to Freud, the abrupt change, in birth, from a quiet, unruffled environment to an entirely different one which overwhelms the helpless infant with a flood of strange sensations creates anxiety and is the prototype of all later anxiety-arousing situations.[1] John Locke's graphic statement, 'I no sooner per-

[1]*The Problem of Anxiety.*

ceived myself in the world than I found myself in a storm',[1] supplies us with a striking example of Freud's claim that birth is a traumatic experience and that it is the model of later fearsome situations, experienced or avoided. For without doing violence to the conscious use Locke made of his words to describe his politically troubled experience, we may read an unconscious complaint into them. They refer to two biographical events, his first forgotten rude experience and the later one which brought a muted echo of the first to his mind. But regardless of whether this reading in depth is correct or mistaken, it is certainly possible that a person who denies the reality of change is secretly using his words to protect himself against remembering an upheaval in his life, the 'gross disturbance'[2] which gave him his first feeling of utter helplessness to cope with a situation, his first feeling of inadequacy. If he has unconsciously made the equation

change = birth,

then his 'demonstrating', to his own satisfaction, that change does not exist constitutes psychologically for him the denial that the event ever took place and that there is a memory of it in his mind. To express this in the language of Parmenides: Being is uncreated. The utterance 'Change is unreal' reports the inner fact that the work of repression is successfully preventing a memory from coming to consciousness; it expresses an unconscious belief that is a bulwark against the invasion of a dreaded remembrance.

It is hard to think that we do not have an unconscious idea of our own extinction, which if quickened into conscious life would bring paralysing terror down on us.[3] And how profound the dread of death must be can be gathered from the following Talmudic tale:—

When Rabbi Nahman was at the point of death, Raba entered into a compact with him to reveal the great secret of life and death after he had passed away. Rabbi Nahman kept his word and appeared before him in a dream.

'Did you suffer any anguish?' asked Raba.

The spirit of the dead man answered, 'The Angel of Death

---

[1]Quoted by W. R. Sorley in his *History of English Philosophy*, p. 104.
[2]Fenichel's expression.
[3]I am not referring to the bloodless residue, i.e., the conscious idea, which is left after the work of repression and which is shorn of nearly all of its affect.

drew my soul away with as light a hand as one draws a hair out of a jug of milk. Nevertheless, I wish to assure you that, even if the Almighty were to order me back upon earth to live my life over again, I would refuse because of my fear of death.'[1]

As in the case of birth, which brings with it the feeling of powerlessness, so in the case of our experiencing the death of someone to whom we are attached we feel impotent to cope with the situation; and the realization that we too will eventually have to yield to death fills us with oppressive gloom. This idea also must go under repression. It should be pointed out that, as against the position taken here, Freud maintained that 'In the unconscious . . . there is nothing to give content to our conception of the destruction of life',[2] that '. . . in the unconscious everyone of us is convinced of his own immortality'[3] and that 'Our own death is indeed unimaginable'.[3] His reason for holding that our own death is unimaginable is that 'whenever we make the attempt to imagine it we can perceive that we really survive as spectators'.[4] This is a peculiar reason indeed for the incomparable discoverer of the unconscious to have given, and it does not seem to me to stand up under scrutiny.

Plainly it is not clinical evidence, nor does Freud offer it as such. If anything, it is a consciously made *Gedankenexperiment*, and can, at best, have no more analytical value than the claim of many people that they cannot imagine themselves doing certain things, that every time they try to imagine themselves acting out wishes which Freud tells us we all have, they only succeed in imagining themselves not doing those things. And their lack of success does not, of course, show in the least that they do not have those wishes or that they do not gratify themselves in unconscious ways. Perhaps if a patient, instead of Freud, had in the course of his analysis claimed that he had no idea of his own death because whenever he tried to imagine it he succeeded only in imagining himself as a

[1]Taken from Nathan Ausubel's *A Treasury of Jewish Folklore*, Crown Publishers. This tale suggests that the psychological mechanism used to cope with the dread of death is that of 'splitting of affect from ideational content'. Raba has the idea of death and, by projection, Rabbi Nahman suffers from the fear of death.

[2]*The Problem of Anxiety*, p. 87.

[3]*Thoughts for the Times on War and Death*, Collected Papers, Vol. IV, The International Psychoanalytical Library, No. 10 (1925), pp. 304–5.

[4]*Ibid.*, p. 305.

spectator, Freud's suspicion would have been aroused by the clever argument. And he might very well have interpreted it as a defence mechanism, on the rule that repressed ideas have opposite, counter ideas in conscious awareness. In connexion with his experiment, Freud observes: 'We were of course prepared to maintain that death was the necessary outcome of life, that everyone owes a debt to Nature and must expect to pay the reckoning—in short, that death was natural, undeniable and unavoidable. In reality, however, we were accustomed to behave as if it were otherwise. We displayed an unmistakable tendency to "shelve" death, to eliminate it from life. We tried to hush it up; indeed we even have the saying, "To think of something as we think of death". That is our own death, of course'.[1] It may, I think without unfairness, be pointed out that if our own death were unimaginable, it is not at all easy to see why there should be a need to 'hush it up', or even how there *could* be a tendency in us to do this. We can no more hush up or shelve an idea that we do not have than we can silence a speaker who does not exist. Freud concludes his study with the words, reminiscent of Socrates in the *Phaedo,* 'If you would endure life, be prepared for death'.[2] Again it has to be pointed out that we can hardly be expected to prepare for what we are unable to imagine. If Freud's *Gedankenexperiment* establishes what he claims it establishes, then he is neither in a position to give his advice nor could anyone understand it. 'If you would enjoy the rainbow, be prepared for the blackness of night' is not the advice that one blind man can give to another blind man.

The introspective experiment we are invited to make, if it shows anything at all, shows that we do have the idea of our own decease. In imagining our death, as Charlie Chaplin does his in *Limelight,* we must, to be sure, remain as spectators. How else could we imagine it? But the fact that we are witnesses does not eliminate what, imaginatively, we are witnessing. The statement, 'Whenever we make the attempt to imagine it we can perceive that we really survive as spectators', throws the spotlight on the wrong actor, so to speak, and keeps the other actor in the shadow. In fact, the statement is metaphysical, rather than psychological, i.e., it

[1] *Thoughts for the Times on War and Death,* Collected Papers, Vol. IV, The International Psychoanalytical Library, No. 10 (1925), p. 304.
[2] *Ibid.,* p. 317.

hides a change in language and has a psychological job. In this connexion the Parmenidean claim comes to mind, namely, the claim that we cannot think of what does not exist. Parmenides rejected the expression 'thinks of what does not exist',[1] and, similarly, Freud rejected the phrase 'imagines one's own death'.

Although we are in conscious possession of the idea of our own death, Freud may, nevertheless, be right in thinking that it does not, as an affective idea, have a place in our unconscious. His own words of advice, 'If you would endure life, be prepared for death', seem to indicate the opposite, however. They are clearly, if by no means conclusively, open to the interpretation, 'If you would endure life, you must resurrect the idea from its grave in your mind, consciously face it and make your adjustments. Wrestling with it under Utgard-Loki's magic, as Thor wrestled with Elli, will only bring you to your knees'. The passage which concludes with his words of advice tends to bear out this interpretation:

Would it not be better to give death the place in actuality and in our thoughts which properly belongs to it, and to yield a little more prominence to that unconscious attitude towards death which we have hitherto so carefully suppressed? This hardly seems indeed a greater achievement, but rather a backward step in more than one direction, a regression; but it has the merit of taking somewhat more into account the true state of affairs, and of making life again more endurable for us. To endure life remains, when all is said, the first duty of all living beings. Illusion can have no value if it makes this more difficult for us.

We remember the old saying: *Si vis pacem, para bellum*. If you desire peace, prepare for war.

It would be timely thus to paraphrase it: *Si vis vitam, para mortem*. If you would endure life, be prepared for death.[2]

I feel tempted to say that what distinguishes man from the lower animals is that he has the unconscious realization that he is some day to die; and I shall proceed on the not wholly unplausible assumption that the idea is in our unconscious. Just as the 'first change' must be rejected and lost to memory, so must the 'last

[1] Its equivalent in Greek, of course.
[2] *Op. cit.*, pp. 316–17.

change' be exorcised from our minds; and with great inventiveness man has contrived in innumerable ways to quiet his troubled
feelings. One of these is the invention of the idea that he has an
immortal 'soul', another is the creation of enduring, living works
bearing his name—sons who have sons, scientific discoveries,
works of art, systems of philosophy, etc. In addition to these the
metaphysician may quite well have discovered a highly intellect-
ualized, linguistic way of comforting himself against a nagging
uneasiness. To describe his discovery in the language of Parmenides, the first great metaphysician of the Unreality of Change,
the philosopher has discovered the path of truth and reason, i.e.,
the way of concealed linguistic alteration, and he rejects the path
of false opinion, i.e., ordinary speech. To the word 'change' is
easily associated the idea of death, the Medusa which if gazed on
turns one into stone, the condition of death; and a metaphysician
who has made the unconscious equation

$$change = death$$

is able to employ his skill with words and his deep insight into the
ways they work to convince himself and others of the unreality of
the final change by 'demonstrating' the non-existence of change.
His demonstration, which is a linguistically perceptive, if an im-
practical, justification for casting out the word 'change', is a
'secondary elaboration' which lends a scientific air to the special
work he assigns to the word on behalf of his unconscious need.

It may be of some interest to note that the view of Heraclitus,
which in one form or another has its contemporary advocates,
namely, the view that 'everything steadfastly changes', lends itself
to a closely similar interpretation. The utterance 'Everything
changes', which means to us that all things perish and pass away,
may for one thing express a psychologically concealed recognition
of the unalterable fate which awaits *all* of us. And those who can
make use of this fact take comfort from the thought that the fate
meted out to us is impartially meted out to everyone: 'Everything
changes' = 'Everyone dies'. Our sense of aloneness and outraged
injustice is lessened by the feeling that our lot is the common lot,
and it also gives us aggressive satisfaction. A headstone in an
American cemetery[1] furnishes confirmation of this; it carries the
inscription

[1]Hatfield, Massachusetts.

77

Death is a debt
To Nature due
I have paid mine
And so must you.

But the word 'change', in addition to being linked with the idea of death, can also have the antithetical meaning *life*. It can, in other words, be made the bearer of both ideas at once. The sentence 'Everything changes' then means that change is lived through, which is to say, death is lived through. The word 'change' is made to stand for the phoenix which springs whole and anew from its own ashes, for death and resurrection. The philosophical sentence robs death of its horror by making it out to be a transitory, if recurrent, condition of life, a disease from which we recover: 'One and the same thing are the living and the dead, the waking and the sleeping, the young and the old; the former change and are the latter, the latter in turn change and are the former'.[1] With the philosophical sentence we tell ourselves that death is real but that it is an aspect of life. We remain alive even in death: 'In the circumference of a circle beginning and end coincide'.[1]

To sum up, the theory that nothing really changes, that despite appearances everything abides unchanged, is to be described as a structure which is composed of three interrelated, interacting strata: the illusion of a theory about the world, at the conscious level; a non-verbal sentence which embodies an alteration of language, at the preconscious level; and a belief (one or more) which satisfies a wish and counters a fear in the substratum of our minds. The metaphysician of permanence has turned out to be, not the *a priori* scientific investigator of all that exists, but a skilful semantic illusionist with the serious purpose of helping us through life. Unlike the physicist who reports and explains physical phenomena, but whose statements may also have private meanings for his unconscious, the metaphysician can with hardly any exaggeration be said to use his statement *solely* to express unconscious material. It can almost without exaggeration be said that *his statement* expresses nothing over and above, nothing in addition to, the unconscious material it denotes. His work, on the one hand,

[1]Heraclitus.

78

is to create the impression that his utterance discloses a deep truth about the nature of things, a truth which takes us to the reality behind the veil of appearance, and, on the other hand, to deny the existence of bogies in the depths of our minds. The philosophical sentence, 'Change is unreal', comes to the same thing as the verbal sentence, 'The word "change" has no descriptive use', which, it should be kept in mind, declares a holiday banishment of the word without denying that it has an established use in everyday language. And because the philosophical sentence is in the ontological idiom, i.e., the idiom in which language is used to describe states of affairs, we are led into thinking that it expresses a proposition about things. The intellectual illusion it creates is strengthened and made all the more difficult to test by the fact that the sentence expresses beliefs for which we have unconscious needs. We might say that our intelligence has discovered an ingenious way of putting language into the service of emotional needs, and at the same time keeps its discovery a secret from itself. A metaphysician is a verbal magician who is taken in by his own tricks; he is both subtle and inventive with words and blind to what he does with them. Heraclitus said, 'It is hard to contend against the heart; for it is ready to sell the soul to purchase its desires'; and Frederick the Great's statement comes to mind to supplement this: 'We are all the sophists of our passions'.

III

THE EXISTENCE OF UNIVERSALS

MANY philosophers have claimed that in addition to objects met with in sense-experience there exist entities of an entirely different and more esoteric kind, technically designated as 'universals'. According to this claim, there are, in addition to such things as tables and white sheets of paper, the utterly different and less well-known objects tableness and whiteness. Universals, in contrast to the changing and passing phenomena perceived with our senses, have been described by many philosophers as being timeless, unchangeable, and exact. But perhaps more important than this, they are intangible to the senses; they cannot be seen with our eyes nor felt with our hands. They are 'intelligible' objects which can be apprehended only in thought. As Plato expressed it: '. . . these, unlike objects of sense, have no separate organ, but that the mind, by a power of her own, contemplates the universals in all things'.[1] Legend has it that Diogenes remarked he could see tables but not tableness, to which Plato retorted that although Diogenes had eyes he had no intelligence.

As is well known, philosophers are by no means in agreement on the question as to the nature of universals. Endless controversies have been carried on about their nature without a theory being arrived at which is acceptable to all competent philosophers. This lack of a generally accepted view may seem surprising, inasmuch as research in the problem has been carried on for so many hundreds of years. What is even more strange, however, is that philosophers have been unable to reach a unanimous opinion about the *existence* of universals. And in the present paper, it will be my purpose to consider the theory that there are universals,

[1]*Theaetetus,* 185. Jowett translation, third edition.

not with the object of establishing or refuting it, but in order to make as clear as possible the nature of the view. For the most part I shall make use of material from the writings of Bertrand Russell, because they seem to me to contain the clearest and most forthright statements of the view in philosophical literature.

It can easily be appreciated that anyone who for the first time comes upon the theory that there are such things as universals will receive the impression that philosophers have discovered a new, hitherto unknown, realm of objects, 'the supra sensible world of universals',[1] that they have made a discovery comparable in general respects to the scientific discovery of microscopic forms of life. Philosophers themselves seem to have thought this. Thus Russell once wrote: 'Seeing that nearly all the words to be found in the dictionary stand for universals, it is strange that hardly anybody except students of philosophy ever realizes that there are such entities as universals'.[2] Many philosophers who have held the theory that there are such entities have done two things. They have claimed, for one thing, to have direct knowledge of them. Russell, for example, has said: 'In addition to our acquaintance with particular existing things, we also have acquaintance with what we shall call *universals* . . .'[3]; and Moore has claimed to have made analyses of some of them.[4] For another thing, they have offered proofs of their existence, if not to strengthen their own convictions, to convince those who are ignorant of the theory and to defend their view against philosophers like Berkeley and James Mill, who have denied that there are any abstract ideas.

All this, the form of words in which the theory is expressed, and the manner in which philosophers have conducted their dispute with regard to it, creates the impression that the theory is about *objects,* of which ordinary people are unaware and the existence of which is in dispute amongst philosophers. One would gather from Plato's remark that those, like Diogenes, who have been instructed in the theory and persist in denying that they ever have the experience of contemplating a universal, suffer from some sort of mental deficiency, a psychological blindness comparable to ordinary blindness. And in the same way, one would gather from Diogenes' statement the sceptical hint that philosophers who claim

[1] *The Problems of Philosophy*, p. 144.   [2] *Ibid.*, p. 146.   [3] *Ibid.*, p. 81.
[4] *The Philosophy of G. E. Moore*, pp. 664–5.

to have contemplated universals have somehow been deluded. An outsider would naturally be led to think that some sort of process of mental looking has convinced many philosophers that the entities in dispute exist while it has led others to deny this. He would quite naturally think that philosophers were engaged in an empirical dispute, one with regard to matter of fact, which some sort of mental looking has not so far been able to settle.

His impression would be further strengthened by Russell's explanation of how it happens that people fail to notice universals.

> We do not naturally dwell upon those words in a sentence which do not stand for particulars; and if we are forced to dwell upon a word which stands for a universal, we naturally think of it as standing for some one of the particulars that come under the universal. When, for example, we hear the sentence, 'Charles I's head was cut off', we may naturally enough think of Charles I, of Charles I's head, and of the operation of cutting off *his* head, which are all particulars; but we do not naturally dwell upon what is meant by the word 'head' or the word 'cut', which is a universal. We feel such words to be incomplete and insubstantial; they seem to demand a context before anything can be done with them. Hence we succeed in avoiding all notice of universals as such, until the study of philosophy forces them upon our attention.[1]

The impression created by these words is that, like a retiring guest at a party where everyone else boisterously clamours for attention, universals have been overlooked by people who understand the words for which they stand. The explanation is expressed in the language of empirical description, in language which purports to describe how it happens that we fail to notice the presence of certain objects.

Now, in the case of the boisterous party, if the attention of people is called to the modest guest, they will see him and acknowledge his presence; they will not, except as a bad joke, get into a dispute about his existence. Similarly, if philosophers are asked to disregard disturbing imagery and the like which may come up when they consider a sentence like 'Charles I's head was cut off', and are directed to contemplate the universals symbolized by 'head' and 'cut', it is to be expected that they will become aware

[1] *The Problems of Philosophy,* pp. 146–7.

of them. It is to be expected that if some such request is made as 'Disregard A's head and B's and concentrate on the *meaning* of "head",' philosophers will think of what is meant by the word and will without exception acknowledge the existence of the universal. But this is not what happens. Instead, what happens is that philosophers get into a *serious* dispute over the existence of universals. Their difference of opinion is unquestionably sincere, and is expressed in language which makes it look to be of such a kind that to its resolution some sort of process of examining the meanings of general words is relevant and should be conclusive, though, strange to say, this does not serve to resolve the disagreement.

A further and unexpected complication has been introduced into this dispute by other philosophers, who have declared the problem to be without literal sense. Thus, for example, in contradistinction to philosophers who have held the theory that there are such objects as universals to be *false*, Prof. Ayer has maintained that it is a pseudo-view, one which, contrary to what it appears to be, is really *nonsensical*.[1] According to him, those who assert the existence of universals, and even devise ingenious arguments to demonstrate this, are not really asserting that anything exists, but are only pronouncing nonsensical combinations of words; and those who deny their existence are not really denying the existence of anything but are likewise pronouncing nonsense. The controversy does not involve a difference of opinion with regard to a theory and is not, therefore, genuine.

Is the dispute empirical, one with regard to whether universals exist, or is it a pseudo-dispute in which no opposing views are really expressed but only nonsense is uttered? How are the theory and the dispute with regard to it to be understood?

It is possible, in the first place, to side at least partly with Ayer and argue that the supposed dispute is only a pseudo-disagreement, one not constituted by any actual difference of opinion between those philosophers who appear to take sides on the problem: that those philosophers who affirm the existence of universals, those who deny their existence, and even those who pronounce the theory nonsensical, are not actually disagreeing, despite the fact that their language and behaviour are appropriate to an actual divergence of beliefs. It is possible to argue, with good reason,

[1] A. J. Ayer, *Language, Truth and Logic,* first edition, p. 36.

that philosophers have not discovered, and are not stating the existence of, entities of a new kind, that the layman is not unaware of the existence of these entities but rather also has knowledge by acquaintance of them, and that those philosophers who deny that universals exist are not disputing the claim of those who assert that there are universals.

For consider how the term 'universal' is used in philosophy. Russell wrote that 'we "conceive" whenever we understand the meaning of an abstract word, or think of that which is in fact the meaning of the word. If you see a white patch of snow, or recall it by means of images, you do not have a concept; but if you think about whiteness, you have a concept . . . The object of your thought, in such a case, is a *universal* or a Platonic idea'.[1] This, quite clearly, is an explanation of how the word 'universal' is used by philosophers. It tells us the term is so used that to say an abstract word, for example, a general name or a verb or an adjective, has a meaning is the same thing as to say it expresses a universal. The meaning of an abstract word is a universal, so that the expression 'the universal for which a word stands' translates into the expression 'the meaning of an abstract word', e.g., 'the universal for which "lion" stands' means the same as what is meant by 'the meaning of "lion"'. In order, then, to know whether there are universals it is only necessary to know the meaning of a general name like 'lion' or the meaning of some other abstract word. And since everyone, layman as well as philosopher, who can understand ordinary conversation knows the meanings of some such words, it follows that *everyone* knows that there are universals.

Philosophers who think that laymen are unaware of the fact that universals exist must be supposed, therefore, to be thinking that laymen are unaware of the fact that abstract words have meanings. But this they *know* to be false, and it is not easy to see how they ever could come to think it. The 'theory' which is expressed by the words 'Universals exist' is also expressed by the words 'Abstract words have meanings'. But no one who understood the sentence 'Prepositions, adjectives, etc., have meanings' would imagine that it expressed a *theory*; and it is difficult to see what happened that could have led anyone to think that 'Universals exist' expressed one, or that philosophers at one time had *discovered*

[1] *Philosophy,* p. 203.

the 'suprasensible world of universals', which implies that they had discovered that abstract words have meanings.

The idea that there actually is a dispute over whether universals exist becomes completely incomprehensible. For what is asserted by the statement 'There are no universals' is also asserted by the statement 'General names, adjectives, etc., have no meanings'. The further statement ' "There are universals" is literally meaningless' expresses what is also expressed by 'It makes no sense to say "Adjectives, general names, etc., have meanings" '. But it is plain, I think, that no one would dream of denying that verbs, etc., have meanings, or of maintaining that it makes no sense to say that they do. All philosophers, those who pronounce the view that there are universals to be without sense, those who merely contend it is false, as well as those who hold it, *know* that abstract words have meaning. They all, therefore, know that there are universals. There is no difference of opinion over whether abstract words have meanings. How then could there be a difference of opinion over whether there are universals? Seen in this light, it becomes plausible to say that, although there appears to be a controversy, there really is none.

Nevertheless, although there is good reason for arriving at the conclusion that there is no divergence of belief, and hence no actual dispute amongst philosophers, and that there is no problem about the existence of universals, to assert this is to deny the obvious. Undeniably philosophers are in intelligible disagreement *of some sort* over universals, even though there is none over whether abstract words have meaning. And unquestionably they are sincere; they are not pretending a dispute. To consider any other possibility would be to explore fantasy rather than fact. The problem, rather, is to find an explanation which will be an explanation of *both* facts: both that there is a dispute about universals and that there is none over whether abstract words have meanings. One may, of course, stop short and take the dispute as merely showing a 'strange thing' about the psychology of philosophers, namely, that they are able to hold '. . . sincerely, as part of their philosophical creed, propositions inconsistent with what they themselves *know* to be true'.[1] But this is not satisfactory.

[1]G. E. Moore, 'A Defence of Common Sense', *Contemporary British Philosophy*, Vol. II, p. 203.

It is psychologically possible, to be sure, for a person to believe what he knows to be false. And it is conceivable that many philosophers, regardless of what they know perfectly well, are nevertheless expressing contrary opinions which they believe. Something strange, psychologically, could have happened to philosophers to arouse beliefs which in normal circumstances they would not have. One is reminded of the man who *knows* his love is untrue to him, has seen her in another man's arms, sees the lie in her face when she denies his accusations, but nevertheless believes her: 'I know she is false to me, and yet I believe her. I *must*'.[1] Something like what happened to this man could, conceivably, have also happened to philosophers, but there is no reason for thinking so. There is no good reason for thinking that any philosophers suffer from some sort of emotional conflict with regard to the fact that words have meanings. The dispute over universals has to be explained in some other way; so far we have not rightly understood it.

The problem is to arrive at an explanation of the theory of universals which will at the same time allow for and be an explanation of the dispute, i.e., will tell us whether the dispute is factual or whether no facts are in dispute but something else is and what it is. Russell has drawn a distinction on the basis of which such an explanation could, perhaps, be constructed. He writes:—

> General words such as 'man' or 'cat' or 'triangle' are said to denote 'universals', concerning which, from the time of Plato to the present day, philosophers have never ceased to debate. Whether there are universals, and, if so, in what sense, is a metaphysical question, which need not be raised in connexion with the use of language. The only point about universals that needs to be raised at this point is that the correct use of general words is no evidence that a man can think about universals. It has often been supposed that, because we can use a word like 'man' correctly, we must be capable of a corresponding 'abstract' idea of man, but this is quite a mistake . . . Consequently there is no need to suppose that we ever apprehend universals, although we use general words correctly.[2]

According to the distinction here implied between the correct

---

[1] I cannot recall the novel from which this is taken.
[2] *Philosophy,* pp. 53–4.

use of general words and their standing for universals or abstract ideas, it follows that the statement which is asserted by some philosophers and controverted by others, that an abstract word, say 'chair', stands for a universal, expresses something new and in addition to the undisputed fact that the word has a correct use in the language. The sentence 'The word "chair" stands for the universal chairness' says something new and in addition to what would be said by a statement explaining the proper use of 'chair' in English, so that in learning the meaning of the second statement a person would not at the same time be learning what was expressed by the first. The distinction thus seems to provide an explanation of how the layman, who knows how to use abstract words like 'cheese', 'walk', and 'not' correctly, could be unaware of the existence of universals, and of how it has happened that even philosophers have disagreed over whether there are any. For we are told that knowing how to use a word correctly, e.g., 'cheese' or 'not', is not the same as, nor does it imply, being able to frame the abstract idea of *cheese* or of *not,* or having acquaintance with the universal it denotes. A person who behaved appropriately on hearing the request, 'Please pass the cheese to me', who knew how to make his own wants known in similar words, and could even talk at length on the differences between cheeses, might not know the abstract idea of cheese, although we should say he knew the correct use of 'cheese' in the language. Similarly, with regard to words like 'five', 'not', 'between', 'white', 'walk', the fact that he has used them correctly on numerous occasions and in different circumstances is not to be counted as any evidence whatever for thinking he knows the universals they denote, or even that there are any such objects. And the philosophical controversy is not about what everyone knows perfectly well, that such words have a correct use in the language; it is a controversy over the purported discovery that *in addition* to their having an ordinary use they *also* stand for entities philosophers have called 'universals'. The possibility of a genuine difference of opinion arising seems to be explained, since those philosophers who have failed to apprehend abstract ideas, even though they know verbal usage, may think the claim that there are universals is false, or even that it is senseless. Thus, although Diogenes could apply the word 'horse' to the right animals, knew the correct use of 'horse', he had failed to frame, perhaps because of mental inability, the abstract idea of horse, and so was led to deny that there were universals.

Another thing that would seem to follow from Russell's distinction is that there are two different processes connected with learning a word: one, of learning its correct use, and the other, a *further* process, of framing an abstract idea, or becoming acquainted with the universal for which the word stands: one process of learning to what animals 'horse' is applicable and another process of framing the abstract idea of horse. The first process is, of course, familiar to all of us; admittedly those of us who know word usage were subjected to it. But what is this further process? What, in addition to teaching us how to use correctly the words in a language, for instance, in the usual, ostensive ways in which children are taught them, is necessary in order to make us *also* know the universals they symbolize?

Russell appears to have answered this question too, to have described the further process: 'When we see a white patch, we are acquainted, in the first instance, with the particular patch; but by seeing many white patches, we easily learn to abstract the whiteness which they all have in common, and in learning to do this we are learning to be acquainted with whiteness. A similar process will make us acquainted with any other universal of the same sort.'[1] One may suppose that 'learning to abstract the whiteness which particular white things have in common or the horseness which particular horses have in common' describes something which has to be gone through in addition to the process of learning the proper use of 'white' or 'horse', so that a person who has learnt to apply 'white' to things that are white and to withhold applying it to things having another colour, and has learnt to apply 'horse' to animals that are horses and to withhold applying it to other animals, could not, merely because he has this knowledge, be said to have gone through the process of abstracting whiteness and horseness, and thereby to have become acquainted with the universals. The description of the process of abstraction gives rise to the idea that becoming acquainted with a universal requires, so to speak, some mysterious sort of mental distillation in which, e.g., whiteness, a non-visual, abstract idea, is derived

[1]*The Problems of Philosophy*, pp. 158–9; see also the following paragraph.

from visual, concrete objects. The attempts in chemistry to obtain a pure substance may come to mind as analogous.

But what would be a test for ascertaining whether a person has achieved acquaintance with a universal? What is to be reckoned as evidence for a person's being acquainted, say, with whiteness or tableness? Philosophers do not explicitly tell us, and Russell denies that the correct use of a word is to be considered as any evidence whatever. Their omission, in conjunction with Russell's denial, is important because, by putting them in a position comparable to that of an explorer who claims to have discovered a strange, new land but has brought back nothing which could serve as evidence for his claim, some philosophers get the idea that the theory of universals is false while others think it is unverifiable and therefore nonsensical.

Nevertheless, there is an ordinary way at hand of finding out whether a person has acquaintance with a universal. In accordance with the philosophical explanation of the word 'universal' to the effect that the meaning of a general word is a universal, it will be plain that knowledge of the meaning of a word is identical with or at least implies acquaintance with a universal. Thus, from the fact that a person knows the meaning of 'white' or of 'table' it follows that he has acquaintance with whiteness or tableness. We do, of course, have a test, which is the only one, for ascertaining whether he knows the meaning of a word. We find out whether a person knows the meaning of 'white' or 'table' by observing how he uses the word. If he continues to use it properly, i.e., in the way in which it is ordinarily used, applies it only to the right things, uses it correctly in assertions and questions, etc., we say he knows its meaning. We take the correct use of 'white' and 'table' as evidence that a person knows their meaning. It follows, then, contrary to what Russell holds, that we do count their correct use as evidence that the person has acquaintance with the universals whiteness and tableness. What could ever have made anyone deny this is not easy to see; though we can, perhaps, see a reason why philosophers should have omitted explicitly stating a test for ascertaining whether a person has acquaintance with universals, since no procedure in addition to the usual one for finding out that people know the meanings of words is necessary.

Furthermore, it will be clear that knowing the meaning of a

word is the same as knowing its proper use. The test for each is exactly the same; it consists in each case of observing how the word is used and what the responses to its use in statements made by others are. There is no test which is a test of one and not of the other; and this is because the expressions 'knows its use but does not know its meaning', 'knows its meaning but does not know its use' are self-contradictory. 'Knows its meaning as well as its use' says nothing different from 'knows its use', because it makes no sense to ask 'Which did you learn first, the meaning of the word or its correct use?' It will be clear, too, that it is not merely false to say that there are two processes connected with learning a word, one of learning its correct use, and a further one, not involved in the first, of learning to abstract a universal, but it makes no sense to say this. Learning to abstract the universal for which a word stands is the same as learning to use the word properly. There is nothing more mysterious about the one than there is about the other.

The attempt to understand the theory of universals by way of the distinction between a general word having a correct use and standing for a universal has not been enlightening. It only leads back to the former unacceptable idea that the dispute about universals is a disagreement over whether general words have meanings. The distinction no doubt has point, however; though what it is remains obscure. Russell would not deny that the correct use of a general word like 'white' is evidence that a person knows its meaning. His denial that it is evidence for a person's being acquainted with the universal for which it stands (a denial which I find hard to think is just a mistake) raises the suspicion that there is a problem about universals which there is not about the meaning of words. It lends justification to the idea that the theory that general words stand for universals does not reduce to the statement that general words have meanings.

Having learned words in the usual ways in which words are learned seems to leave many people unsatisfied. It leaves them with the feeling, apparently, that it is not enough, that the ordinary ways have not given them knowledge of what the words really mean. Moore has given explicit expression to this dissatisfaction: 'What, *after all,* is it that we mean to say of an action when we say that it is right or ought to be done?'[1] And in the attempt to

[1] *Ethics,* p. 8. Italics my own. See also C. D. Broad, *Scientific Thought,* Introduction.

answer this question Moore, who knows the ordinary use of the word, thought it necessary to try to *discover* a property common and exclusive to all right actions. Again, as in the case of Russell's distinction of which the present expression of dissatisfaction is a continuation, knowing how to apply 'right' to actions to which the word is commonly applied is not to be taken for knowing its meaning. In order to know what the word means it is necessary to know a property, one that is common and exclusive to all actions to which the word would ordinarily be applied. The meaning of 'right' is a common property, which a person may not know even though he knows the ordinary use of the word. In general with regard to abstract words, Plato tells us: 'Whenever a number of individuals have a common name, we assume them to have also a corresponding idea or form.'[1] And from Russell we have the statement: 'Let us consider, say, such a notion as *justice*. If we ask ourselves what justice is, it is natural to proceed by considering this, that, and the other just act, with a view to discovering what they have in common. They must all, in some sense, partake of a common nature, which will be found in whatever is just and in nothing else. This common nature, in virtue of which they are all just, will be justice itself, the pure essence the admixture of which with facts of ordinary life produces the multiplicity of just acts. Similarly with any other word which may be applicable to common facts, such as "whiteness" for example. The word will be applicable to a number of particular things because they all participate in a common nature or essence.'[2]

The idea that the meanings of abstract words, or universals, are common properties is one which seems natural and invites ready acceptance. It seems to account for the difference between proper names and general names, etc., e.g., between 'Edward' and 'boy'. And it provides us with an explanation of how it is that after having had pointed out to him a number of things to each of which the same word is applied a person can go on by himself to apply the word correctly to new things: of how it is that after having been shown applications of a word W to *a, b, c* he can go on by himself and apply it correctly to *d, e,* etc. If in the course of being taught ostensively the use of W, all he learned were the

[1] *Republic,* Book X, 596.
[2] *The Problems of Philosophy,* p. 143.

separate facts that *a* was called W and that *b* also was called W, he would not have learned anything which would enable him to proceed independently to new applications, i.e., to applications which had not been explicitly made for him, any more than after being told that this boy was called 'Edward' and that boy, too, he would have been told anything which would justify him in calling other boys 'Edward'. If, however, we suppose that W is applied to *a, b,* and *c* in virture of their having a given property ϕ in common, we can understand how a person who has learned this, namely that W is applicable to *a, b, c* because they have ϕ in common, can go on by himself to make further applications of W to *d, e,* etc. What enables him to make independently the new applications is knowledge of the *general fact* that W is applicable to anything which has ϕ: he applies W to *d* and *e,* etc., by noting that in common with *a, b,* and *c* they have ϕ. The general fact that W is applicable to anything which has ϕ, which he learns from the separate applications of W, is equivalent to the fact that ϕ is the meaning of W, so that in knowing the meaning of W he knows to what it is applicable. It is natural, thus, to think that 'the meaning of the term will be what is common to the various examples pointed out as meant by it'.[1]

Despite the naturalness of this account of the meanings of words, some philosophers have disagreed with the theory that the meanings of words are common properties. Locke's well-known challenge may be recalled: 'For I demand, what are the alterations [which] may or may not be in a horse or lead, without making either of them to be of another species? . . . he will never be able to know when anything precisely ceases to be of the species of a horse or lead'.[2] This challenge is unanswerable. Imagine a horse changing by imperceptible gradation into a swan. Clearly, we can distinguish three stages in the process of transformation: one with regard to which everyone would say the animal was a horse, another with regard to which everyone would say it was neither a horse nor a swan, and still a third with regard to which everyone would say it was a swan. But these stages, which themselves involve an undetermined amount of latitude, are connected by imperceptible gradation with each

[1] C. I. Lewis, *Mind and the World-Order,* p. 78.
[2] *Human Understanding,* Book III, Chap. III, 13.

other, so that there is no sharp line of division between any of the stages and no way of ascertaining where one ends and the other begins. Like a person going from one army to another facing it and separated from it by no-man's-land, one can imaginatively proceed from the horse to an animal which is neither horse nor swan, and finally to the swan without being able to know where precisely he left one and arrived at the other. If, on the other hand, there were a property ϕ, simple or complex, in virtue of having which the animal was a horse and in virtue of failing to have which the animal ceased to be a horse, and another property ϕ', on the possession of which depended whether a thing was a swan or not, it would be possible to know at *exactly* what point in the process of transformation the animal ceased to be a horse, at what point *exactly* it became neither a horse nor a swan, and at what point *exactly* it became a swan. It would cease to be a horse at precisely the point when it lost ϕ, and it would become a swan precisely at the point of transformation when it acquired ϕ'. But this is made impossible by the fact that the change proceeds by imperceptible gradation. The fact that there are no sharp lines of demarcation shows that there is no property common and unique to all things, actual or imaginable, to which the word 'horse' is applicable and lacking which makes the word inapplicable. The meaning of the word is not an essence, a common property.[1]

Without instancing other words to illustrate the point, it can be seen that with regard to any abstract word W there are things which we should correctly and without hesitation call W; there are things from which we should correctly and without hesitation withhold application of W; and there are things, actual or easily imaginable, with regard to which a person who knew all there was to be known about the ordinary, actual use of W would not know what to do, whether to apply it or withhold it. His knowledge of actual usage would be of no help to him. This is not, as C. D. Broad seemed to think,[2] due to inadequate knowledge of the rules for the use of W, but obtains in spite of knowing all there is to be known about the actual use of the word. And to search for *exact* rules, or what is equivalent to this, to search for a set of

[1]This is not to deny that there are common properties in the ordinary sense of 'common property'.

[2]*Scientific Thought,* Introduction.

common properties in virtue of which a word is applied and in the absence of which application is withheld, would be like trying to discover rules for a game in addition to the well-known ones, while knowing perfectly well that the usual rules were all the rules that had ever been invented for the game. There are no sharply defined criteria for the use of a word, in the sense that if we knew the criteria we could never conceivably be in the position of not knowing whether it is correct or incorrect to apply the word, given also that we knew all the relevant facts concerning the thing to which the word is to be applied, so that further observation would be of no help.

It is worth while to bring out Locke's point somewhat differently. If Russell's account is the right explanation of the condition under which a general name like 'horse' is applicable to each of a number of things, it is to be supposed that anyone who has applied the word correctly and continues to use it properly under a variety of circumstances will know the common property in virtue of which it is correct to apply it. If the reason why each of a number of animals is called 'horse' is that they have a common property ϕ, it would be a miracle if in continuing correctly to call more of the right animals 'horse' we nevertheless did not know ϕ. It would be as if a person in his everyday transactions made purchases with pound notes, never accepted the wrong change in coins, etc., but, in spite of this, did not know the monetary value of pound notes. The fact, however, that philosophers think a *search* for common properties is necessary, and that finding one in any particular case will constitute a *discovery,* implies exactly this. It implies that, at least frequently, and perhaps always, we do not know the common properties which make it correct for us to apply words to each of a class of individuals. It becomes difficult in such cases to see what the explanation of continued correct application could be. The Mormons once thought, when a person in a state of religious exaltation suddenly began to speak in strange syllables, that he was divinely inspired and talked sense; and when someone else in the congregation began to translate his words to the others, they thought that he too was divinely inspired and understood the words. Their explanation of what happened was intelligible, though undoubtedly false. And one might hold, in explanation of what happens in the case of the continued correct application of a

word, that this is due to divine assistance or to a mysterious influence the property exerts over our pens and tongues, or that it
just happens that we continue to use the word correctly while
remaining in ignorance of the property which makes our use
correct. It is hardly to be supposed, however, that philosophers
would offer any such explanation or find it acceptable. The only
remaining possible explanation of continued correct use of a word,
on the Platonic assumption, is that those who use the word know
the property for which it stands.

But then the idea that a word is applicable to each of a number
of things because they participate in a common essence, together
with the idea that some sort of search is necessary in order to discover the essence symbolized by the word, which we already are
able to use in everyday life, leads to a paradox. If in knowing how
to use the word correctly we must know the property ϕ in virtue
of which it is applied to things, there can be no problem of search-
ing for or discovering ϕ: to know the correct use of the word is
the same as knowing that ϕ is its meaning. If, on the other hand,
a *search* for a supposedly unknown property is necessary, then
there is no common property for which the word stands, no property
which is its meaning. Even if an examination of all the things to
which the word is applicable were to end in the discovery of a
property ϕ, common and unique to the things to which the word
is applicable, ϕ could not have been the property in virtue of the
possession of which by each of a number of things the word was
applicable to them.

In sum, if a word is applicable in virtue of ϕ, ϕ must be known;
and if, *in knowing its use,* we don't know of any common property
in virtue of which the word is applicable, we do then *know* that
it is not because the things have such a property that it is applicable to them. In neither case is a search sensible, or a relevant
discovery possible. It is a paradox, in view of this fact, that philosophers have thought a search was necessary and that after so
many years they apparently have failed to realize that it is not a
genuine search but is rather a pseudo-search. By asserting both
that abstract words stand for common properties and that the
properties are unknown and have to be discovered by a process
additional to the process of getting to know the use of words,
philosophers have, to all appearances, held a view according to

which *words have meanings which they were never given by anyone nor were known by anyone to have.* It is difficult to suppose that philosophers have really thought anything of this sort; and more directly with regard to the dispute over whether the meanings of words are common properties, it is difficult to see why Locke's familiar challenge should have had so little influence on other philosophers.

The *fact* with regard to abstract words is that they are applicable to each of a number of things because the things resemble each other more or less, without there being anything common to all of them to set exact boundaries which would mark off correct from incorrect applications of the words. And it is entirely reasonable to think that if the dispute concerned whether the things to which a word was applicable all had something in common, or were exactly similar in some respect or set of respects, it would have been resolved long ago in favour of Locke and others, instead of ending in a stalemate. It is to be expected as a *normal* thing that philosophers would come in time to see and admit the facts. How, then, is the apparent failure on the part of many philosophers over a long period of years to see and admit the facts to be understood? In only one way: as not actually constituting any such failure at all. In order to reach an understanding of what philosophers are saying, we must take into consideration the fact, which we have to take seriously, that they persist in apparently not seeing, what seems plain to us, that the adduced facts are inconsistent with their theory. When continued confrontation with plain fact does not make philosophers give up their theory, it is safest to proceed on the assumption, not that their intelligence is weak, but that somehow the facts do not count against the theory. Their behaviour clearly shows that they do not reckon the facts as constituting a reason for giving up the view that *they* are holding. Hence we are driven to conclude that the view which has naturally been attributed to these philosophers because of the manner in which they have expressed themselves, the view against which the facts do count, is *not* the view that they are holding. Their words have to be reconstrued in such a way that the facts do not refute what they are intended to express.

When philosophers assert that a word W is applicable to each of a number of things because they have a property in common, and continue to insist on this in face of the fact that the things to which W is applicable only resemble each other more or less without there being anything common to all of them *in virtue of which* W is applicable to each, they do not by their words wish to controvert fact. They mean, rather, to tell us something about their use of an expression, although they do this in an indirect and misleading way. A more explicit statement of what they assert is the following: A word is applicable to each of a number of things because *it stands for* the property which they all have in common. This, in an indirect way, informs us that to say a word is applicable to each of a number of things *is the same as* to say it stands for a common property.

Now we can see what they are doing: they wish, regardless of the facts, to *use* 'stands for a common property' to mean the same as 'is applicable to each of a number of things'. This explains why the facts do not count against what they are saying, and why the dispute over common properties ends in a stalemate. Some philosophers wish to use, and in their philosophical writings do use, 'stands for a common property' synonymously with, so that it means no more than, 'is applicable to each of a number of things', while other philosophers, like Locke, are opposed to their use of the expression. And since matter of fact is not in dispute, neither can win, and each can go his own way.

We are also now in a better position to see what the dispute over the existence of universals comes to. There is no controversy, no divergence of opinion, with regard to whether words have meanings, and there is no factual controversy over whether the meanings of words are common properties. But the tendency of many philosophers to use 'stands for a common property' synonymously with 'is applicable to each of a number of things' throws some light, as will later be seen, on the nature of the view that there are universals and the dispute regarding it.

Connected with the philosophical idea that the meanings of abstract words are common properties is the idea that common properties, or universals, are *entities,* different in kind from the things they are said to 'characterize' and such that they could exist even when characterizing nothing. It is not by an accidental use of language or merely for the purpose of expressing themselves more colourfully that some philosophers have asserted: 'Universals can be in many places at one time'. The statement 'Whiteness is now in many places' is not merely an unusual way of expressing the commonplace fact that there are many white things; it serves to bring out the point that, though they are very queer, universals are entities. By way of parenthetical observation, it may be remarked that philosophers like Stout, who seem to have been outraged by what they took to be a flagrant misuse of the word 'entity', a misuse in violation of the necessary proposition that nothing can be in several places at the same time and according to which we should have to say that there were self-contradictory entities, have argued that no object could be in 'local separation' from itself. It is self-contradictory to say 'Jones is now in two different parts of the world', and, as 'entity' is ordinarily used, it is self-contradictory to say 'The *entity* whiteness is now in a number of different parts of the world'. Thus, Prof. G. F. Stout let himself be governed by the ordinary, non-contradictory use of 'entity' and proposed a view according to which characters are particular.[1] Other philosophers, however, have not felt the force of the objection from the logical impossibility of 'local separation'. This, I think, is noteworthy. For if 'Some entities can be in many places at one time', rightly understood, were self-contradictory, one would expect that philosophers who have asserted it would give it up. Read in terms of ordinary usage, it is self-contradictory; and there is no particular difficulty in seeing this, no complicated chain of reasoning is involved. There is, therefore, some reason for thinking that it is *not* self-contradictory, that philosophers mean something different by it from what a literal interpretation of the words would make one think.

To return to the theory that there are such entities as universals, this theory implies that the meanings of abstract words, i.e., the meanings of general names, adjectives, etc., are entities. Since it is not to be supposed that the fact that abstract words have meanings is being asserted as a theory or is in question among philosophers, it may be gathered that what some philosophers have intended to convey is the theory that the meanings of such words are *entities*. Accordingly, what now would seem to be in dispute is not whether there are universals, but whether universals are entities, or, to include Ayer's position, whether it makes sense to

[1]'Are Characteristics Universal or Particular?', *Proc. Arist. Soc.,* Supp. Vol. 3.

say they are objects. It would appear to be a factual dispute about the nature of the meanings of words.

Is this a possible construction? Have some philosophers really claimed to have discovered a further fact, unknown by most people and disputed by others, the fact, namely, that the meanings of abstract words are objects? There is, in the first place, an air of absurdity about supposing that any philosopher has actually meant to hold this. No philosopher, or group of philosophers, would think of saying, 'Jones, like most men, knew his wife for thirty years, but never did know that she was not just a shadow, never did know that she was made of flesh and bones and had a temper'. And it is not easy to think that philosophers have ever held a theory of such a sort that they might naturally be imagined as saying, 'Like most men, Jones knew the meaning of "horse" for thirty years or more, but, oddly enough, he never did know it was an entity'. Were Diogenes alive we could hardly imagine him refraining from remarking that after thirty years and better of assurance based on knowledge by acquaintance Russell himself has become uncertain: 'I conclude, therefore, though with hesitation, that there are universals, and not merely general words.'[1] One might very appropriately ask what happened that an assurance based on *acquaintance* with universals, similar to acquaintance with sense-data, should have dissolved into uncertainty. Without labouring the point, it becomes justifiable to suspect that the view that universals are objects is not an empirical theory about the nature of the meanings of words. Berkeley and others, who appear to have placed a straightforward interpretation on the words philosophers have used to express this view, made the *Gedanken-experiment* of attempting to envisage 'abstract ideas', and came to the conclusion that there were no such entities, that is, that the meanings of words are not objects, over and above the tangible things, etc., to which the words are applicable. It would be absurd to think that what Russell has called a natural oversight could not be corrected by a serious effort. But it is a mistake to take the theory as empirical, to be established or refuted by some sort of examination of the meanings of words. 'Coming to know that universals are entities' describes no conceivable process of learning anything about the meanings of words.

[1] *An Inquiry into Meaning and Truth*, p. 436.

This, and at the same time what the theory comes to, can be seen if we keep in mind both the connexion of the idea that universals are entities with the contention, which is also the main source of the idea, that the meanings of general words are common properties, and also the form of speech philosophers sometimes use to express the relation between words and their meanings, viz., general words *stand for* universals. The view that universals, and therefore common properties, are entities of an abstract sort, when considered in conjunction with this form of speech, is readily seen to lead to the further statement that 'General words stand for abstract entities'. Nevertheless, in spite of their description of universals as being less tangible than the concrete things they characterize, as being non-sensuous, abstract objects to be gazed on only with the mind's eye, philosophers so use the phrase 'stands for a common property', or (to call attention to another of Russell's expressions) 'denotes a universal', that a word that is said to stand for or denote a common property does not stand for anything in addition to the things or events, etc., to which it applies. Also, thus, to say that a general word stands for an abstract entity does not mean that it denotes anything other than the concrete, particular things to which it is applicable.

It can now be seen that 'Universals are entities' does not, nor is it intended to, express a theory about the nature of the meanings of words, any more than to assert that general words stand for common properties or for abstract entities is to state a theory about the meanings of words. 'Universals are entities' means no more and no less than the expression it naturally brings to mind, namely, 'General words stand for abstract entities', which itself is only an alternative form of words for 'General words are applicable to each of a number of things'. But the intermediate expression has a further point.

'Abstract words stand for abstract entities' leads to 'Abstract words are the *proper names* of abstract entities'. Thus Russell speaks of universals as being *named* by words.[1] In effect philosophers may be construed as arguing: A word that is applicable to each of a number of things, events, etc., *stands for* the property they have in common; it therefore stands for an abstract entity; consequently, in addition to being the general name of each of

[1] *The Problems of Philosophy,* p. 147.

the things, etc., to which it is applicable, it is also a proper name, the proper name of an abstract object.[1] And since to be the proper name of an *abstract object* is not to be the name of an *object,* in any ordinary sense, we can see that in an indirect way what philosophers are saying is that abstract words are proper names, without their being the proper names of any things. Philosophers whom we may suppose to be saying this know, of course, that words like 'white', 'horse', 'running', 'similarity' are not commonly classified with proper names like 'Plato' and 'London'; and it is therefore natural to suppose that they are recommending, for various reasons, such a classification. By asserting that universals are entities, they are not, in an indirect way, making the obviously false statement that abstract words, as a matter of ordinary classification of parts of speech, are proper names. Rather, to put the matter provisionally, they are making in concealed form the *linguistic proposal,* 'Let us classify such words with proper names'. The statement 'Universals are entities' hides the linguistic proposal to reclassify, formally, abstract words with proper names.

I expect that the theory I am here stating or, for that matter, any modification of it, will hardly impress itself favourably on the minds of most philosophers. Nevertheless, with the help of this hypothesis a number of puzzling things connected with the philosophical view, which otherwise remain unexplained, can be cleared up. For one thing, it is completely puzzling to think what could have happened that would have made anyone *think* that universals have been discovered or that hardly anybody except students of philosophy know that there are universals. On the theory that the philosophical view is a linguistic proposal to reclassify abstract words with proper names it is not difficult to see what the 'discovery' refers to. Philosophers have actually discovered a new *possible* way of classifying words, and those people who are unaware of the existence of universals are merely unaware of this possibility. In a similar way it is possible to explain anyone's *thinking* that knowledge of the correct use of an abstract word does not imply knowledge of a universal; what he thinks but expresses in a misleading manner is that knowledge of the correct use of 'horse', for example, does not imply recognition of

[1]See C. I. Lewis, 'The Modes of Meaning', *Philosophy and Phenomenological Research,* Vol. IV, No. 2, pp. 238–9.

the possibility of classifying the word 'horse' with 'Dobbin', say. Also we can now understand why the controversy over universals should have continued without resolution for so many hundreds of years, which if it had been empirical or *a priori* would be astonishing beyond belief. If the dispute consists of counter-proposals with regard to altering linguistic conventions, then we can understand why the dispute should continue without resolution, although, it must be admitted, this does not explain the intense and recurrent interest in the problem. Perhaps further investigation, following John Wisdom's hint that philosophical views are the vehicles for expressing unconscious fantasies, will lead to an understanding of this point also. Furthermore, an increasing hesitation, after years of certainty about the existence of universals, like that in the case of Russell, can be made intelligible as an uncertainty about the appropriateness of the proposed verbal reclassification, an uncertainty induced by the fact that the *differences* between abstract words and proper names have come, for some reason, to impress themselves more on his mind; indecision would be reached when both the differences and similarities between abstract words and proper names impress themselves with equal force.

Finally, to cut matters short, we can understand why philosophers who hold that universals exist should be unmoved by the argument from the logical impossibility of an entity being in local separation from itself. The necessary proposition that no entity can be in more than one place at any given time does not deny the physical possibility of something happening which can be imagined or conceived as happening. If 'No entity can be in several places at one time' denied the possibility of a situation *described* by 'Entity a is in several places now', it would not express a necessary proposition, one which could not be false under any conceivable or describable circumstance. We make it express a necessary proposition by preventing 'Entity a is now in several places' from describing anything. Its import, if not its form, is thus verbal, to the effect that as 'entity' is actually used it makes no sense to say with regard to a named or described object that it is in several places at a given time: it tells us that such a sentence as 'Moore is now in Cambridge and also in Northampton' describes no state of affairs, makes no sense. Now, the merely *formal* reclassification of abstract words with proper names, without depriving them of their ordinary use as abstract words, carries with it the possibility of sensibly writing such sentences as 'Whiteness is now in many places', which are only bizarre expressions for familiar sentences like 'There are now many white things'. But the necessary proposition that no entity can be in several places at one time together with the philosophical proposition that universals can be in several places at the same time implies that universals are not entities. And one thing, although not the only one, which those who raise the objection from the logical impossibility of local separation are doing, is to point out that since the substitution of the proper name of an entity, e.g., a name like Russell, for x in 'x is now in many places' results in nonsense, whereas the substitution of 'whiteness', 'chairness', etc. does not, these words are not proper names of entities. They are not proper names at all, as 'proper name' is ordinarily used. Philosophers who make the reclassification proposal know, of course, that abstract words are not proper names. Their indifference to the objection is therefore to be construed as indicating an academic willingness to give up a necessary proposition for the sake of their proposal. They wish to classify abstract words with proper names without converting them into proper names of *entities*. And doing this involves changing the meaning of 'proper name' in such a way that from the fact that a word is a proper name it no longer follows that it is the name of an object; that is, the philosophical use of 'proper name' is no longer determined by the prevailing use of 'entity'. Berkeley's *Gedankenexperiment* can be seen as coming to nothing more than pointing out that abstract words are not proper names of entities, which fact he covertly urges against the formal reclassification of abstract words with proper names, against *calling* them proper names.

The fact that on the reclassification-proposal hypothesis it becomes possible to explain a number of otherwise puzzling features connected with the philosophical theory of universals is a positive reason in its favour. What Wisdom has pointed out about typical linguistic proposals,[1] however, shows that it is an *exaggeration* to characterize the theory as a proposal. For one thing, a philosopher

[1] John Wisdom, 'Philosophy, Anxiety and Novelty', *Mind*, April, 1944, p. 173.

who holds the theory of universals does not say 'Let us classify abstract words with proper names'. Instead he uses the language of assertion: 'There *are* such entities as universals', or, the assertion which it masks, 'Abstract words *are* proper names'. In view of this, it is undoubtedly closer to the facts to describe him as stating the notational classification of abstract words with proper names to be a fact, i.e., as actually asserting that abstract words *are* proper names, though in a subtly disguised way. His classification is not to be thought incorrect or improper,[1] through failing to correspond to the prevailing classification, but is to be viewed as a reclassification which, for some reason, he prefers. That is, it is not based on a mistake; it issues from a preference which may be determined by a hidden purpose, or by nothing more than considerations of convenience in developing a uniform notation for logic. It will be obvious that the preceding explanations of the various puzzling features connected with the view remain, with slight modifications, the same.

For another thing, in the usual case of a person making a verbal recommendation the intention is that the change be adopted for ordinary use as a regular thing. This, in the present case, the philosopher undoubtedly does not intend; he is not interested in having grammar books or the grammatical structure of ordinary sentences changed. It could be said that he is making an academic proposal, for esoteric adoption only. But again, it seems closer to the facts to describe what he does as making or maintaining an actual though academic reclassification of abstract words with proper names. And what he does is concealed from himself as well as from others. The view is an instance of linguistic magic, which, if we are to take seriously the panegyric expressions of philosophers over universals, gives rise to feelings which are appropriate to objects more wonderful and satisfying than those met with in sense-experience.

Wisdom also points out that it is usual in the case of an ordinary recommendation to give a reason for the proposed change. But this, in the present instance, is done in the form of 'proofs' advanced for the theory. These are actually statements which call attention to analogies that obtain between the use of expressions,

---

[1] For a different point of view see Norman Malcolm's paper, 'Moore and Ordinary Language', in *The Philosophy of G. E. Moore*.

on the basis of which philosophers feel justified in making the reclassification. The following brief argument will serve to illustrate this point. The meaning of a word is something different from the word. For instance, the meaning of 'horse' in English is the same as the meaning of the different word 'cheval' in French, i.e., the two different words have one and the same meaning, so that two people, each of whom knows one word and not the other, will know the same meaning. It must therefore be something over and above the words which express it. Like the case of a person who is called 'Jacques' by his French friends and 'James' by his English friends, the meaning of a word in English is an object named by the word, and either is or could be named by other words in different languages. What this proof *actually* shows is, not that the meaning of a word is an entity or, what comes to the same thing, that 'meaning' is a general name denoting abstract objects, but that 'meaning' is a substantive the grammatical use of which bears some resemblance to the use of general names denoting things. The argument calls attention to a linguistic similarity which is used by some philosophers to justify their classification of 'meaning' with general names of objects. In turn, this regulates the further reclassification of other abstract words with proper names.

The view expressed in this paper concerning the nature of the theory that there are such entities as universals is, of course, an interpretation which has been arrived at indirectly, by inference from certain assumptions that seemed to me to be reasonable but which may not impress others in the same way. It is, therefore, of interest to find independent confirmation in the form of a statement[1] from a philosopher which, except for the fact that it is combined with the Platonic theory, is a linguistically unconcealed expression of the reclassification view set out in this paper: 'It is convenient, however, to regard such general terms ["wise", "city"] as names on the same footing as "Socrates" and "Paris": names each of a single specific entity, though a less tangible entity than the man Socrates or the town Boston'.[2]

[1]Pointed out to me by Prof. Alice Ambrose.
[2]W. V. Quine, *Mathematical Logic*, p. 119.

IV

THE POSITIVISTIC
USE OF 'NONSENSE'

IN a recent paper in MIND[1] I developed a theory about the *nature* of the philosophical view that there are such objects as universals, which makes it out to be completely different from what it appears to be. The long-standing dispute over this view, a dispute into which positivists have in recent years entered with the contention that 'There are such entities as universals' is literally nonsensical, was given an explanation according to which it is not the factual disagreement it gives one the impression of being. Owing to an oversight, however, only the traditional part of the controversy was discussed, i.e., the controversy between those who deny and those who assert the existence of universals; there was no discussion of the positivistic contention. This omission it is my present purpose to rectify.

According to the theory arrived at in the paper, the words 'There are such entities as universals', though they create the semantical illusion[2] of stating the existence of objects, described by philosophers as being less coarse and more exact than the familiar objects of sense-experience, come to no more than does the statement 'Abstract words are proper names'. This statement is to be understood as describing an unorthodox classification of abstract words, made by people who know perfectly well that they are not proper names. Hence it is not to be taken as saying what is false, but as stating an alternative arrangement to the usual one of some parts of speech. Academically, and probably for psychological

---

[1]'The Existence of Universals', January, 1946.
[2]I owe this expression to Prof. Herbert Davis.

reasons, it is a reclassification which many philosophers prefer, with the established one being recognized as doing adequately the work required of it in ordinary discourse. The traditional dispute over the existence of universals thus turns out not to be factual, but what makes it irresolvable is *not* that not all the facts are known which are relevant and necessary for the conclusive establishment of either of the contending claims. The irresolvability is constituted by a difference in preference, and is comparable to the irresolvability of an aesthetic disagreement over a work of art. Some philosophers find the established classification satisfactory, and resist any innovation, even though the new classification is meant for contemplation rather than for practical use. Still others make up a different arrangement of their own. Thus, Prof. G. F. Stout, who holds that characters are particular, reclassifies adjectives with general names, for instance, 'tawny' with 'lion', and resists the further classification of both with proper names.

Many, if not all, positivists, contend that the view that there are universals, as well as the traditional disagreement with regard to it, is without any literal significance whatever. This claim, which extends to all of metaphysics, starts a new dispute in philosophy: one in which traditional philosophers insist that the sentence 'There are universals' is perfectly intelligible to them and that it does express something about which they can intelligibly disagree, while positivists hold that the sentence is really unintelligible and that the controversy with regard to what, supposedly, it expresses is nonsensical, though conducted in all seriousness. According to positivists philosophers have been 'duped by grammar' into 'the more inglorious kind of metaphysics which comes from a failure to understand the workings of our language'.[1] In turn, traditional philosophers fear the 'threatened catastrophe'[2] of 'the sombre conception of metaphysics which they have espoused'.[3]

The question thus comes up whether this new dispute is constituted by a straightforward difference of opinion about the *fact* with regard to 'There are universals', whether it is nonsensical or

[1] A. J. Ayer, *Language, Truth and Logic*, p. 39.
[2] E. A. Burtt, 'What is Metaphysics?', *The Philosophical Review*, Nov., 1945, p. 533.
[3] *Ibid.*, p. 557.

not. On the theory I have constructed about the view regarding universals two possibilities are open to me. I can hold that positivists have simply made a mistake, or I can hold that their view has an explanation similar in general respects to that of the traditional belief in universals. The first alternative lends itself more naturally to acceptance; but the second, nevertheless, seems to me to be the correct one. In any case it is the more interesting possibility to pursue; and it is interesting on its own account to see what evidence can be brought forward in its favour.

Ayer undoubtedly *thinks* that the positivistic assertion states a fact. He even goes to the length of trying to show 'how easy it is to write sentences which are literally nonsensical without seeing that they are nonsensical',[1] in order to defend himself against the charge that his view involves 'incredible assumptions about the psychology of philosophers'.[1] It seems to me, if we take the positivistic assertion as a factual linguistic statement which uses 'nonsense' in the way in which philosophers, both positivistic and traditional, appear to think it is being used, we must suppose that an incredible assumption about the psychology of philosophers *is* being made. One need only consider the duration of metaphysical problems and by what subtle reasoning philosophers have been led to their views in order to realize how entirely incredible the assumption really is. Nonsense does not have such a remarkable career. And it seems to me that the reason positivists do not feel that the assumption is incredible is that they are not really making it. It seems to me the assertion that the philosophical view about universals is nonsensical says something quite different from what it appears to be saying. Their use of language, which successfully conceals even from the positivists what they are doing, produces a semantical illusion similar to that produced by the traditional dispute. I propose to argue that the reasons they give for concluding that the view is nonsense constitute *true* statements about the view, but the 'conclusion' that it is nonsense is not a *conclusion*; it is something quite different.

Ayer writes:

It should be mentioned here that the fact that the utterances of the metaphysician are nonsensical does not follow simply from the fact that they are devoid of factual content. It follows

[1] *Language, Truth and Logic*, p. 36.

from that fact, together with the fact that they are not *a priori* propositions . . . We may accordingly define a metaphysical sentence as a sentence which purports to express a genuine proposition, but does, in fact, express neither a tautology nor an empirical hypothesis. And as tautologies and empirical hypotheses form the entire class of significant propositions, we are justified in concluding that all metaphysical assertions are nonsensical.[1]

This says two things about metaphysical sentences in general, both of which are true of 'There are such entities as universals'. For one thing, it says that the sentence fails to express an empirical proposition about the existence of objects of a certain kind. It must be admitted, of course, that the form of expression philosophers have used, from Plato on and including those who have disagreed with the view, leads one quite naturally to think that the existence of objects of some sort is being stated, for which 'a special non-empirical world is invoked to house them'.[2] But this is only a deceptive feature of their choice of language. Unlike 'Ghosts exist', 'There are such entities as universals' expresses no empirical proposition about entities. To agree with positivists on this point it is not necessary to adopt their special philosophical view about the nature of contingent propositions, the view, namely, that it is of their 'very nature'[3] to be hypotheses.

For another thing, the sentence does not express an *a priori* proposition. What we know in knowing an *a priori* proposition, e.g., the proposition that every effect has a cause, are facts about the established ways in which words are used in a language. Unlike what we should know if we knew that every event had a cause, namely, a fact about nature, what we know in knowing that every effect has a cause are the linguistic facts that 'effect' and 'cause' are so used that application of the word 'effect' to an event which would be described as not having a cause would be withheld. In other words, what we know is the linguistic fact that 'uncaused effect' has no use, that it describes nothing, either actual or imaginable. And when, in place of 'logically impossible', philosophers use 'logically inconceivable', as for example in 'It is logically inconceivable for any thing to be an effect which has no cause', it is not to be imagined that 'effect which has no cause'

[1] *Language, Truth and Logic*, pp. 31–2.　　[2] *Ibid.*, p. 35.　　[3] *Ibid.*, p. 23.

describes a state of affairs which, owing to some psychological limitation, we are unable to conceive; what prevents us from conceiving an uncaused effect is the linguistic fact that 'uncaused effect' is a senseless expression. The sentence 'Every effect has a cause', or its equivalent 'It is logically impossible for anything to be an effect and not have a cause', is *made* to express a necessary proposition by the fact that nothing is *called* an 'effect' to which the description 'has a cause' does not apply. But this is not to say that the sentence 'Every effect has a cause' *expresses* this fact, or, in general, that *a priori* propositions are verbal.

In this connexion Ayer has written: 'Thus if I say "Nothing can be coloured in different ways at the same time with respect to the same part of itself", I am not saying anything about the properties of any actual thing; but I am not talking nonsense. I am expressing an analytic proposition, which records our determination to call a colour expanse which differs in quality from a neighbouring colour expanse a different part of a given thing. In other words, I am simply calling attention to the implications of a certain linguistic usage'.[1] Ayer has remarked an important similarity between *a priori* and empirical linguistic propositions, between, for example, 'Nothing can be blue all over and also orange' and 'It makes no sense to say "x is blue all over and also orange".' The feature they have in common is that what we know in each case are facts about word usage. This led him to assimilate *a priori* with empirical linguistic propositions. Apparently positivists have been so impressed by this feature of similarity that in order to emphasize it they felt themselves justified in *stretching* the word 'verbal' to cover *a priori* propositions.

But this exaggerates a similarity at the expense of a formal difference, the difference between '*a priori*' and 'empirical', which impresses other philosophers. They in turn proceed to discover a contradiction in the view that *a priori* propositions are verbal: '*p* is a verbal proposition' implies that *p* is empirical, hence the view that *a priori* propositions are verbal entails the contradictory consequence that *a priori* propositions are empirical. It will be obvious that philosophers who argue in this way wish to emphasize not the similarity, but the difference between *a priori* and ordinary linguistic propositions. This they succeed in doing, as

[1] *Language, Truth and Logic*, p. 104.

their argument shows, by regulating the use of 'verbal' by reference to the feature of dissimilarity between the sentences for the two sorts of propositions, i.e., by reference to the fact that, unlike sentences for ordinary linguistic propositions, sentences for *a priori* propositions *do not express* facts about the ways words are used.[1] Thus, although what we know in knowing that nothing can be blue all over and also orange is that 'being blue all over and also orange' has no descriptive use, the sentence, 'Nothing can be blue all over and also orange' nevertheless does not *express* this linguistic fact. In short, if with positivists, we are impressed by one feature of *a priori* propositions we shall be inclined to call them 'verbal', and if, with other philosophers, we are impressed by the other feature we shall be inclined to deny them that designation. But regardless of the view we adopt both features are actual features of *a priori* propositions.

It will be clear now that the view that there are such entities as universals, taken as non-empirical, is nevertheless not *a priori*. In order for 'There are such entities as universals' to express an *a priori* proposition, 'Abstract words are proper names' would have to express a true empirical one. The first sentence would then be *made* to express a necessary proposition by the fact that abstract words were as a matter of established practice called 'proper names'; and what we should know in knowing that universals exist is that abstract words are grammatically classified as proper names. The facts of the case, with which philosophers who hold the view are not at all concerned, are, however, other than what is required to make the view *a priori*.

'Universals exist' expresses neither an *a priori* nor an empirical proposition. And since it 'purports to express a genuine proposition', i.e., since, for one thing, it is a sentence in the indicative, it is, according to Ayer's definition of 'metaphysical', a metaphysical sentence. Therefore it is nonsense. But how is 'nonsense' being used? It looks as though the word has its ordinary connotation, such that to say a metaphysical sentence is nonsensical is to say it is an unintelligible combination of words. It looks as if Ayer has

---

[1]The following paraphrase of the argument helps make this point clear: If an expression for an *a priori* proposition expressed linguistic facts (i.e., the facts we know in knowing the *a priori* proposition) the *a priori* proposition would be empirical.

arrived at the *conclusion* that the sentence with regard to universals is literally unintelligible as a result of having discovered certain facts about it. And when traditional philosophers disagree with positivists, it looks as if the disagreement is over the question whether in fact sentences, which all philosophers would agree state metaphysical views, are unintelligible or not. Ayer argues that because they express neither *a priori* nor empirical propositions he is 'justified' in concluding that they are without sense. Other philosophers, for whatever reasons they may give, disagree with this.

Let us look more closely at what Ayer has done. He defines a metaphysical sentence as one which purports to express a genuine proposition, but which actually expresses neither an empirical nor a necessary one; and from the fact that necessary and empirical propositions constitute the sum total of 'significant propositions' he feels justified in concluding that metaphysical sentences are nonsensical. It will have been noticed that in his demonstration he uses the *new* expression 'significant proposition' (as well as 'genuine proposition', apparently used synonymously with it), which he nowhere thinks it necessary to explain.[1] We may gather, therefore, that when he says that 'tautologies and empirical hypotheses form the entire class of significant propositions', he is *defining* 'significant proposition' and its equivalent, 'genuine proposition'. By this definition it means the same as 'tautologous or empirical proposition'. This explains why, with complete assurance and without the uncertainty induced by the suspicion that perhaps he has overlooked some propositions, he was able to assert that 'tautologies and empirical hypotheses form the *entire* class of significant propositions'. The demonstration thus proceeds directly from the fact that metaphysical utterances express no significant propositions (in the defined sense) to the conclusion he thinks that fact justifies him in drawing, namely, that they are nonsensical. But what does the conclusion tell us about meta-

[1]Ayer does not use 'proposition' and 'indicative sentence' synonymously, so that 'significant proposition' does not translate into the known expression 'significant sentence'. See *Language, Truth and Logic*, p. 121; also his *Foundations of Empirical Knowledge*, pp. 93–102, especially p. 102, where he writes: 'In general, we use the word "proposition" rather than "sentence" whenever we are concerned, not with the precise form of an expression, or the fact that it belongs to a particular language, but with its meaning'.

physical utterances in addition to what we already know about them from knowing the facts which are used to justify the conclusion?

It seems quite plain to me, in the first place, that Ayer is not making an empirical inference. It is not that from the fact that metaphysical sentences express neither *a priori* nor empirical propositions he concludes it to be *very likely*, or even certain, that they are nonsensical, in the usual sense of 'linguistic nonsense'. He gives the impression that perhaps he is doing this when he writes: 'Of course it is possible that the author of such a remark ["The Absolute enters into, but is itself incapable of, evolution and progress"] is using English words in a way in which they are not commonly used by English-speaking people, and that he does, in fact, intend to assert something which could be empirically verified. But until he makes us understand how the proposition that he wishes to express would be verified, he fails to communicate anything to us.'[1] This remark, together with the view he actually does hold about metaphysics, would lead one to think he was, perhaps, a stranger to a special language spoken with mutual understanding by others and that he concluded the language made no sense because he failed to understand anything said in it. Ayer's acquaintance with metaphysics prevents us, however, from thinking that he is in the situation of a person who knew just enough arithmetic to know that '$\sqrt{2}$' represented neither an integer nor a rational fraction and went on to make the mistaken empirical inference that it was senseless.

We should be closer to what he is saying if we supposed the conclusion to be *entailed* by what he states with regard to metaphysical utterances. And if we suppose this we should have to think that to say 'S is an indicative sentence which expresses neither an *a priori* nor an empirical proposition but S is not nonsensical' is to say something self-contradictory. But there is no ordinary use of 'nonsense' in English which makes the statement self-contradictory. If we look upon what Ayer has said as constituting a logical demonstration of the positivistic view we shall have to conclude that he mistakenly attributed a meaning to 'nonsense' which it does not have, and that the demonstration is invalid because it is based on this mistake. The author of an elementary book on mathematics wrote: 'Mathematics is not simple

[1] *Language, Truth and Logic*, p. 22.

in the sense of being non-mathematical', from which it follows that not even the easiest parts of mathematics are simple, even to God. And if the positivistic argument that because metaphysical sentences express neither *a priori* nor empirical propositions they are nonsensical is viewed as a logical demonstration, they may, without serious distortion of their position, be regarded as thinking that metaphysical utterances are nonsensical *in the sense* that they are indicative sentences which express neither *a priori* nor empirical propositions. But there is no such sense in English of 'nonsense', just as there is no sense of 'simple' according to which 'simple' means 'non-mathematical'.

It is difficult for me, however, to believe that Ayer and other philosophers have made the mistake of thinking that 'nonsense' has a meaning which in fact it does not have in English. It is not too much to expect, if they did make a mistake of this sort, that they would have corrected it by now, especially in view of the fact that so many philosophers have protested against their claim. Nor is it easy to see, supposing this is their mistake, why other philosophers have not in so many words pointed it out to them. In the case of the writer on mathematics we should not be inclined to say that he committed the error of attributing to 'simple' a meaning it does not have in English usage. We should rather be inclined to say he *gave* it that meaning. And in the case of the positivistic use of 'nonsense', it seems to me that the same thing has happened, i.e., that positivists have given a new use to 'nonsense'. It seems to me more likely that a number of philosophers have unconsciously agreed upon a new use of the word than that they have made a mistake in common.

It will be recalled that in his demonstration 'significant proposition', was introduced via a concealed definition, and it seems to me to be not at all unplausible t o suppose that he repeats this procedure, or something like it, with the word 'nonsense'. On this assumption, his 'demonstration' turns out to be both an explanation of and the justification for a new use of 'nonsense', which, because it is stated in the form of a demonstration, effectively conceals what is being done, from himself as well as from others. His 'conclusion', then, turns out to be a linguistic innovation. It introduces us to the positivistic use of 'nonsense', according to which 'nonsensical indicative sentence' means the same as 'indicative sentence which expresses neither an *a priori* nor an empirical proposition'. And when in his demonstration he states that 'we are justified in concluding . . .' he is 'justifying' an extension of the application of 'nonsense' to metaphysical statements. The fact that a given indicative sentence expresses neither an *a priori* nor an empirical proposition is a necessary condition for saying that the sentence is nonsense, and Ayer wishes to make it also a sufficient condition. He wishes to make 'expressing no significant proposition' the sole criterion for the application of 'nonsensical' to indicative sentences. And from the fact that without being compelled by the logical requirements of his demonstration to introduce into the statement of it the expression 'significant proposition' (which carries with it the connotation of importance), we may gather what he considers to be a justification for the new use of 'nonsense'. There is an important similarity between, e.g.:—

'7 is a more nearly circular number than 2'.

'There are such entities as universals'.

The first expresses no proposition whatever; it says nothing at all and is nonsensical. The second expresses neither an empirical nor a necessary, i.e., no *significant,* proposition. The difference between the two sorts of sentences Ayer apparently counts as being so insignificant, or unimportant, as to feel justified in bringing out their similarity, which he does by changing the meaning of 'nonsensical' so as to make it applicable to both.

If, now, after having decided to call them both 'nonsense', the difference between them impresses itself upon the attention of a philosopher, he may proceed to mark the difference by calling one 'important nonsense'.[1] In a slightly different connexion some positivists, against the protest of others, have actually done this sort of thing: '. . . if we adopt conclusive verifiability as our criterion of significance, we are logically obliged to treat these general propositions of law [e.g., "arsenic is poisonous" and "a body tends to expand when it is heated"] in the same fashion as we treat the statements of the metaphysician. In face of this difficulty, some positivists have adopted the heroic course of saying that these general propositions are indeed pieces of nonsense, albeit

[1]Some positivists have done this by characterizing metaphysics as a kind of poetry. This is enlightening.

an essentially important type of nonsense. But here the introduction of the term "important" is simply an attempt to hedge'.[1] Ayer instead proposes to be more 'liberal'[2] with expressions for general propositions; he thinks they 'should be allowed'[3] the designation 'factually significant'. We may very well be curious about what kind of liberality and what kind of allowing these are. It does not require much imagination to see what they come to. It is plain to be seen that, in the case of expressions for general propositions, Ayer is being *liberal* with the application of 'factually significant'. And it is also plain to be seen that he prefers not to be so liberal in the case of metaphysical sentences.

The philosophical view that metaphysics consists of statements that are devoid of sense is not the view it gives one the impression of being. It only states the fact that metaphysical sentences do not express either empirical or necessary propositions. But at the same time it uses a familiar word in a new way, so that it looks to be saying one thing, while it actually says something else. It is this new, and as yet not established, use of 'nonsense' that is in dispute. Some philosophers wish to *call* metaphysical utterances 'nonsensical', and they attain their end by covertly redefining the word, without being explicitly aware of what they are doing. The *sting* in what they say about metaphysics is in the selection of the word upon which they bestow their special meaning. Undoubtedly their choice of the word 'nonsense' indicates an attitude of disapproval of anyone doing metaphysics: behind the linguistic screen we can detect the emotional evaluation, 'Metaphysics is trivial and absurd'. We can glimpse the same thing behind the definition of '*significant* proposition'. And when other philosophers protest that metaphysics is not nonsense, they are protesting against both the evaluation and the philosophical use of 'nonsense'.

[1]*Language, Truth and Logic,* pp. 23–4. See also comment by F. P. Ramsey, p. 263, *The Foundations of Mathematics.*
[2]*Ibid.,* p. 26.
[3]*Ibid.,* pp. 24–5.

V

STRONG AND WEAK
VERIFICATION I

THE class k of non-*a priori* declarative sentences formulable in a given language, i.e., sentences of such a form that if they express anything they express empirical propositions, consists of the classes k', of sentences having literal significance, and k'', of sentences lacking literal significance. Sometimes (and always, according to some philosophers, when we are doing metaphysics) we talk nonsense, under the illusion that what we say is intelligible. In order to obviate this sort of confusion, especially with regard to metaphysical sentences which, if they belong to k'', at least do not obviously lack meaning, these philosophers have formulated a criterion by the use of which we are enabled, supposedly, to decide with regard to any k-sentence whether it is a member of k' or of k''. This is to the effect that any k-sentence s is literally significant if and only if the proposition expressed by s is verifiable.[1] [$\phi(p) = p$ is verifiable, $\psi(s) = s$ is literally significant, $e(s, p) = s$ expresses p]:

$$(s, p): s\varepsilon k \; . \; e(s, p) \; . \supset . \; \psi(s) \equiv \phi(p) \qquad \text{.............(I)}$$

In a previous paper,[2] I attempted to show that this could not be taken as a criterion of literal significance for k-sentences. For if a k-sentence s fails to express a proposition, and so is meaningless, by application of the criterion solely we could not decide whether s is literally significant. That is, its application under these circumstances would be vacuous. But if s does express a proposition,

[1] A. J. Ayer, *Language, Truth and Logic*, pp. 19–20.
[2] 'The Principle of Verifiability', *Mind*, Vol. XLVI, N.S., No. 183.

thereby being subject to non-vacuous application of this principle, it could be the case, as this criterion allows, that p is *unverifiable*, from which it would follow both that s had meaning, since it expresses a proposition, and that it lacked meaning, since p is unverifiable. I understand now,[1] that A. J. Ayer is prepared to reformulate this criterion, to the effect that any k-sentence is literally significant if and only if s is verifiable:

$$(s) : s\varepsilon k \:.\: \supset \:.\: \psi(s) \equiv \phi(s) \qquad \dots\dots\dots\dots\dots\dots\dots\text{(II)}$$

But I fail to see what could be meant by saying that a *sentence* is verifiable, nor what could be meant by saying that a *sentence* is true or false, though some philosophers say this sort of thing.[2]

In this paper, however, my object is to discuss a further point, in connexion with the principle of verifiability, which is independent of either form I or form II. This concerns the distinction between 'weak' and 'strong' verifiability. It is my intention to show that this supposed distinction is a pseudo one, i.e., that there is in point of fact no distinction between 'strong verifiability' and 'weak verifiability', not because 'strong verifiability' and 'weak verifiability' mean the same but because they are so used that they have no meaning at all. In order not to prejudice what follows with respect to the version, (I) or (II), which one may hold with regard to the principle of verifiability, I shall use the term 'statement', rather than either 'proposition' or 'sentence'. The term 'statement' may be used indifferently, so far as the discussion is concerned, to mean either sentence or proposition.

k'-statements (i.e., literally significant k-sentences, or propositions expressed by such sentences) are, in the first place, to be distinguished with respect to being either 'practically verifiable' or 'theoretically verifiable',[3] where of course any practically verifiable statement will also be theoretically verifiable, but not conversely. This distinction is required in order to avoid condemning as meaningless such obviously significant statements as 'There are mountains on the dark side of the moon' and 'There are human beings on Venus'. Thus, for example, the statement 'There are

---

[1]As the result of a conversation with him.

[2]In discussing this point with a logical positivist who 'dispensed' with propositions I was offered the following definition of 'true sentence': a sentence is true if it expresses a true proposition!

[3]*Language, Truth and Logic,* pp. 20–1.

human beings on Venus' is theoretically verifiable only, because 'we lack the practical means of placing ourselves in the situation where relevant observations could be made';[1] whereas 'There is an inkspot on the underside of my sheet of paper' is practically verifiable because no such means for making relevant observations are lacking. Now according to Ayer, if such obviously significant statements as 'arsenic is poisonous' are also not to be condemned as meaningless, 'a further distinction which we must make is the distinction between the "strong" and the "weak" sense of the term "verifiable".'[2] He then proceeds to define 'strong verifiability' and 'weak verifiability'.

Before considering his definitions, however, it is important to notice a certain point about his statement. It may look as if he is intending to make a distinction, perhaps for the sake of avoiding confusion, between two *different senses* of 'verifiable', one to be designated the 'weak' sense and the other to be designated the 'strong' sense. This, however, does not seem to me to be his intention. It does not seem to me that he wishes to distinguish between different senses of 'verifiable'; but rather that he wishes to distinguish between the meanings of the expressions 'strongly verifiable' and 'weakly verifiable', where in each expression 'verifiable' is to have the *same* meaning. I.e., 'a statement S is verifiable means 'S is such that relevant observations could be made with respect to it', and to say that S is 'strongly' or 'weakly' verifiable is to say something *in addition* to this. His statement might be misleading in the way it would be misleading for someone to say that he was going to distinguish the 'black' and the 'white' sense of 'men', when what he wanted to do was to distinguish between 'black men' and 'white men'. It is important to notice this point. For if it is *also* his intention, as it seems to me to be, to use 'strong' and 'weak' in such a way that they are *opposite* in meaning, so that the assertion 'S is weakly verifiable' would be inconsistent (in some or other respect) with the assertion 'S is strongly verifiable', then his definitions of 'strong verification' and 'weak verification' will not be *independent,* in the sense that one could have meaning while the other lacked it. That is, if he is using 'strongly verifiable' and 'weakly verifiable' in such a way that 'S is strongly

[1]*Language, Truth and Logic,* p. 21.
[2]*Ibid.,* p. 22.

(or weakly) verifiable' entails both that S is verifiable and that it is *not,* in some or other respect, weakly (or strongly) so, then if he is using 'strongly verifiable' unintelligibly he will also be using 'weakly verifiable' unintelligibly.

Ayer's definitions are the following: 'A proposition is said to be verifiable, in the strong sense of the term, if, and only if, it could be conclusively established in experience. But it is verifiable in the weak sense, if it is possible for experience to render it probable.'[1] We may gather from this that he wishes so to use 'strongly verifiable' and 'weakly verifiable' that 'S is strongly verifiable' is to mean 'S could be conclusively established in experience' and 'S is weakly verifiable' is to mean 'S could be rendered probable in experience'.

It is easy enough, first, to see what Ayer means by the expression 'in experience'. He means looking, feeling, and the like, i.e., making our *own* observations, as opposed, for example, to asking someone else to look, etc., for us, and then accepting his word as evidence for the truth of a statement. Accordingly, 'conclusively established in experience' may be supposed equivalent in meaning to 'conclusively established by looking, feeling, etc.'; and similarly for 'rendered probable in experience'. We do of course verify statements in both ways, *directly,* by looking ourselves, as well as *indirectly,* by having others look for us and accepting their reports. And Ayer does not, it may be supposed, exclude the latter form of verification, since every statement which is verified for us (e.g., newspaper reports about conditions in remote regions of the world) *could* be directly verified by us, at least in principle. It would now be an easy matter to see what he means by 'strongly' and 'weakly' verifiable if we could see how he was using 'conclusively established' and 'rendered probable'.

Ordinarily 'conclusively established' and 'rendered probable' (in experience) are so used that we say we conclusively establish a statement S by looking, feeling, and doing various other things, where after doing a number of such things, one or more as the circumstances require, further observations will be unnecessary; and if circumstances are such that S can be conclusively established only by looking, feeling, etc., we say we can render S probable only, when, e.g., we just look. According as circumstances re-

[1] *Language, Truth and Logic,* p. 22.

quire, by looking, feeling, etc., we *make certain,* or get to *know,* that a statement is true, whereas sometimes by looking alone, or feeling alone, we fail to make certain, although we may thus make relatively certain of the statement, or get to know that it is probably true. 'The way to find out whether one has seen a thing right, if one is in doubt, is to get nearer and try to touch it, pick it up, use it, etc. E.g., there may be a dish of fruit before me: my hosts are known practical jokers: are those real apples or not? I cannot tell by looking only, or even by picking one up, but must try biting one. (I can only find out their nature through practice.) Or again, is that a pen on my desk or just a shadow; I tell by what I feel on putting out my hand. I.e., by further activity I tell whether I was right or wrong in taking there to be a pen there, or the apples to be real ones'.[1] It will be clear that in those cases where we cannot get to know, or establish conclusively, that a certain statement S is true, because we are prevented in one way or another from doing more than looking, for example, it will nevertheless be possible, *in principle,* by further activity, to establish S conclusively.

But is Ayer using 'conclusively established' and 'rendered probable' (in experience) in these ways? Is he using them in such a way that it is proper to say, after a certain amount of investigation, that we have rendered a statement probable, have fallen short of establishing it conclusively, but that further investigation *could* establish it conclusively? It seems to me that he is not using the terms in this way, and furthermore that he is using them in such a way that they lack meaning altogether, with the consequence that he fails to give meaning to 'strong' and 'weak' verification.

Originally, in opposition to the view that in order to be literally significant *k*-statements had to be conclusively verifiable,[2] Ayer held that 'no proposition is capable, even in principle, of being verified conclusively, but only of being rendered highly probable'.[3] Accordingly, he held that 'the question that must be asked about any putative statement of fact is not, Would any observations make its truth or falsehood logically certain? but simply, Would any observations be relevant to the determination of its truth or falsehood?'[4] From these statements, as well as from others

---

[1] G. A. Paul, 'Lenin's Theory of Perception', *Analysis,* vol. 5, no. 5, p. 72.
[2] *Language, Truth and Logic,* p. 23.   [3] *Ibid.,* p. 214.   [4] *Ibid.,* pp. 25-6.

he makes,[1] it is very difficult to ascertain what precisely he is trying to say. It looks as if he intends to assert that there *could be no k'*-statement which was open to conclusive verification, even in principle, i.e., that it is *impossible* for there to be a statement which is both a member of *k'* and also conclusively verifiable. Thus he says: 'Empirical propositions are one and all hypotheses, which may be confirmed or discredited in actual sense-experience. And the propositions in which we record the observations that verify these hypotheses are themselves hypotheses which are subject to the test of further sense-experience. Thus there are no final propositions'.[2]

If it is correct to inpute to him the view that no possible *k*-statement could be both literally significant and conclusively verifiable, then it seems to me that he is holding something from which it follows that the *distinction* between 'strong' and 'weak' verifiability is unintelligible. For the only reason for which one could suppose that there could not be, or that it is *inconceivable* that there should be, such statements, is that it *did not make sense* to say that there were. And the only reason for which one could suppose it does not make sense to say that there are conclusively verifiable *k'*-statements is that the expression 'conclusively verifiable' is devoid of literal significance. That is, if 'conclusively verifiable' were a literally significant expression it would have to make sense to say that there were conclusively verifiable statements, although it might be false to say that there were. Moreover, if the assertion 'There are conclusively verifiable statements' failed to make sense I do not see how 'There are *inconclusively* verifiable *k'*-statements (i.e., statements which could be rendered probable)' could be an intelligible form of words.

Prof. Braithwaite, however, supposes Ayer to hold merely that there are no conclusively verifiable *k'*-statements, and not that there could not be: 'Now in his book Ayer gives no instances of strongly verifiable or of strongly falsifiable propositions—for the very good reason that, at the time when he wrote the book, he did not believe that there were any instances of such propositions'.[3] From this I take it that Braithwaite supposes him to hold

---

[1]*Language, Truth and Logic*, pp. 132–5.   [2]*Ibid.*, p. 132.
[3]R. B. Braithwaite, 'Propositions about Material Objects', *Proc. Arist. Soc.*, Vol. XXXVIII, p. 270.

an *empirical view about statements* of a certain sort, to the effect that *there are none*. If he is right, it seems to me that Ayer is asserting something which is philosophically irrelevant, as being concerned with matter of fact. And if he is holding that there could be such statements one might suppose that a little ingenuity on his part would have sufficed to produce *examples* of the sort of statements he had in mind and so saved him the trouble of holding a view to the defence of which he devoted a good deal of time. At any rate 'he has since been converted to the more reasonable view that there are such propositions, and in his paper to the Aristotelian Society last year he gives instances of them'.[1]

One thing which may now be seen with regard to the purported distinction between 'strong' and 'weak' verification is that it is to be used as a distinction by reference to which the class *k'* of verifiable *k*-statements is to be divided into the mutually exhaustive sub-classes:—

(α) the class of strongly verifiable statements

(β) the class of weakly verifiable statements.

Moreover, it is not to be used as a distinction, like the one between practical and theoretical verification, according to which all *k'*-statements are verifiable in principle, although only some are verifiable in practice. That is, it is not to be used as a distinction by reference to which *all k'*-statements are to be supposed open, in principle, to strong verification, while only some are to be supposed open to it in practice. Rather, it is to be used in such a way that at least some, if not all, weakly verifiable statements could not with literal sense be said to be strongly verifiable, even in principle.

It might be supposed that no *k'*-statement S could be weakly verifiable (i.e., it would not make sense to say it was) unless it were verifiable conclusively, at least in theory. It might be supposed that although I could not conclusively establish S in my present circumstances I nevertheless could conceive myself to be in circumstances in which I could establish it conclusively. For to suppose that S could be rendered probable, that there could even be 'overwhelming reasons for believing' S, but that it could not in principle be established conclusively, would be to suppose

[1] R. B. Braithwaite, 'Propositions about Material Objects', *Proc. Arist. Soc.,* Vol. XXXXIII, p. 270.

that there is a goal, viz., the conclusive establishment of S, to which we can get closer and closer but which, because of the *nature* of S, we could not even in conception attain. But this does not seem to me to make sense.

Ayer, however, seems to think otherwise, but I do not propose to pursue this point further here. At any rate, it will obviously not make sense to say that there are weakly, or inconclusively, verifiable statements unless it also makes sense to say that there could be conclusively verifiable ones. Ayer now holds that there are such statements. He writes:'. . . my being in pain will verify the proposition that I am in pain. Why? Because when I say "I am in pain" I mean I am in pain, and if *p* then *p*. But how do I establish *p*? How do I know that I really am in pain? Again the answer can only be "I feel it"'.[1] Similarly, but with greater generality, Braithwaite writes: 'Any proposition about a present experience of mine is verified by my having the experience or falsified by my not having the experience. And this sort of verification is strong verification: the proposition that I am now seeing blackish patches is "conclusively established" in my experience, the proposition that I am now in pain is conclusively disestablished in my experience'.[2]

Braithwaite holds this, namely, that 'there are propositions which are strongly verifiable in Ayer's sense',[3] because he thinks that sometimes he has 'knowledge of empirical propositions which is *direct*'.[3] It will be clear from this more precisely what sort of statements Ayer intends *a*, the class of conclusively verifiable statements, to consist of. It is to consist *solely* of *k'*-statements of which we can have 'direct knowledge', i.e., statements about

[1] A. J. Ayer, 'Verification and Experience', *Proc. Arist. Soc.,* Vol. XXXVII, p. 154.

[2] 'Propositions about Material Objects', p. 271.

[3] *Ibid.,* p. 271. Braithwaite speaks also as if propositions about past and future experiences of mine are strongly verifiable. But his account is too brief and unclear for me to see what he is trying to say. For example, he uses the expression 'direct knowledge by memory' (p. 272), to which I can attach no meaning. If I understand his use of 'direct knowledge', it seems to me nonsensical to speak of *direct* knowledge of propositions about past or future experiences. And if he wishes to hold that only those propositions are strongly verifiable of which he can have direct knowledge, then it must be supposed that only propositions about present experiences of mine are to be taken as strongly verifiable, on his view. See 'Verification and Experience', p. 155.

'present experiences of mine'. And β is to consist of all other k'-statements.

Both Ayer and Braithwaite are using 'strongly verifiable' in such a way that whenever it is true to say that we have strongly verified in experience, or conclusively established, a given statement, it will also be true to say that we *know* it to be true. And it is plain, of course, that I can be said to know whether such statements as 'I am now having a pain' and 'I am now seeing blackish patches', i.e., statements 'about a present experience of mine', are true. But does it make sense to say that I could *verify* such statements, in the sense that by verifying them I obtain knowledge, which I should otherwise lack, *as the result of making certain observations*? It looks as if in attempting to verify the statement 'I now have a pain' I should have to start with a statement the truth of which I do not know and then proceed to establish it by making certain *observations,* as if, e.g., I could start in ignorance of the pain I am now having and then make certain that I was having it by 'feeling it'! But this obviously does not make sense. It does not make sense to say 'I am going to verify whether I am now having a pain' or 'I am going to verify a statement about a present experience of mine'—as if I were intending to find out whether I am now having a certain experience, which I was not aware of having before looking, and could only find out as a result of looking.

Braithwaite, although he holds that we can verify statements about our present experiences, nevertheless, gives substantially the same sort of reason, it seems to me, for supposing that it does not make sense to say that we could. For he maintains that my knowledge of any statement about my present experience is such that '*I can give no reason* for it (except by repeating that I know it, if that is to be called a reason)'.[1] By these words, I take it, he intends to convey that sentences of the form 'I know, for the following reasons . . ., that I am now having a pain' are lacking literal significance, not because reasons are difficult to find, but because none *could* be found, i.e., it does not make sense to say there are any. Similarly, therefore, such sentences as 'I have conclusively verified that I am now having a pain' will also fail to have sense.

It seems to me, thus, that statements about present experiences of mine (to which we may now understand a-statements to be

[1]'Propositions about Material Objects', p. 271. Italics my own.

confined), though obviously literally significant, are such that to assert with regard to them that they are verifiable conclusively, or for that matter, inconclusively, is simply to say something which is devoid of sense. It appears to me that Braithwaite and Ayer have been misled into talking such nonsense as a result of using the word 'verify' in two different senses, viz., the sense of *make true*, and the different sense of *establish by relevant observations,* while supposing that they were using 'verify' in the latter sense alone. Thus in the sentences 'My being in pain will verify the proposition that I am in pain' and 'Any proposition about a present experience of mine is verified by my having the experience' the word 'verify' is used, if intelligibly, to mean 'make true'. That is, the first sentence, for example, means the same as 'My being in pain will make true the proposition that I am in pain'. And these sentences will be nonsensical if we use 'verify' to have the other meaning: It does not make sense to say 'My being in pain will establish by relevant observations the proposition that I am in pain'. In holding that it is possible to verify such statements as 'I am now having a pain' it seems to me that Ayer and Braithwaite are simply confusing these senses of 'verify'.

It will be clear, then, if Ayer's supposed distinction between 'strong' and 'weak' verification is to be made understandable, that it must be taken as a distinction holding exclusively with respect to statement of (β), such that at least some will be strongly verifiable, either practically or theoretically. For the statements of (β), namely, those not 'about present experiences of mine', i.e., statements about physical objects, other people, laws of nature, etc.,[1] will be the only possible k'-statements left with regard to which it could be significantly said that they are verifiable. It may be remarked here, that the principle of verifiability, even if it could be taken as a criterion of literal significance for k'-sentences, could not be supposed to be such a criterion for *all* k'-sentences, but for those of β only.

But with regard to β-statements, which Ayer thinks are all hypotheses,[2] he holds that they are not 'capable, even in principle, of being verified conclusively, but only at best of being rendered highly probable'.[3] He writes: 'I cannot carry out all the tests which

---

[1]*Language, Truth and Logic,* pp. 23, 147, 203, 214.
[2]*Ibid.,* p. 132.   [3]*Ibid.,* p. 214.

would bear upon the truth of even so simple a proposition as that my pen is lying on my desk. In practice, therefore, I accept such a proposition after making only a limited number of tests, perhaps only a single test, which leaves it still possible that it is false'.[1] Braithwaite argues in the same vein: 'Moreover, these propositions cannot be strongly verified by any finite number of experiences: it is possible that there should not, in fact, be a clock on the mantelpiece now even if there appears to be one whenever I (or indeed other people) look. I may acquire by looking, feeling and consulting other people overwhelming reasons for believing the proposition, reasons so adequate that (if the proposition is true) it is better English to say I know the proposition than that I merely believe it. But my knowledge is always corrigible in the sense that it is logically possible that I am mistaken: the proposition can never be verified in Ayer's strong sense of verification'.[2]

We might ask 'What *prevents* me from carrying out all the tests which bear upon the truth of "there is a pen on my desk"?' Apparently a large number of tests won't establish it conclusively, and neither will any *finite* number of observations enable me to know with certainty that there is a pen on my desk. If, however, a finite number is not sufficient, will an *infinite* number do—so that after an infinite number of observations I shall know (incorrigibly) that there is a pen on my desk? But Braithwaite and Ayer deny that it is *logically possible* to make an infinite number of observations, as if there were a *logical obstacle* which prevents me from making them. There is nothing, however, no task which I cannot *conceive* myself as doing, even though circumstances may be such as to prevent me from actually doing it. So if it made sense to say 'after an infinite number of observations I conclusively established that there is a pen on my desk' then I *could* (in conception) establish it conclusively. But Ayer holds that such statements are not open, even theoretically, i.e., in conception, to conclusive verification. He may hold this because he thinks either that it does not make sense to talk about an infinite number of verifications,[3] or, if it does make sense, that even an infinite number of observations

---

[1] *Verification and Experience,* p. 147.
[2] 'Propositions about Material Objects', pp. 273–4.
[3] A. Ambrose, 'Finitism and "The Limits of Empiricism",' *Mind,* Vol. XLVI, No. 183, pp. 383–4.

won't establish the statement conclusively. For I could be suffering from a consistent hallucination with respect to all my senses, and if a finite number of observations might be hallucinatory[1] in an internally coherent way there is no reason to suppose that an infinite number could not similarly be hallucinatory. It looks as if the possibility of having hallucinatory experiences or the impossibility of making an infinite number of observations were obstacles which prevent me, *in principle,* from ever conclusively establishing β-statements. But there could only be *such* obstacles—obstacles of such a sort that I could not conceive what it would be like to overcome them (and not because of some mental deficiency on my part, but because of the *nature* of the obstacles)—if to assert 'I have conclusively established S' was to assert something devoid of literal significance. For to assert 'I shall conclusively establish S' would be to assert something the attainment of which is inconceivable, i.e., I could not know what it would be like to attain it. And if that is the case, it does not make sense to say they are obstacles, as if their presence prevented me from attaining a certain goal. For there is no goal.

Braithwaite, indeed, seems to me to hold in effect, at least with regard to those β-statements which are about material objects (and I think also with regard to all β-statements), that they could not intelligibly be said to be conclusively verifiable. He asserts: 'This "corrigibility" is not an accidental feature of this proposition about the clock: it is an *essential* feature of all propositions about material objects'.[2] And he would thus seem to hold it to be *unthinkable*[3] that they could be strongly verified, i.e., that it does not make sense to say that they are.

I do not, therefore, see that 'strongly verifiable' has been given any meaning whatever. Apparently it is not being used in the way it is used in ordinary discourse, namely, in the sense in which we should say that we 'have conclusively established' that there is a pen on my desk if we have looked at it, felt it, and used it in various ways. Braithwaite seems to be aware of this fact. He writes: 'There is a clock on my mantelpiece now is not strongly verifiable. In ordinary language it is *natural* to say that I verify this

---

[1]'Propositions about Material Objects', p. 273.
[2]*Ibid.,* p. 273. Italics my own. See also, *Language, Truth and Logic,* p. 23.
[3]L. Wittgenstein, *Tractatus Logico-Philosophicus,* 4. 123.

proposition by looking. But this is not Ayer's strong sense of verification.'[1] It would appear thus that Ayer and Braithwaite intend to use it *unnaturally* in such a way that nothing we could *conceivably do* would be sufficient to verify conclusively a β-statement. This use of 'conclusively verifiable' is not merely unnatural but also senseless. And if it is senseless I do not see that 'weakly verifiable' has sense as they use it; nor do I see how Braithwaite could hope to give an account of 'a "weaker" verification of material-object propositions . . . *in terms of* strong verification in my experience'.[2]

[1] 'Propositions about Material Objects', p. 273. Italics my own.
[2] *Ibid.*, pp. 272–3.

VI

STRONG AND WEAK
VERIFICATION II

IN his introduction to the second edition of *Language, Truth and Logic* (1946) Professor Ayer attempts to meet objections[1] to his view that non-basic empirical propositions are, in principle, only weakly verifiable by resorting to two moves. First, he exchanges the position that basic statements are not propositions for the position that they are empirical propositions which are open to conclusive verification. And second, by holding that basic propositions are strongly verifiable he tries to reinstate the usual distinction between strong and weak verification, or rather he tries to secure the legitimacy of his application of the term 'weakly verifiable' to non-basic empirical propositions while withholding application of 'strongly verifiable' to them by contending now that the term 'strongly verifiable' has an application to basic propositions. To the casual reader these moves might seem to strengthen the paradoxical position that non-basic empirical propositions are at best weakly verifiable, e.g., that the truth-value of the statement 'There is a restaurant in the London School of Economics' can be rendered probable but cannot be established conclusively. To more careful readers these moves might seem to be downright mistakes. But if they are, they are very curious mistakes. For they are so transparent that it is not easy to see how a careful thinker could possibly have made them. And it is unsatisfactory to say, 'Well, he just made them and that is all there is to it'.

The words 'transparent', 'obvious', 'clear' are, to be sure, psychological words which are often used to cajole or intimidate or to

[1] Made in the preceding study, 'Strong and Weak Verification I'.

make a display of one's mental quickness. There is a story that G. H. Hardy passed over a step in the proof of a mathematical theorem he was lecturing on to his class with the comment, 'This is obvious'. His students objected that it was not obvious to them and asked for the explanation. Hardy, who apparently was taken aback by the objection, left the lecture room to look over the omitted step and after a few minutes' deliberation returned and announced to the class, 'Yes, it is obvious. We shall go on'. Whichever of the three motives the tale about Hardy illustrates, my intention in saying that Ayer's mistakes are transparent is none of these. When I say they are obvious I mean that he knows everything necessary in order to know that they are mistakes, but makes them anyway. They are perverse in the way in which all philosophical 'mistakes' of any duration seem to be perverse: they go against what everyone knows perfectly well, including the people who make them. And this is something which requires explaining.

My plan in this paper is first to discuss Ayer's views with re-regard to basic propositions and the distinction between strong and weak verification as if they are mistakes and then proceed to construct a hypothesis according to which they are not mistakes but are unconsciously made revisions of language. It can easily be seen that this hypothesis, though it may come as a shock to many people and lead them to think me a metaphysical Cassandra, has the merit of explaining the perverseness of the 'mistakes', of explaining how a person could make mistakes, and persist in thinking them not to be mistakes, while knowing everything necessary to prevent his making them. For if the views constitute linguistic revisions expressed in the form of statements of fact, then we can see both why they look to be mistakes and also why they can be maintained in the face of known fact with which they appear to be in conflict. The points I wish to discuss are in the following quotation:—

To begin with, it will be seen that I distinguish between a 'strong' and a 'weak' sense of the term 'verifiable', and that I explain this distinction by saying that 'a proposition is said to be verifiable in the strong sense of the term, if and only if its truth could be conclusively established in experience', but that 'it is verifiable, in the weak sense, if it is possible for experience to render it probable'. And I then give reasons for deciding that it is only the weak sense of the term that is required by my principle of verification. What I seem, however, to have overlooked is that, as I represent them, these are not two genuine alternatives. For I subsequently go on to argue that all empirical propositions are hypotheses which are continually subject to the test of further experience; and from this it would follow not merely that the truth of any such proposition never was conclusively established but that it never could be; for however strong the evidence is in its favour, there would never be a point at which it was impossible for further experience to go against it. But this would mean that my 'strong' sense of the term 'verifiable' had no possible application, and in that case there was no need for me to qualify the other sense of 'verifiable' as weak; for on my own showing it was the only sense in which any proposition could conceivably be verified.

If I do not now draw this conclusion, it is because I have come to think that there is a class of empirical propositions of which it is permissible to say that they can be verified conclusively. It is characteristic of these propositions, which I have elsewhere called 'basic propositions', that they refer solely to the content of a single experience, and what may be said to verify them conclusively is the occurrence of the experience to which they uniquely refer.[1]

It can be seen that Ayer wishes, with a number of other philosophers, to hold that empirical propositions like 'There is a restaurant in the London School of Economics' and 'The Serpentine is in Hyde Park' are *permanent* hypotheses, which are intrinsically, by their very nature, incapable of being established conclusively. Experience can render them more and more probable, but never certain. No Londoner really knows that the Serpentine is in Hyde Park, and no student at the London School of Economics knows that there is a restaurant there, no matter how many times he has lunched there and argued about the Labour Government. To resort to an analogy, with respect to establishing such propositions conclusively we are in the position of a person who tries to reach the horizon: like him we can get farther and farther away from our starting point in the direction of the goal but the goal itself remains forever out of our reach. Or to use a stricter analogy, we are in the position of a person who tries to arrive at 1

[1] *Language, Truth and Logic,* Introduction, pp. 9–10, second edition.

by going out in the sequence $\frac{1}{2}, \frac{3}{4}, \frac{7}{8}, \frac{15}{16}, \frac{31}{32}, \frac{63}{64}, \ldots$; no matter how far he goes out in the sequence generated by $\frac{2^n - 1}{2^n}$, an infinity of fractions remains between him and 1.

Regardless of how this view may strike one it is easy to see that the more general view that *all* empirical propositions are only weakly verifiable cannot be maintained. For this view implies that the term 'strongly verifiable' applies to no proposition whatever. And this, in turn, implies that 'strongly verifiable' has no literal use, that it is a term without sense. Now, it can be seen that if 'strongly verifiable' had no use, then the connected term 'weakly verifiable' could have no application to propositions either. For if 'strongly verifiable' had no conceivable application to propositions, such that the expression '*p* is strongly verifiable' made no sense, then the term 'weakly verifiable' would fail to distinguish in any way between empirical propositions and would become a useless term. The sentence 'All empirical propositions are only weakly verifiable empirical propositions' reduces, thus, to the uninformative, pointless sentence 'All empirical propositions are only empirical propositions'. Like the inhabitants of Emerald City, who experience no colour but green and, consequently, cannot in their language intelligibly say 'All things are green', a philosopher who maintains that 'strongly verifiable empirical proposition' is a senseless expression rules himself out from being able to say, with literal significance, 'All empirical propositions are only weakly verifiable'. He cannot say this with sense any more than, as language is at present used, he can say with sense, 'All empirical propositions are *meekly* verifiable'. Some words are connected to each other in the way in which the wheel of a ship is connected to its rudder, and one cannot destroy the rudder and insist that the wheel has its old function. If 'strongly verifiable', is deprived of its use as a contrast term to 'weakly verifiable' it is not the case, as Ayer puts it, that there is no *need* to 'qualify the other sense of "verifiable" as weak'; rather *there is no other sense* to qualify.

Seeing this makes Ayer try to remedy the predicament of his theory in the following way. Basic statements, referring 'solely to the content of a single experience', for example, the statements 'I have a pain' and 'There looks to me to be an elephant in the distance', which formerly he had supposed non-basic and only weakly verifiable,[1] he now holds to be open to conclusive verification by 'the occurrence of the experience to which they uniquely refer'. In this way, as he imagines, the required distinction between strong and weak verifiability is reinstated. Allowing the application of 'strongly verifiable' to basic statements is plainly designed to prevent the application of the term 'weakly verifiable' to non-basic statements from becoming illegitimate. For by allowing a use to the first term he can, it would seem now, distinguish between statements which can be established conclusively and those which experience can render probable only, and so is no longer committed to holding the self-stultifying view that *all* empirical statements are hypotheses. Instead he can now say that some are hypotheses and that others are strongly verifiable.

Two questions have to be discussed. One is the question as to whether it is 'permissible' to say that basic propositions are strongly verifiable, or that they can be conclusively established. The other is whether the required distinction between the pair of terms 'strongly verifiable' and 'weakly verifiable' has been retained by the linguistic manœuvre of allowing an application of the term 'strongly verifiable' to basic propositions. I call what has been done 'a manœuvre with language' because it is designed to protect the main position, which is that non-basic empirical propositions are permanent, or it would perhaps be better to say infinitely permanent, hypotheses. This is the linguistic citadel, whatever the psychological reasons that make holding it important, for the defence of which linguistic outposts are given up.

Let us first consider Ayer's change of mind which makes him grant that it is 'permissible' to say that basic propositions are open to strong verification. It is hardly necessary to point out that the verb 'verify' denotes a process, the process, namely, of establishing the unknown truth-value of a proposition. By going through the process of verifying a proposition p, either weakly or strongly, we obtain information about the truth-value of p which we did not have prior to our going through the process. In other words, the process is one of obtaining new information with regard to the truth-value of p; and it makes no sense to speak of verifying what we already know. We can proceed to confirm by observation or an experiment what we believe or what we feel certain of; but to

[1] *Op cit.,* pp. 90–3.

say that we are verifying what we already know is to imply the self-contradictory thing that we do not know what we already know, that we both do and do not know that p is probable, or that it is certain.

To come now to the question whether it is permissible to apply the term 'strongly verifiable' to basic propositions. I can think of no other meaning of the word 'permissible', in the context of the present discussion, than 'allowed by proper usage'. And if 'permissible' is being used in this sense, then it is not permissible to apply 'strongly verifiable' to basic propositions. It is not English usage to say with regard to any basic proposition that it can be established conclusively in experience, by making tests of any sort or by making introspective observations, because it is not English usage to speak of *establishing* basic propositions. It makes no sense to say, 'I have established that I have a pain', any more than it makes sense to say, 'I probably have a pain'. We should think a person was using language in a queer, improper way if he said, 'I probably have a pain, but I have yet to establish this conclusively', and we should think the same thing of a person who said, 'I have conclusively verified in experience that I have a pain'. It is possible, of course, to suspect a person who claims to have a pain of lying, but it is impossible to think that he might not know whether he has a pain. It is, of course, possible to think that he might not know whether he has a shilling in his pocket, but having a shilling is radically different from having a pain. For a person who has a pain cannot have it without knowing that he has it. And not only this: his knowledge that he has a pain is not arrived at by a process of verification. It is to be noted that feeling his pain, unlike feeling the shilling in his pocket, does not *establish* that he has a pain. For 'I feel a pain' and 'I have a pain' mean the same. You cannot have a pain and not feel it or feel it and not have it. There is, thus, no *getting* to know, or conclusively establishing, that you have a pain by feeling it, as if *in addition* to having it, you have to feel the pain in order to know that you have it. Knowledge of the truth of a basic proposition is had *without being arrived at* by a process of verification. By tests you can satisfy yourself that your tooth or your ankle is the cause of your pain, but there are no conceivable tests for establishing that you have a pain.

It is the same with the basic proposition 'There looks to me to be an elephant in the distance'. By further tests, by rubbing your eyes, getting closer to the place where there appears to you to be an elephant, asking other people, etc., you can satisfy yourself whether or not you are actually seeing an elephant. But there is no process of establishing that there *looks* to you to be an elephant in the distance. It makes perfectly good sense to say, 'What I see is probably an elephant' or 'I have conclusively established that what I see is an elephant'; but it makes no sense, so far as normal English is concerned, to say 'It is probably the case that it looks to me as if there is an elephant in the distance', or to say 'I have conclusively established that it looks to me as if there is an elephant in the distance'. And in general with regard to basic propositions, it is not only the case that we could not say 'there will never be a point at which it is impossible for further experience to go against it', but it is also the case that there could be no further experience a person might have, over and above his experience of having a pain or his experience of something appearing to be so and so to him, which would establish for him the fact that he was having the experience.

If Ayer, as it seems, mistakenly thinks that it is permissible to apply 'strongly verifiable' to basic propositions, then we shall have to charge him with confusing two different senses of the word 'verifies', of confusing 'verifies' in the sense of 'makes a proposition true' and 'verifies' in the entirely different sense of 'establishes a proposition to be true'. Ayer's own words give this charge the semblance of plausibility; for he says, 'It is characteristic of these propositions, which I have elsewhere called "basic propositions", that they refer solely to the content of a single experience, and what may be said to verify them conclusively is the occurrence of the experience to which they uniquely refer'. The experience to which a basic proposition refers, like the state of affairs to which a non-basic proposition refers, is what makes the proposition true, and not the process by which its truth is established. Thus, my having a pain is what makes the proposition that I have a pain true; but what would verify the proposition, if there were any sense in speaking of verifying it, would be an experiment or a series of observations which ended in my knowing that I had a pain. The distinction is made clear in the genuine case of verifying a non-basic proposition. What verifies, in the sense of 'makes true', the assertion that a shilling is round is the shape of a shilling; but what verifies, in the sense of 'establishes', that a shilling is round is not the shape of a shilling, but perceiving its shape, looking at it, feeling it, etc.

Let us now look at Ayer's second claim, which is that the term 'weakly verifiable' has a literally significant application to an entire class of empirical propositions, because, as he thinks, the term 'strongly verifiable' is applicable to a different class of empirical propositions. And let us, for the sake of the argument, grant that 'strongly verifiable' is meaningfully applicable to basic propositions. The question to decide now is whether, even allowing this, it can be granted that the proper distinction between the terms has been retained. That is, it has to be determined whether by restricting the applicability of 'conclusively established in experience' to basic statements and confining the use of 'rendered probable by experience' so that it applies exclusively to non-basic empirical statements the proper relationship between the two expressions has been preserved.

In the case of some pairs of terms which function as alternatives to each other, such that the applicability of one of the terms of a given pair depends on the fact that the other has a possible application, the ranges of the terms are mutually exclusive. Thus, consider the designations 'even number' and 'odd number'. These are so related to each other that if 'even number' described no number, 'odd number' would describe none either. A people whose number system we should, in *our* language, describe as consisting of the odd numbers only would not be able, in *their* language, to say with meaning, '3 is an odd number'. But more specifically than this, these designations are exclusive alternatives, in the sense that neither has a theoretically possible application to any number to which the other is significantly applicable. There is no theoretically possible circumstance in which any even number could, without self-contradiction, be said to be odd, or an odd number even. Or to put the matter with greater care, there is no number with regard to which it would be possible at one time to say, without self-contradiction, that it was even and at a later time to say, without self-contradiction, that it was odd—the use of 'odd', 'even', and the numerals meanwhile remaining unchanged. The same is true for other genuine alternatives: 'rational number' and 'irrational number', '*a priori* proposition' and 'empirical proposition'.

Ayer apparently conceives the relation between the terms 'strongly verifiable' and 'weakly verifiable' to be like that between 'even number' and 'odd number'. It would seem that he thinks the terms are exclusive alternatives, such that under no logically possible condition could a proposition, which at a given time is only weakly verifiable, be said to be strongly verifiable. And if this is what he in fact maintains, if he actually holds that he has correctly described the relationship between the terms, as he has defined them, then he has made a mistake. For no proposition can, with sense, at any time be said to be weakly verifiable unless it is, in principle if not in fact, open to strong verification. It is only possible for experience to render an empirical proposition p probable, to establish it with more or less certainty, if it is theoretically possible for experience to establish p conclusively. There is no sense whatever, so far as established linguistic usage is concerned, in saying that p can be rendered more or less probable, and thus that it approximates in some or other degree to certainty, if it is logically impossible to establish p conclusively. The linguistic fact, if there is such a fact, which would make it *logically impossible,* as opposed to physically impossible, for p to be established with certainty, would be the *senselessness* of stating 'p is conclusively established'. And it does not take much thinking to see that if it were really the case that the words 'p is conclusively established' constituted an improper use of language, the words 'p is probable, but less than certain' or the words 'The probability of p is closer to certainty than is the probability of q' would also have to constitute an improper use of language—which they do not. For if it made no sense to speak of p being certain, it would make no sense to speak of p being *less than* certain.

It can be seen, thus, that even if we grant that basic propositions are strongly verifiable, it remains impossible to say with sense that non-basic empirical propositions can be rendered probable but cannot, logically, be established conclusively. The attempt to explain the relationship between 'strong verification' and 'weak verification' as being like the relationship between 'even number' and 'odd number' or like that between '*a priori*' and 'empirical' fails to make one term a genuine alternative of the other. And also, of course, it cannot actually be admitted that 'conclusively established' applies to basic statements. Thus Ayer's two moves are not a satisfactory defence of the view that non-basic empirical statements are permanent hypotheses.

Norman Malcolm, in his ably argued paper, 'Certainty and Empirical Statements',[1] maintains that the philosophical theory that non-basic empirical statements cannot be known with certainty is mistaken. And I have argued as if Ayer's moves are errors, one consisting of a misapplication of the term 'strongly verifiable' and the other consisting of a misconstruction of the proper connexion between the use of 'rendered probable by experience' and the use of 'established conclusively in experience'. Malcolm's claims, like those I have made, are that the theories reduce to mistaken claims about the proper use of language. I think, however, that it is unsatisfactory to view the theories in this way, for doing so throws no light on the perverseness of the mistakes. It gives us no satisfactory explanation of how it could come about that anyone should make such mistakes, and chronically persist in them, while being perfectly well acquainted with the linguistic facts which should have prevented his making them, and should certainly prevent his persisting in them. In ordinary life a person who knows English usage would not, except as a joke, dream of saying to someone who complained of having a pain, 'Have you verified conclusively that you have a pain? Have you made sure that you really have one?' He would know that to ask this would not be to ask a question but to do something whimsical with language. Yet the same person in his philosophical talk will insist that it makes good sense and is not a misuse of language to say that we establish, by a process of sense-verification, that we have a pain. It is this sort of discrepancy between what a philosopher knows about proper linguistic usage and how he chronically misdescribes it when doing philosophy that is not satisfactorily explained by supposing that he just makes mistakes.

Freud has explained that an illusion, i.e., a conviction which exists without the support of evidence or one which persists in the presence of confuting evidence, has its source in an unconscious wish. And it seems to me that what I have characterized as Ayer's perverse mistakes can most satisfactorily be explained not

[1] *Mind*, January, 1942.

as being mistakes about language but as being changes he unconsciously wishes to make in language. We might say that he is an unconscious linguistic reformer, whose reforms are perhaps not intended for practical adoption. What he does he conceals from himself by the form of speech in which he expresses his re-editing of language. And not only does he achieve concealment by the form of speech he uses; by it he also creates the wished for illusion that he is doing a sort of science, discovering facts about the nature of empirical propositions.

Consider the first error which Ayer apparently makes, of thinking that basic, or experiential, statements are strongly verifiable. Earlier he had contended[1] that they were not propositions, and he now describes what he had *really* done in holding this view in the following way: 'My reasoning on this point was not in itself incorrect, but I think that I mistook its import. For I seem not to have perceived that what I was really doing was to suggest a motive for refusing to apply the term "proposition" to statements that "directly recorded an immediate experience"; and this is a terminological point which is not of any great importance.'[2] It requires no great perspicuity to see that what Ayer, in so many words, is telling us is that he was changing language and not simply using it in a mistaken way. His reasoning, as he rightly claims, was not incorrect, for it consisted of no more than a description of the difference between the use of statements that directly record an immediate experience and the use of empirical statements which go 'beyond what is immediately given'.[3] When this difference in use impressed him with its importance he *refused* to call any utterance which registered a sense-content a 'proposition'; and when the difference lost its importance for him and a similarity impressed him more his resistance against applying 'proposition' to basic statements vanished. Once insight is gained into what was really being done it becomes a 'terminological point which is not of any great importance', but before that it certainly did not seem terminological and was felt to be of considerable importance. To put the matter briefly, the problems about strong and weak verifiability are problems of bringing out and emphasizing various similarities and dissimilarities between different kinds of propositions, similarities and differences which are not made

---

[1] *Op cit.*, pp. 90–2.　　[2] *Ibid.*, pp. 10–11.　　[3] *Ibid.*, p. 91.

explicit and are even concealed by the usual way we talk about the propositions. If we read in the light of his self-analysis what he writes about the difference between empirical and *a priori* statements, we can realize that in holding statements like 'The Serpentine is in Hyde Park' to be hypotheses he is dissatisfied with the ordinary language used in connexion with them. He writes: '. . . no general proposition whose validity is subject to the test of actual experience can ever be logically certain. No matter how often it is verified in practice, there still remains the possibility that it will be confuted on some future occasion . . . And this means that no general proposition referring to matter of fact can ever be shown to be necessarily and universally true. It can at best be a probable hypothesis. And this, we shall find, applies not only to general propositions, but to all propositions which have a factual content'.[1]

Of course no proposition which is subject to the test of experience can be logically certain, or be shown necessarily true. It is logically impossible for p to be empirical and also necessarily true. But what is the point of remarking this except to give a motive for refusing to preface non-basic factual statements with phrases like 'It is certain that', 'I know that', and in this way marking the difference between logically certain propositions and empirically certain propositions? In ordinary conversation, if a person who had rowed a number of times on the Serpentine and strolled along its banks were asked whether he was certain that the Serpentine is in Hyde Park, he could quite properly answer, 'I know that the Serpentine is in Hyde Park'. And he might very well say that he was as certain about the Serpentine as he was about $2 + 3$ being equal to 5.[2] The use of the same language with both ordinary empirical statements and *a priori* ones covers a difference between them felt to be important, and this is a source of dissatisfaction to some philosophers, especially if their respect for mathematics is very great. They then resort to the linguistic expedient, which they restrict to philosophical discourse, of refusing to use 'It is certain that' with non-basic empirical statements and, instead, apply 'hypothesis' and 'weakly verifiable' to them. They know perfectly well that, if it did not indicate a pathological state of

[1] *Op cit.*, p. 72.
[2] A mathematician once said this sort of thing to me.

mind, it would be an outrage of language for a student who frequently ate in the restaurant of the London School of Economics to say that it is a probable hypothesis that there is a restaurant there. But their *philosophical* view is not an outrage of language; it constitutes a *change* of language for the purpose of bringing out the dissimilarity between logical certainty and empirical certainty and also for the purpose of emphasizing the likeness between empirical certainty and probability. The difference between the first two is more plainly marked by their new nomenclature as a difference in kind, and the difference between the second two is marked as a difference in degree only.

Once the term 'weakly verifiable' is stretched so as to cover all empirical statements which go beyond what is immediately given, it is soon realized, or it would be if this new mode of speech were put into practice, that the old distinction between being conclusively established in experience and being rendered probable by experience will have to be reinstated in some way.[1] One way to accomplish this would be to introduce further terminology to do the work of the old. On the highways of New York State there are signs which read 'Stop' and others which read 'Full Stop'. New York automobile regulations apparently recognize two kinds of stops. In a similar way, if we adopted the new terminology, we could mark the ordinary distinction between 'establish conclusively in experience' and 'render probable by experience' by introducing the expressions 'fully weakly verified' and 'partly weakly verified', the first to apply to established empirical propositions and the second to those which are rendered only probable.

But Ayer, apparently, is not interested in *working out* the requirements of his new way of speaking. One receives the impression that his revision of language is motivated by emotional rather than by practical considerations, and that one of his objects is to throw statements which go beyond what is immediately given into an unfavourable light. This he achieves, not only by making linguistically more pronounced the difference between them and *a priori* propositions, but also by making more pronounced the

[1] See John Wisdom's 'Philosophical Perplexity', *Proc. Arist. Soc.,* Vol. XXXVII.
[2] *Op cit.,* p. II. I: 7.

difference between them and basic propositions. He 'chooses'² to classify basic statements as empirical propositions which are open to *conclusive* verification, and so creates a contrast which is not favourable to non-basic propositions. In its new usage, 'conclusively verified', like 'weakly verified', no longer has its usual meaning; it no longer has any connexion whatever with verification. In the new way of speaking, *a priori* and basic propositions are to count as being certain and non-basic propositions as being only probable. And the unfavourable light in which non-basic statements are thus thrown is increased by not working out the requirements of the new use of 'weakly verifiable'. The term 'strongly verifiable' is not used as the required alternative to the term 'weakly verifiable', if the latter is taken to mean what is ordinarily meant by the phrase 'could be rendered probable by experience'. In their new use the two terms function as genuine alternatives, but not as alternatives which correspond to the pair of everyday expressions, 'could be conclusively established in experience' and 'could be rendered probable by experience'. For 'strongly verifiable proposition' means empirical proposition which is not subject to the process of verification, and 'weakly verifiable proposition' means empirical proposition which is subject to the process of verification. But Ayer wishes to use the terminology of *strong* and *weak* verifiability for the purpose of creating an unfavourable contrast. And achieving this end is made possible for him by the fact that the terms, in their new use, carry with them former emotional associations.[1]

[1]For a study of the persuasive use of language see Prof. C. L. Stevenson's 'Persuasive Definitions', *Mind*, July, 1938.

VII

SUBSTRATUM

ONE of the most troublesome problems in the literature of philosophy concerns 'the ancient and honourable notion of substance'. As is well known, the metaphysical problem about the nature of material things, the question, that is to say, as to the *ultimate* constitution and structure of such objects as books and pennies and soap bubbles, has given rise to different theories none of which has, in essentials, turned out to be universally acceptable to professional philosophers. It has to be pointed out in this connexion that each theory has its convinced adherents and that the arguments for each theory, though not convincing to some philosophers, are accepted as conclusive by others. This is a bewildering state of affairs and we may well wonder what has happened to create it: we may well be curious to discover what it is about some demonstrations that makes it possible for one group of able philosophers who have studied the problem to reject them and another group to accept them. In this paper the main object is to examine the theory which Aristotle expressed by saying that 'matter is unknowable in itself'. And I wish to examine it in connexion with only one of the sources from which it derives. The theory has one source in the conception of a thing as being the invariant subject of change: 'The thing, to be at all, must be the same after a change, and the change must, to some extent, be predicated of the thing'.[1] It has another source in the distinction between a thing and its appearances, and still a further one, which is perhaps the basic source, in the distinction between

---

[1] F. H. Bradley, *Appearance and Reality* (1925), p. 72.

144

a thing and its attributes. Only the last source will be of concern to us here.

According to what we may call the substratum theory, a thing such as an apple or a pebble is composed of a substance in which a variety of attributes inhere, or which supports them or is their bearer or their owner. The substance itself is held to be something distinct from the sum of its properties. It is also held that our 'experience' of a thing is confined to its qualities, so that it is possible for us to know what attributes the thing has; but what the possessor of the attributes, the substratum itself, is, remains hidden from us. Substratum lies beyond the bounds of possible experience: 'We cannot say anything at all about its nature'.[1] When a philosopher says 'We do not know what things really are',[2] one cannot help feeling that he utters these words with deep regret. It is not too much to imagine that some people feel them- selves to be living in a world of impenetrable mystery and have the intolerable thought, though it may also give them a certain amount of pleasure, that their curiosity about the world can never be satisfied.

Not all philosophers have been able to accept this theory. Instead, some have been attracted to a different view about the composition of physical things, one from which it follows that there are no unknowable substances. This view is to the effect that a thing is composed of nothing more than the properties which, in ordinary language, 'it' is said to have: 'What would commonly be called a "thing" is nothing but a bundle of co-existing qualities such as hardness, redness, etc.'[3] On this theory we can know what things really are, because there are no sub- stances distinct from the experienceable qualities. There is noth- ing behind the barrier of knowable attributes, nothing to be an inner mystery which forever frustrates our curiosity.

Philosophers who adopt the view that a thing is just a bundle of properties sometimes reject the substratum theory in a way which throws it into an unexpected light. We quite naturally take the theory that a thing is made up of a substance together with a

[1]G. Watts Cunningham, *Problems of Philosophy* (1924), p. 167. It is not to be supposed that this is Prof. Cunningham's view.
[2]A. E. Taylor, *Elements of Metaphysics* (1912), p. 131.
[3]Bertrand Russell, *An Inquiry into Meaning and Truth* (1940), p. 120.

collection of attributes inhering in it to be a hypothesis with regard to the material facts about such things as tables and inkwells. And undoubtedly most philosophers, regardless of whether they hold the theory or reject it, conceive it to be about 'the structure of reality'. Some philosophers, however, appear to view it in a different light, which, if that is the right way to view it, makes it out to be utterly different from what we take it to be. Thus, one philosopher has written: 'The introduction of an unknowable can generally, perhaps always, be avoided by suitable technical devices, and clearly it should be avoided whenever possible'.[1] The sort of device by the use of which unknowables are to be avoided or 'got rid of' consists of making up a new form of speech, one not found in the language of ordinary conversation, and substituting it for the familiar, common form of speech which, it is claimed, introduces unknowables:—

> Common sense regards a 'thing' as having qualities, but not as defined by them; it is defined by spatio-temporal position. I wish to suggest that, wherever there is, for common sense, a 'thing' having the quality C, we should say, instead, that C itself exists in that place, and that the 'thing' is to be replaced by the collection of qualities existing in the place in question. Thus 'C' becomes a name, not a predicate.[2]

Our interest in the question as to what the metaphysical theory actually comes to, what its *nature* is, is justifiably aroused when we learn that some philosophers think it to be of a kind that can relevantly be dealt with by the use of a linguistic device, which consists in altering a current mode of speech. If the introduction of a new way of speaking will 'get rid' of the unknowables claimed to exist by the theory, then the theory is only apparently about things, not actually about them at all. For no sort of change in language could, by itself alone, alter the inaccessibility to us of facts about material things, just as no tinkering with our language will make accessible to us information about the topography of the dark side of the moon. The idea that behind the experienceable attributes we meet with in our everyday perception of things there exist unknowable substrata could only be got rid of by

[1] Bertrand Russell, *An Inquiry into Meaning and Truth* (1940), p. 122.
[2] *Ibid.*, pp. 121–2.

linguistic means if the idea of such substrata were produced by the language we used, not by the things we perceived. An appropriate change in language may very well destroy an illusion produced by the use of words, but it will not remove an idea genuinely connected with the perception of things. Thus, the ordinary sentence 'This is red', which seems to ascribe an attribute to something referred to by the subject word 'this', creates, according to some philosophers, the misconception that the substantive stands for an unknowable something, a bare particular behind the attribute 'red': 'One is tempted to regard "this is red" as a subject-predicate proposition; but if one does so, one finds that "this" becomes a substance, an unknowable something in which properties inhere, but which, nevertheless, is not identical with the sum of its properties'.[1] The way to dispel this unreal notion, which has no relation to the facts about the 'structure of reality', is to replace expressions like 'this is red' by expressions of the form 'redness is here' and treat adjectives like 'red' as names, not as predicates.

According to this conception of the source and nature of the theory, many thinkers have been deceived by language into holding a *Scheintheorie*; while labouring under the notion that they were advocating a deep hypothesis about the constitution of things, they were taking a verbal shadow for an actual theory about the ultimate nature of material objects. What has happened has been summed up in the following way: 'It happens to be the case that we cannot, in our language, refer to the sensible properties of a thing without introducing a word or phrase which appears to stand for the thing itself as opposed to anything which may be said about it. And, as a result of this, those who are infected by the primitive superstition that to every name a single real entity must correspond assume that it is necessary to distinguish logically between the thing itself and any, or all, of its sensible properties'.[2] Another philosopher has put it in this way: ' "Substance", in a word, is a metaphysical mistake, due to transference to the world-structure of the structure of sentences composed of a subject and a predicate'.[3] Like a chronic psychological obsession

[1]Bertrand Russell, *An Inquiry into Meaning and Truth* (1940), p. 120.
[2]A. J. Ayer, *Language, Truth and Logic,* (1936), p. 32.
[3]Bertrand Russell, *A History of Western Philosophy* (1945), p. 202.

which cannot be removed by confrontation with fact, the transference persists despite our familiarity with chairs and the like. And the explanation of the stubbornness with which the delusive idea persists is, apparently, that the source of the idea does not lie in the perception of things or in experiments conducted on them. The conception of substratum is a *metaphysical* mistake, not a scientific one, and is not correctable by scientific means.[1] It would seem that the technique designed to destroy the transference and cure the linguistic delusion consists of reframing language in such a way that it will no longer offer the temptation to make the transference. One is reminded of Freud's comments about some neurotic people who become well only after changing their environment. The linguistic neurosis, so to speak, is also to be cured by changing the linguistic environment, by making part of the language aseptic, to use John Wisdom's expression.

By no means, of course, are all or even most philosophers in agreement with this version of what the substratum theory of the nature of material things comes to. Where it is maintained that the substance theory is an illusion caused by the subject-predicate structure of language, many other philosophers make the claim that the established language in everyday use is itself the natural result of an antecedent belief about the composition of material things. They, instead, explain the fact that language has a subject-predicate structure by reference to a prior hypothesis about reality. Thus: 'When we ask how, if a "thing" is merely the series or sum of its attributes, and possesses no underlying unity to which the attributes belong, the whole of our ordinary language about things comes to be constructed on the contrary assumption, how it is that we always talk and think as if every "bundle" of attributes were owned by something of which we can say that it *has* the quality . . .'[2]

Some philosophers maintain that the substratum theory is only the semblance of an empirical hypothesis into which we are tricked by language; others maintain that the theory is an actual hypothesis about the structure of things and that it determined the form of our language about things. How is one to decide between

---

[1]'If science keeps to its own sphere, it cannot clash with any metaphysical theory'. J. McT. E. McTaggart, *Some Dogmas of Religion* (1906), p. 91.

[2]Taylor, *op. cit.,* p. 133.

these two versions of what it comes to? What sort of observation or experiment or purely intellectual consideration will show that the words 'Material things are constituted by substances in which attributes inhere' express a theory about material objects or that they are a verbal fraud which successfully masquerades as a theory? A little thought leads to the disconcerting conclusion that perhaps there is no way of definitely and conclusively deciding between the two versions. For those who insist that it is a theory about things are in no better position to make relevant observations than those who deny this: the disagreement does not arise because of any difference in observation or from different results of experimentation. And those who maintain it is a verbal counterfeit know no more facts about grammar and the accepted usages of words than those who hold the opposite view; there is no linguistic fact about ordinary discourse they can point to of which the others are not aware, and such that their acquaintance with it would compel them to give up their view. Neither knowledge of actual language nor sense-observation of things seems adequate to settling the matter, and it would consequently seem that there is no way of settling it. For what else is there to turn to?

Where different hypotheses have been proposed without agreed success, it is certainly permissible to try out still another hypothesis. The worst thing that can happen is that we shall again fail to arrive at an acceptable solution, which is something we are all hardened against in philosophy. I propose to take the view, in partial agreement with one of the two contending versions, that the substance 'theory' is only the verbal imitation of a theory and entirely different from what we are inclined to think it is. But I shall argue that it is not ordinary, everyday language that causes us to think this. Instead, I shall try to show that the illusion of its being a theory about things is produced by a concealed *revision* of ordinary subject-predicate sentences, by a manœuvre with language, and not by the subject-predicate form of discourse itself. It is what *metaphysicians* have done with words, their metaphysical artistry, that creates the appearance of a theory about the structure of things; but what they have done is hidden from our conscious awareness, as well as their own. The theory may be compared to a dream; indeed, in this case, the metaphysician may be said to dream with words. As in the case of an ordinary dream, the linguistic metaphysical dream is consciously enjoyed or disliked but only secretly understood. And in order to see how the illusory effect of a theory about the nature of things is produced, the language of the metaphysical fantasy has to be interpreted.

It is important, first of all, to see that the theory is not factual; i.e., it is important to see that it is not a theory about the constitution of material objects. Consider what Locke said:—

It is the ordinary qualities observable in iron or a diamond, put together, that make the true complex idea of those substances, which a smith or a jeweller commonly knows better than a philosopher; who, whatever substantial forms he may talk of, has no other idea of those substances than what is framed by a collection of those simple ideas which are to be found in them. Only we must take notice, that our complex ideas of substances, besides all these simple ideas they are made up of, have always the confused idea of something to which they belong and in which they subsist. And therefore, when we speak of any sort of substance, we say it is a thing having such or such qualities . . . These and the like fashions of speaking intimate that the substance is supposed always something besides the extension, figure, solidity, motion, thinking, or other observable ideas, though we know not what it is.[1]

Not imagining how these simple ideas can subsist by themselves, we accustom ourselves to suppose some *substratum* wherein they do subsist, and from which they do result, which therefore we call *substance*.[2]

So that if any one will examine himself concerning his notion of pure substance in general, he will find he has no other idea of it at all, but only a supposition of he knows not what support of such qualities which are capable of producing simple ideas in us; which qualities are commonly called accidents. If any one should be asked, what is the subject wherein colour or weight inheres, he would have nothing to say, but the solid extended parts: and if he were demanded, what is it that that solidity and extension inhere in, he would not be in a much better case than the Indian before mentioned . . .[3]

Hume's challenge, which seems based, in a soundly empirical manner, on the sense-observation of things, is well known:—

[1] *An Essay Concerning Human Understanding*, Bk. II, Ch. XXIII, Sec. 3.
[2] *Ibid.*, Sec. 1.   [3] *Ibid.*, Sec. 2.

I would fain ask those philosophers, who found so much of their reasonings on the distinction of substance and accident, and imagine we have clear ideas of each, whether the idea of *substance* be derived from the impressions of sensation or reflection? If it be conveyed to us by our senses, I ask, which of them, and after what manner? If it be perceived by the eyes, it must be a colour; if by the ears, a sound; if by the palate, a taste; and so of the other senses. But I believe none will assert, that substance is either a colour, or sound, or a taste. The idea of substance must, therefore, be derived from an impression of reflection, if it really exist. But the impressions of reflection resolve themselves into our passions and emotions; none of which can possibly represent a substance.[1]

At first glance, Hume appears to have rejected the idea of substance as a 'fiction' on the basis of observation. He seems to have come to his conclusion as the result of a closer, more careful, examination of things, a process comparable to inspecting a box to see whether it has a secret compartment. It looks as if he has made a thorough inventory of his sense-experiences of such a thing, say, as a table, experiences we should express by saying 'This table is brown', 'This table feels smooth', and the like, and discovered that he actually experienced *only* brownness and rectangularity, smoothness and hardness, etc. He never, in connexion with any of his senses, perceived the *thing* that is brown and smooth and rectangular, the substance in which the perceived attributes inhere. His description of what happened is the description of a person who in no instance of the sense-perception of objects comes upon anything over and above and in addition to attributes, a further something which owns them, and who in consequence rejects the notion that any such entities as substances exist. The impression his words give is that they describe the rejection of an empirical claim on empirical grounds, a rejection based on reasons similar to those which finally make us give up the belief in ghosts; we have never come upon one, not even its shadow. But this impression is erroneous.

It may first be noted that if the substratum hypothesis regarding the constitution of material objects is empirical and if what Hume did, to test it, was really to make a series of observations,

---

[1] *A Treatise of Human Nature*, Bk. I, Pt. I, Sec. 6.

then his rejection of the theory was quite unwarranted. For if this was his procedure, we have to suppose that he looked for what he should have realized, if the theory were correct, he would not be able to find and, after looking for substance and not finding it, that he concluded that it did not exist. Those who hold the theory claim that we 'experience qualities but not the substance in which they inhere'. How, then, could his failure to perceive substance have led Hume to make the claim of having demonstrated the notion of substance to be a fiction? How can one refute a hypothesis by not finding what the hypothesis states one cannot find? No scientist would think of rejecting the atomic theory because he failed to see an atom through the microscope, and it is hard to believe that it was something like this that Hume was actually doing. It is hard, in spite of the empirical descriptive language he used, to think that his claim is empirical and that he based it on processes of looking at things, feeling them, tasting them, and so on.

Locke would certainly not have found his consideration impressive. For he *agrees* with Hume about what we discover from an examination and inventory of our experiences of things. In his own words:—

> Everyone upon inquiry into his own thoughts will find, that he has no other idea of any substance but what he has barely of those sensible qualities, which he supposes to inhere, with a supposition of such a substratum, as gives, as it were, a support to those qualities or simple ideas, which he has observed to exist united together. Thus the idea of the sun, what is it but an aggregate of those several simple ideas, bright, hot, roundish, having a constant regular motion, at a certain distance from us, and perhaps some other?[1]

How, then, is the difference of opinion between the two philosophers to be explained? Is it to be explained as resulting from the fact that not all information relevant to the refutation or establishment of the substratum hypothesis is available, so that the lack of complete information leaves room for a divergence of beliefs? Is it to be hoped that examinations through future supermicroscopes, refined experiments, etc., will ever bring the metaphysical

[1] *Op cit.,* Bk. II, Ch. XXIII, Sec. 6.

problem of substratum to an end? It is not difficult to see that laboratory science holds out no hope for its solution in the future. If physicists and chemists had satisfied themselves that at last they had reached the end of their quest and knew everything about matter, philosophers could show that the *metaphysical* problem of substance still remained unsolved. Nor would more ways of sensing things than the usual five be of the slightest help. A new and yet further way of perceiving a thing like an orange would only reveal new *qualities* of the thing; we still would not be able to perceive the substance itself, and the controversy over its existence would remain.

Consider again what Hume appears to have done, namely, to have looked for something by means of a series of careful observations. In the case of an actual search for anything we always have *some* idea of what it is we are looking for. We know, for example, what it would be like to look for and discover (or fail to discover) the unknown cause of a disease. But if we had no idea whatever, however rough, no inkling, of what it is we were trying to discover, we should not know where to begin nor where to turn, nor should we be able to recognize the thing as answering to what we want. The experiment Hume invites us to make is utterly different in this respect from an ordinary instance of looking for something. In this case, not finding what we are looking for implies that we had, to begin with, no idea whatever of what we were trying to discover. And it implies, moreover, that no process of looking had been resorted to. The search was only a sham. For when Hume points out that the supposed idea of substance derives neither from sensation nor reflection, which both he and Locke are agreed are the only sources of our ideas, he in effect tells us, not that it, like the idea of a centaur, is *fictitious,* but that there is *no such idea*. He tells us that the phrases 'substance in which attributes inhere', 'owner of attributes', 'support of qualities' describe nothing actual or imaginable and are literally empty phrases to which no application has been given. Of course, then, there can be no looking for a bearer of properties, no examination of anything for the purpose of trying to discover a substratum, any more than there can be a search for binomial scarlet or for a slithy tove.

When it is claimed that none of our senses acquaints us with substance, that they all fail to reveal to us a support of such experienced qualities as shape, colour, and taste, what this claim has to be construed as coming to is that it is *logically impossible* to perceive in any way the subject of attributes. When it is said 'We experience qualities but not the subject in which they are supposed to inhere', what these words must be taken to be stating is that under no conceivable circumstances could we ever experience substance, that this is a logical impossibility, however much they look to be asserting an empirical fact about what we fail to perceive. No one could seriously be supposed to be maintaining that we do not perceive substratum because as a matter of fact it does not exist or that we are prevented from experiencing it by a physical obstacle or some sort of physiological inadequacy. Nothing can be said to be a goal if we cannot describe what it would be like to attain it, and nothing can be said to be a barrier preventing us from attaining a goal unless we can describe overcoming it and reaching the goal. And what makes it certain that the inaccessibility of substance is not to be explained on physical or physiological grounds is that there are no descriptions in philosophy of what it would be like to perceive substance or of what it is that prevents our experiencing it.

A familiar argument, which is substantially Hume's, helps make clear what it is that stands in the way of our experiencing the substratum support of attributes. It goes as follows. If, in our imagination, we take away the various properties of a thing, for example, the shape, size, and other attributes of an orange, we find that there is nothing left; there is no residue, which is the owner of properties and distinct from them, for us to imagine. There is no difficulty about imagining Voltaire deprived of all his possessions, his garments, his money, books, and snuff box: bare Voltaire remains after this process. But when Voltaire's attributes are taken away from the substance in which they inhere, nothing whatever, no bare something, is left. This shows that the seemingly descriptive expression 'substance in which properties inhere but which is distinct from them' is not used to describe anything. The impossibility of imagining substratum is a logical impossibility, which has its source in the linguistic fact that the word 'substratum', in the sense of something 'in which properties inhere but which is distinct from them', has been given no application.

It might, of course, be urged that 'substratum' does denote something, though what it denotes eludes us; but then we should have
to accept the absurd consequence that the word has an application
which it has never been given and is not known to have. It is
clear, then, that we cannot perceive substratum for the same
reason that we cannot see binomial scarlet: 'perceives substratum',
like 'sees binomial scarlet', is a literally senseless expression.
Hence, when a metaphysician says, 'We do not know what things
really are', his plaint would seem to be against language, namely,
that to say such a thing as 'A knows what it is, the substratum,
that attributes ϕ_1, ϕ_2, ϕ_3 . . . inhere in' is not to say anything.
And when another metaphysician states that 'we cannot say
anything about its nature', he seems to be remarking that there do
not exist words for describing substratum, which is to say that
the word 'substratum' is connected with no descriptive phrases.

It would appear now that the explanation of the substance
hypothesis which construes it to be the distorted recognition of a
linguistic fact, the recognition of such a fact displaced, so to speak,
on to the world of things, is correct. The idea that the theory is a
mistake due to the transfer to the world-structure of the structure
of subject-predicate sentences needs, apparently, to be qualified in
the following way: it is this sentence structure take in conjunction
with the linguistic fact that it makes no sense to speak of knowing
what it is that is the subject of attribution which is responsible for
the mistake. Can this explanation be the right one, however? It is
sufficiently plain that the theory is not an account of the nature of
things and that its appearing to be such is an illusion due to the
form of words used to express it. But is the source of the theory
to be found, as is claimed, in the language we use in everyday
conversation, the language of ordinary discourse?

The claim would be correct if in ordinary language it made sense
to speak of perceiving colours, shapes, etc., but did not make sense
to speak of perceiving things. But this is not the case at all; and it
must be a mistake to think that the metaphysical idea of unknowable substance could be produced by the subject-predicate structure of *ordinary* sentences like 'The dog is barking' or 'This table is
heavy'. For it makes perfectly good sense to speak not only of
hearing the barking of the dog and feeling the weight of the table
but also of seeing the dog and of seeing the table, i.e., of perceiving

the *thing* that is barking and the *thing* that is heavy. Moore has said: 'Some people may no doubt think that it is very unphilosophical in me to say that we *ever* can perceive such things [as doors and fingers]. But it seems to me that we do, in ordinary life, constantly talk of *seeing* such things, and that, when we do so, we are neither using language incorrectly, nor making any mistake about the facts—supposing something to occur which never does in fact occur'.[1] Ordinary, *unphilosophical* people who speak in subject-predicate sentences do not have the idea that things, as opposed to attributes, are unknowable. How then could it possibly produce such an idea in the minds of metaphysicians? It seems plain that ordinary language could not have produced the idea; the source has to be discovered elsewhere. When a person who maintains that we do perceive things and that to say that we do is not a misuse of language is condemned as being unphilosophical, then we have to think that being *philosophical* consists in doing something unusual with words, not mistakenly, but with purpose, whether or not with awareness. It becomes highly plausible to think that metaphysicians have, if not consciously then with unconscious skill, *introduced* 'linguistic unknowables'. If substratum is unknowable, then the word 'substratum' does not mean what is ordinarily meant by the phrase 'subject of attribution'. In some way that is obscure to us, language has been altered; and it is this altered language which is responsible for the theory that things are unknowable substrata in which attributes inhere.

What has happened? How has the metaphysical dream been produced? Fortunately, there are statements to be found in the literature which give us insight into what has taken place. Consider the following statement:—

Those who maintain that there is an ultimate plurality of substances, and yet hold that characters are, as such, universals, seem logically bound to deny that a substance is the complex unity of all its qualities and relations. Thus Mr. McTaggart, who occupies this position, asserts in his *Nature of Existence,* Ch. V, that the complex unity is itself only a complex adjective, and therefore presupposes a subject ultimately distinct from itself.[2]

[1]G. E. Moore, *Philosophical Studies* (1922), p. 226. Moore said this in a different connexion.
[2]G. F. Stout, *Studies in Philosophy and Psychology* (1930), p. 394.

And also this statement:—

> If we . . . suppose that his kind and all his particular attri-
> butes as well *belong* to the individual, the individual, to which
> they all belong, becomes a mere uncharacterized *something*. For
> in saying *what* it is, we should merely assign to it a fresh pre-
> dicate; whereas we want to get not at its predicates but at that
> which 'has' them. Thus we should reach a new way of consider-
> ing the subject of predication. Originally it was the concrete
> individual, Socrates or Plato; but of what he is, one part was
> distinguished as what he is essentially, and the rest reduced to
> attributes or 'accidents' of him, not necessary to his being, and
> not to be included in an account of his essence. Now, what he is
> essentially is also reduced to the position of attribute and mere
> predicate, and the subject becomes a mere subject of which as
> such nothing more can be said except that it exists and is unique
> in each individual.[1]

What these quotations, on careful reading, can be seen to tell us
is that the substratum theory expresses the linguistic result of
juggling with words. The illusion that things are unknowable in
themselves has its source in a linguistic creation. In almost so
many words, these quotations explain the mechanics of the illusion
as consisting of the change brought about in language by *reducing*
general names to the status of 'mere adjectives', that is to say, the
change brought about by reclassifying general substantives as
'complex adjectives' while retaining the subject-predicate form of
sentence.

It appears that some metaphysicians wish to recompose language, for some reason or other. Ordinary grammar does not
satisfy them; and they wish to change it by depriving general substantives of their grammatical noun function and give them the
status of adjectives without, however, giving up the subject-
predicate form of sentence. In order to do this, it is quite plain
that linguistic reparations will have to be made. If the substantive
'penny' is counted as a 'complex adjective' which 'presupposes a
subject ultimately distinct from itself', then, since in English there
is no term distinct from it which it presupposes as a subject term,
a new term will have to be invented to supply the need. If we
wish to deprive 'penny' of its noun place in the sentence 'The

[1] H. W. B. Joseph, *An Introduction to Logic* (1931), p. 54.

penny is round' and at the same time wish to keep the grammatical structure of the sentence intact, without replacing the noun by a synonym, then our only resort is to find a structural replacement for the deleted term. For obviously there cannot be a sentence which has a subject-predicate structure but fails to have some sort of subject term, if only one which plays the rôle of subject in purely formal respects. A subject-predicate sentence *must* have a subject; this is the 'necessity of thought' of which Locke speaks.

The introduction of a term which is only a formal, and not a material, substitute for a general noun is made possible by the fact that general names have two distinct functions. A word like 'mouse' has, for one thing, a literal meaning; in this respect it has a semantic function which enables us to say *what* a thing is, e.g., that a thing is a mouse, or that a thing is a ball or a penny. In addition to this, it also has the formal syntactical function of serving as the subject of predication in sentences. If, now, general names are deprived of the syntactical use to which they are at present put, and given adjectival classification under parts of speech, the subject-predicate form of sentence in which they occur as subjects can nevertheless be preserved by introducing a term that will do part of the work of a general name, i.e., do its syntactical work without doing its semantic work. It will be sufficient if the new term is made to behave syntactically like an ordinary subject term and is otherwise a pseudo term, having no application to phenomena. Thus, to revert to the former example, the *structure* of the sentence 'The penny is round' can be kept intact after its noun has been deleted, by letting the mark 'x' occupy the place of 'penny'. We then have the new subject-predicate sentence 'The x is round',[1] where 'x' differs from ordinary subject terms in respect of having been given no application. It is the failure to give 'x' a meaning that makes it a 'mere subject' or, to use Bertrand Russell's word, a *hook* on which to hang adjectives.

One philosopher seems to have divined what has happened when he observed that 'Our idea of a substance, in fact, turns out to be no more than an unknown x, to which we refer the contents of experience'.[2] The new subject term *is* an unknown x, which is

---

[1] 'x' is not to be taken as representing a variable.
[2] James Gibson, *Locke's Theory of Knowledge and its Historical Relations* (1917), p. 95.

to say it is a symbol that has no known meaning assigned to it; it has no semantic use, though it has the appearance of having such a use. It is a term by means of which we cannot say *what* a thing is, although, in the subject-predicate sentences of the substratum language invented by metaphysicians, it supplants words with which we can, and in ordinary language do, say what things are. It is this new form of subject-predicate language that causes the idea of unknowable substratum: the new term is a 'linguistic unknowable'. The complaint that we cannot say anything about the nature of substance, about what things really are, is not the factual complaint about things it may at first have seemed to be, nor is it about our everyday language, which, of course, contains general names. It is the expression of dissatisfaction with the substratum language of metaphysics and is of the same order as complaining that we cannot say what a 'tove' is. The term 'x' tells us nothing, conveys no information, about the thing described by the adjectives of a sentence in which it occurs as subject. Nor, of course, can we explain its meaning, in the way in which we can explain the meaning of a general name. If we are asked what a kangaroo is we can answer the question by describing the animal to which the word 'kangaroo' applies, which is to say, by giving roughly the meaning of the word. This is impossible in the case of the metaphysical subject, which has no application; there is no explaining what an x is. The observation that on the substratum theory 'the individual . . . becomes a mere uncharacterized *something*. For in saying *what* it is, we should merely assign to it a fresh predicate; whereas we want to get not at its predicates but at that which "has" them'[1] comes to the same thing as the above complaint. It is easy to see why we cannot 'get at' substance with a language in which general names have been reduced to adjectival status and have had their former position taken over by a term which does only their syntactical work. We can state what attributes a thing has but we cannot say what it is in which they inhere, except that it is an x, an 'uncharacterized something'. We can 'get at' some animals with the word 'kangaroo', but we get at nothing with the term 'x'.

The idea of substance as being that which remains after a thing has been stripped bare of its qualities—the idea, in other words, of

[1] Joseph, *loc. cit.*

159

'bare substance' or the 'bare particular'—turns out to be a disguised expression of a linguistic fact. That which remains, after a general name has been deprived of its application to things by depriving it of the meaning it has in common with an indeterminate set of adjectives, is a term which has only a syntactical use, an equivalent of the formal subject term of substratum metaphysics. 'Bare substance' is nothing more than a 'bare' substantive word, the metaphysical ghost of a general name. This is the conception of substratum as something *distinct* from its properties and in which they inhere. And this conception is nothing more than the conception of a subject-symbol which is *completely* distinct from its predicates by virtue of the fact that it has no meaning of its own, a fact which also makes impossible our saying, by means of it, what things are. It is possible in this language to say what properties a thing has, but not what it is. This fact, it may be noted, rids philosophers of the need of trying to distinguish the essence of a thing from its accidents. For without the ordinary distinction between general substantive words like 'penny' and 'horse' and adjectives like 'round' and 'roan'—a distinction which can be destroyed either by eliminating general nouns or by changing them into adjectives—there is no distinction between the essence and accidents of a thing. There is left only the distinction between a term which is a 'pure' subject term (the pure abstract being of medieval metaphysics) and adjectives.

Consider, again, the familiar argument used to demonstrate the unknowability of substance, the argument, namely, that we cannot envisage the entity that is left after a thing has been stripped of its attributes, or, what amounts to the same thing, Hume's argument that in addition to the perceived qualities of colour, shape, odour, taste, and the like we never experience the thing which has them. This argument rests on and, indeed, is a distorted way of calling attention to actual points of difference and similarity between general names and adjectives. General names differ in their formal, syntactical use from adjectives, but also they are like them in important respects. For one thing, like adjectives, they have multiple applicability; or, to express this fact in metaphysical language, the universals for which they stand are capable of having a number of instances or of being possessed in common by a number of things. Thus, we can say that many things are grey and we can say that there are many mice. Also, and what is more specifically relevant in connexion with the argument, the application of a general noun is determined by a variable set of adjectives, not sharply defined or specified. To put it roughly, as regards their meaning, general names are 'complex adjectives'. This is what Locke was pointing out when he remarked that 'everyone upon inquiry into his own thoughts will find, that he has no other idea of any substance but what he has barely of those sensible qualities, which he supposes to inhere . . . Thus the idea of the sun, what is it but an aggregate of those several simple ideas, bright, hot, roundish . . .?' Hence, to speak of an experiment, conducted in the imagination, of stripping a thing of its attributes is a disguised and more colourful way of expressing the linguistic fact that the meaning of a general noun like 'mouse' is the same as that possessed by a complicated set of adjectives, so that by 'stripping away' its adjectives, i.e., by depriving the noun of its adjectival meaning, we deprive it of its application to things. Noticing the impressive similarity between general nouns and adjectives makes some people wish to assimilate them to the class of adjectives. It is much as if, by their argument, they were to say: 'See, the difference between general nouns and adjectives is mainly a difference in the way they function syntactically in sentences. By comparison with their semantic similarity, this difference is trivial, but it hides their similarity'. And to correct this state of affairs and bring out what is hidden by the structure of subject-predicate language, general nouns are reduced to adjectival status. The syntactical function of nouns is turned over to a new symbol, and in this way the structure of subject-predicate sentences using general names as subjects is preserved and also the mystifying illusion of a deep theory about the structure of reality is created. Undoubtedly, the motivation for the change goes deeper than the linguistic considerations; we may well think that psychological needs play an important rôle in the production of the illusion.

Metaphysicians who find the substratum theory unacceptable also feel the importance of the semantic similarity that grammar tends to conceal, and are dissatisfied with the grammar that conceals it. What impresses these philosophers seems mainly to be the fact that both sorts of words, adjectives and nouns, have multiple applicability, that, e.g., 'white' and 'snow' are each applicable to a number of things. They see, however, the possibility of a different reconstruction, to which they are attracted. They see the possibility of assimilating adjectives to the class of substantive words. Instead of reducing general names to complex adjectives they change adjectives into abstract nouns, 'red' into 'redness', 'round' into 'roundness', and so on, and dispense altogether with the subject-predicate form of sentence. In this way they get rid, not of linguistic unknowables in ordinary language (which has none), but of the pseudo unknowables, the introduced metaphysical subjects of the substratum language. Instead of having philosophical sentences like 'The x is white', they have philosophical sentences like 'Whiteness is here', or 'Whiteness, here, now'.

VIII

THE PARADOXES OF MOTION

I WISH to consider Zeno's celebrated arguments against the existence of motion. I propose to examine at length and in considerable detail the flying arrow paradox and shall conclude my paper with a more general discussion of the remaining three paradoxes of motion: the stadium, the dichotomy, and the Achilles and the tortoise. My purpose is not only to try to say something new about the paradoxes, but also to bring forward for consideration some general claims about the nature of metaphysical theories and demonstrations. For one may well wonder what sort of things metaphysical theories and demonstrations are. The Cartesian complaint about the condition of philosophy still holds good, and its condition has even been aggravated by the claims of Logical Positivism; and there seems to be no prospect of improvement. A well-known philosopher once remarked in the course of a conversation that he was *tired* of a certain view about what metaphysical theories and proofs come to and now *preferred* to talk differently about them. And it would seem that without exaggeration we may say his remark epitomizes the real method employed in philosophy, the method behind the verbal scenes, so to speak. It would seem that *emotional* preferences and aversions determine the acceptance and rejection of theories, and that any other supposed determinant is a fraud and a magician's show. For with hardly any exceptions, views go out of fashion rather than are rejected because they have been shown to be false, and new views which come into fashion go out in the same way. This, at any rate, is the impression left on many people. To other people, of course,

163

metaphysics appears the deepest of the sciences. One may well wonder which is the appearance and which the reality.

Instead of saying that I wished to consider the argument of the flying arrow against the existence of motion, I should have phrased myself more cautiously and said I wished to consider what *purports* to be an argument in demonstration of the impossibility of motion. For it may be that the real work of the argument is something else, however strong the impression it gives of being a *refutation* of physical motion. Undoubtedly Zeno himself laboured under this impression, but it may nevertheless be mistaken. The style of language in which the argument is expressed is the style of scientific demonstration, but this may be a linguistic façade behind which different work, work other than to establish matter of fact, is being done. On the other hand, the argument may have been designed to do just what it seems designed to do, namely, to demonstrate that motion does not exist, that rivers do not really flow and galloping horses are in fact motionless, held in immobility by mighty chains, as Parmenides expressed it.

There are several versions of the paradox and I shall take the one that is clearest and, for my present purpose, simplest to deal with. This is stated as follows: 'Everything, when it is behaving in a uniform manner, is continually either moving or at rest, but what is moving is always in the *now,* hence the moving arrow is motionless'. The view that motion is impossible is a consequence, according to this, of the contention that 'what is moving is always in the *now*'. It follows, in other words, from the notion, which is felt by many people to be inescapable, that a moving body must effect a change of place in an instant of time. In a somewhat expanded form the paradox might be restated to read: Motion implies change of position, the transition from one place to another, in an instant of time; therefore, since nothing can happen in an instant of time or in the *now,* motion is impossible.

What is one to make of this argument? There is no denying that it *looks* like a demonstration, correct or fallacious, of the impossibility of bodies changing their location by moving through space. But can it really be this? Can it be imagined that its work is to establish the non-existence of such a pervasive and well-known phenomenon in nature as the motion of bodies? The most frequent point of view taken is that it is a proof but that it contains a hidden mistake. Those who take this point of view insist that it is a completely obvious fact that physical bodies do move, that the wind does sway trees and that birds do fly. They insist that the philosophical proposition denying this is unmistakably shown to be false by our everyday sense-experience, and therefore that the proof given for it *must* contain an error of reasoning. It is worth pointing out that so far in its very long history nothing has been discovered which all experts would agree was a *mistake*.

Other points of view are also taken. Some philosophers think, if we are to take them at their word, that the proof is correct and demonstrates the unreality of motion, unmasks it as 'mere appearance'. Others still maintain it is correct but that it does not prove the impossibility of motion. Instead they take it to be the true explanation of a physical phenomenon. Thus, according to Russell, it explains the phenomenon of the motion of a body as consisting '*merely* in the occupation of different places at different times'[1] and compels us to 'reject the notion of a *state* of motion'.[1]

One opinion has it that the philosophical theory is false and, therefore, that the proof given for it contains a mistake; another that the theory is true and the proof correct; and a third opinion has it that the proof is the right explanation of a phenomenon of nature, of what motion 'consists in'. Which of these opinions is one to accept, and is there a rational procedure for deciding between them? I propose to try to show that none of these meta-theories is the true explanation of the import of the paradox. On the hypothesis that the paradox is about a fact of nature and its proof either correct or incorrect we get nowhere. Philosophical mathematicians have remained deadlocked for a surprising number of centuries. It therefore cannot be amiss to try out a different hypothesis. A philosopher some time ago made the remark that ordinary language should be changed because it permits the concoction of such wild things as the Zeno paradoxes, because it gives birth, so to speak, to such linguistic monsters. This seems to me to get closer to what the paradox comes to than do the three opinions held about it. In any case, this is still a further opinion regarding the nature of the paradox, namely, that in some way it is linguistic and has its source in *a fault in ordinary language*. In view of this variety of ideas about its nature, it is certainly

[1]Bertrand Russell, *Principles of Mathematics* (1938), p. 473.

reasonable to apply in an explicit way what may be called 'meta-philosophical tests' to the paradox, in order to try to get at the facts about its nature: whether it is about the physical universe or whether, in some way, it is linguistic, or whatever else it may be.

Let us look at the proof in relation to the proposition it is supposed to establish, the proof, namely, that motion implies change of position in an instant of time, hence, since nothing can change its place in an instant, motion is impossible. This argument is of the form 'p implies that q implies r', where p validates the inference of r from q. That is, the proposition 'Nothing can change its place in an instant or in the *now*' plays the logical rôle of validating the inference of 'Motion is impossible' from 'Motion implies change of place in an instant of time'. There is no denying that the proposition 'Motion is impossible' strongly appears to state a fact of nature, i.e., it looks like an empirical proposition, which, moreover, most people would immediately and unhesitatingly reject as incontrovertibly false. In fact, one might well say that it is too patently false for it to be what it is natural to take it to be, or for people with eyes with which to see the world around them and the intelligence with which to relate their thoughts to their experiences to have taken it seriously and even to have accepted it as true. And perhaps it is not taken seriously in the way in which ordinary statements of fact are. A tale handed down about the Sophist Diodorus illustrates the attitude taken to the theory. Diodorus was well known for his lectures against the existence of motion. Having put his shoulder out of joint he went to a physician to have it set. 'How?', said the doctor, 'your shoulder dislocated! That cannot be, for . . .' The tale does not go on to say, but undoubtedly Diodorus was not persuaded by the doctor's words that it could not be and insisted on and received medical treatment.

With the proof, however, it is a different matter. The validating proposition, to the effect that no change of place can occur in an instant of time, is clearly not an inductive generalization. It is not based on sense-observations of any sort nor is it an hypothesis constructed on the basis of evidence deriving from experimentation. No one, of course, would dream of claiming to have observed what happens in the course of an instant of time. And not only that; it is plain that no temporal microscope, no imaginable quickening and refinement of our optical apparatus, would enable us to make such an observation. No matter how quick the flash and sharp the eye, the time in which the flash happened could not have been an *instant*. This is so not because flashes always take longer and human sense-perception is always too gross, but because phrases like 'happened in an instant of time', 'moved from here to there in the *now*', are not *used* to describe anything whatever. Unlike the expression 'takes only a ten-thousandth of a second', the phrases 'photographed at a shutter speed of an instant' and 'photographed in the *now*' describe no conceivable occurrence. The 'cannot' in the validating proposition is the 'cannot' of logic, not of physics. What prevents a body from effecting a change of position in the *now* is a fact of language, not a fact of physical nature: the fact, namely, that the terms 'instant', 'moment', 'the *now*' have a definition according to which it makes no sense to speak of something occurring in an instant or of a change of place happening in 'the *now*'.

When a philosophical mathematician describes an instant by saying, 'the instant does not last for a finite time, and there is not a beginning and an end with an interval between them', he tells us in a misleading way something about the use of the word 'instant' which makes it senseless to speak in certain ways. He tells us that an instant has no duration, which is to say that the word 'instant' has no application to time-intervals. This is the *obstacle* that prevents a thing's moving from one place to another in the *now*. Of course, if 'instant' does not apply to parts of time, then it will make no sense to speak of a body changing its place in the course of an instant. The validating proposition is *a priori*, in knowing which we understand something about the use of 'instant'.

Like the validating proposition, the conclusion that motion is impossible is not empirical. The words 'Bodies are incapable of motion; meteors don't really fall nor do arrows actually fly' are in the language of material fact, but this is a deception. Consider the famous proposition of Heraclitus that everything flows. This also looks to be an astonishing statement about nature, but it is in fact only a linguistic creation, a deceptive manœuvre with familiar words that appeals to our imagination. For no observation and no describable phenomenon will be acceptable evidence, actual or theoretical, of the falsity of the theory to anyone who holds it. It can readily be seen that if we were to say, 'Water flows and so does honey in hot weather. But what about granite mountains and iron ships? Certainly they don't flow', our words would not move in the slightest anyone who holds the Heraclitean view. Nor would he seriously think to tell us, 'Look more closely and carefully and you will see what I have seen. You will see that granite mountains and iron ships do flow, only they flow even more slowly than does honey just before it congeals'. It is not that he has somehow been able to see in things what we haven't been able to see which makes him say that everything flows; granite mountains present the same appearance to his eyes that they do to ours. Moreover, it is not possible to describe any phenomenon with regard to which he would say, 'Well, if it existed, then, to be sure, not everything would flow'. A person who lives in the world that we live in and uses the language that we use but, nevertheless, says, 'Everything flows, water flows and sharks' teeth flow, too', is not using language to describe the world. This is a conclusion that will be plain to anyone who does not suffer from what we might call a metaphysical blind-spot.

What the philosopher does with language is not difficult to see, though why he does it is not, perhaps, so easy to understand. It is clear that the sentence 'Everything flows' would be a true or false description of things, if the word 'flows' were used in it to distinguish between those phenomena which flow and those, which we should perhaps have to imagine, that did not flow. Otherwise, the sentence 'Everything is a flowing thing' would no more be descriptive of things than is the tautologous sentence 'Everything is a thing'. And since a person who holds the view is unable to describe a situation which would, if it existed, render his view false and make him give up saying, 'Everything flows', he is not using the word 'flows' in the ordinary way to modify the word 'thing'. He is not using 'flows' in any way to give us information about phenomena nor to distinguish between things. Consciously or unconsciously, but purposefully, he is not using language to describe a conditions of things. We can see, though his motivation remains obscure, that he has decided to make 'flows' a descriptively *functionless* word. His statement is secure against any criticism which makes use of either fact about nature or fact about actual usage, because his purpose is not to describe either nature or language but only *to change language*. And we may suspect that he has a deeper motive than mere linguistic whimsy for doing this.

In the same way, it can readily be seen that the words 'Motion is impossible' are not being used to express a proposition about things, however strong an impression to the contrary they may create. For if flowing rivers, galloping horses, and flying arrows are to be taken as bodies in a state of rest, what then are we to imagine or describe over and above and in addition to such phenomena that would constitute an instance of a thing being in motion? The question, of course, is rhetorical. The *philosophical* sentence 'Motion is impossible', unlike the ordinary sentences 'Water cannot turn into ice at a temperature below 32° F' and 'Birds cannot fly', is not being used to describe, as in these cases, falsely, a condition of things.

It is the same with the statement, which seems to be the explanation of a familiar phenomenon, that motion 'consists merely in the occupation of different places at different times'. This statement entails the denial that motion involves the *transition* of a moving body from one place to another. No one who denies this would think of denying that moving bodies *appear* to be in a state of transition and that they do not appear to be in a series of 'static states of rest'. We thus have to suppose him to be saying something like this: 'A particle in motion looks to be in a state of transition in the path along which it is moving, but its motion, nevertheless, consists of a succession of static states of rest. It does not get from one place to another; it simply *is* in one place at one time and in another place at another time'.

Now, there is no difficulty about seeing that what only *looks* to be the case could be conceived to *be* the case. Any expression that describes an appearance, visual or otherwise, also describes a theoretical reality; and if it describes an appearance, it will make sense to say it describes a reality, however fantastic it might be to assert that there is such a reality. And if we can say, with sense, that a moving body looks to be in a process of transition, we shall, in our language, have to be able to say, with sense, that it *is* in a process of transition. We cannot intelligibly say the one thing without being able with sense to say the other. But when a philosopher tells us that not only neon sign arrows (which look to pass from one place to another) but also actual arrows in flight are in a succession of states of rest, we are compelled to suppose him to be denying that *any* conceivable phenomenon would answer to the description 'is in a process of transition' or to the description 'is passing from place p_1 to place p_2'. For if flying arrows and shooting stars are not to count as answering to such a description, what on earth are we to reckon as coming under it? Arrows in flight are not neon sign arrows, and how must an arrow behave, other than the way it behaves in flight, in order to be said to be 'passing from one place to another'?

Again, the question is rhetorical. Anyone who denies that a moving body is in a process of transition, anyone who denies that it is in a *'state* of motion' or in process of *getting* from one place to another, is in no position to give a satisfactory answer to the question. In some way, he has ruled himself out from being able to distinguish between the real thing and the illusion. Whatever it may be, his use of 'looks to be in a state of transition' cannot be to describe an appearance, in the way in which the words 'The neon arrow appears to be moving' are used to describe one. In consequence, his purported explanation cannot be an explanation, either right or wrong, of what motion 'consists in'. The sentence 'The motion of a body consists merely in its occupying different places at different times' is in what we might call the 'ontological idiom'. The style of language in which the sentence is written, which makes its outward form like that of the factual explanatory sentence 'The motion of the figures on the film screen consists merely in their occupying different places at different times', deceives us into thinking that this sentence, too, is factual explanatory, whereas, as reflection shows, it cannot be.

If, like the validating proposition, the conclusion of Zeno's proof is not with regard to material fact, it is unlike the validating proposition in not being *a priori* either. We cannot, with reason on our side, think that Zeno wished to prove that motion is a *logical* impossibility, that it is logically impossible for moths to flutter and for eagles to swoop, in the way in which it is logically impossible for a thing to be green all over and also pink. An *a priori* statement may be compared with paper money that is backed by gold, the gold in the case of an *a priori* statement being some linguistic fact with regard to accepted usage. If the sentence 'Motion is impossible' expressed an *a priori* proposition, there would have to be a fact about language to the effect that the word 'motion' had no application to anything that happened and that phrases like 'galloped down the highroad' and 'floated down the stream' described nothing at all.

Now, to try to prove that motion is logically impossible is in effect to try to demonstrate that the word for motion has no literal meaning in the language in which the demonstration is conducted. But how, by the farthest stretch, could anyone be imagined attempting to do such an utterly ridiculous thing? His attempting this, in view of the fact that he knows the use of the word as well as anyone, would be as incomprehensible to us as would be the behaviour of a trained astronomer who, while in the full possession of his senses, tried to reach for the moon. If we restrain our hostile tendency to be scornful of others, we can realize that, whatever it is that he is doing, he cannot be trying to do this. His assertion that motion is impossible can with no more plausibility be supposed *a priori* than it can be supposed to be with regard to material fact. Our intelligence can give its assent to neither. Everyone, probably, has had the experience of observing behaviour which from a distance seemed senseless but which on his drawing nearer and learning more about it became intelligible to him. This was once my experience with the hand language used by deaf-mutes. We may say that our problem is to draw nearer and discover the sense in the apparently senseless verbal misbehaviour in the present case.

It is the same with the claim that the motion of a body consists merely in the body's occupying a series of different places, without passing from any one place to any other. Whatever it is he is doing, a philosopher who says this cannot be so eccentric, and commit such an outrage against our intelligence, as to be declaring that the word 'motion' *means the same as* the phrase 'succession of static states of rest'.

The validating proposition of the argument is *a priori,* and the conclusion is neither *a priori* nor about the behaviour of physical bodies in space. What is the right construction to be placed on the premise, the proposition, namely, that 'Motion implies change of place in the *now*'? If the implication is an entailment, the linguistic gold backing this proposition will have to be some fact to the effect that the combination of words 'is moving but fails to be in motion throughout any instant or moment of time while it is moving' describes no condition of any material thing. More specifically, what would make it logically impossible for a thing to be in motion and not be moving in the *now* would be the fact that the word 'moves' applies to no phenomenon to which 'is changing its position in the *now*' or 'passes from p_1 to p_2 in an instant of time' fails to apply. But by what magical rule of language or logic is anyone able to deduce from the conception of motion the conception of transition from one place to another being effected in the *now*?

According to the validating proposition, no expression of the form 'took only an instant of time to move from p_1 to p_2', or of the form 'moved $\frac{1}{n}$ of an inch in the *now*' applies to any theoretically possible occurrence. According to the philosophical-mathematical dictionary, as it were, the terms 'instant' and 'the *now*' have a definition which prevents their having a descriptive function in combination with the words 'moves', 'runs', and the like. Hence, if 'being in motion' entailed 'effecting a change of position in the *now*,' the term 'motion' would have no application to anything that happened in the physical world. But the word does, of course, have a known and accepted use in the language in which the entailment is stated. It has already been seen that the paradoxical conclusion of the proof, i.e., 'Motion is impossible', could not with any sort of plausibility be construed as being intended to convey the linguistic information that 'motion' is a word which has no application in the language of everyday speech. The proof, therefore, could not be intended to demonstrate this. We are thus led to the idea that the words 'Motion implies a change of position in the *now*' are not, by some unaccountable and persistent mistake, intended to express an entailment which does not exist. Instead, we are forced to think that they have a different purpose. It is purposeful, if unconscious, artistry with language, and not a mere mistake, that creates the paradox.

We get more insight into what has happened linguistically when we notice that, whereas the validating proposition leads in one direction, the premise by itself, considered apart from the validating proposition, leads in an opposite direction. By itself, the proposition that motion implies change of place in an instant of time implies the further proposition that an instant (as well as the *now,* etc.) has *duration.* We could reason in this way: It takes some time, however little, for a body to move from one place to another, however short the distance between the two places; hence, if motion implies change of place in the *now,* then (since motion does take place) the *now,* an instant, and the like *will have to have duration.*

It is to be noticed that the same consequence obtains from the supposition that a body remains *at rest* in the *now.* An instant, which 'does not last for a finite time, and there is not a beginning and an end with an interval between them', has no duration, of course, which is to say that 'instant' is not the name of a very brief unit of time. But it is a fact that the word behaves syntactically like a substantive of a special category, viz., the category of names of time-intervals. We may say that like the word 'point' in the language of geometry, the use of 'instant' has two aspects. Semantically, as regards its use in expressions to convey information, 'instant' is not the name of a time-interval. This is what the validating statement actually informs us. Syntactically, as regards the mode of its use in sentences, 'instant' is a substantive that belongs to the class of words denoting units of time. This is what is indicated by the premise: in an oblique way, the statement 'Motion implies change of place in an instant of time' tells us that 'instant' is *formally,* if not materially, classified with time-interval substantives.

To restate briefly the results with regard to the three propositions. The conclusion that motion is impossible is neither a factual statement about the behaviour of bodies in space nor is it one that in any way tells us something about the established use of the word 'motion'. The premise in an indirect way calls attention to the fact that 'instant' functions syntactically like a substantive that denotes a small unit of time. And the validating proposition calls attention to the fact that the term is not the name of a time-interval.

The problem now is to discover what the conclusion *does* come to and how the facts about the use of 'instant' brought out by the proof are relevant to it. In what way do these facts constitute a proof and what do they 'prove'?

It is to be kept in mind that if the sentence declaring the

impossibility of motion did state an *a priori* proposition, the word 'motion' would then lack application to physical phenomena. The word does, to be sure, have a well-known use; but we can easily understand the *wish,* for some reason or other, to get rid of it. This sort of wish is by no means rare outside of philosophy, and is sometimes expressed without any attempt at concealment. A political scientist, for example, once expressed the wish to have the word 'nation' deleted from our vocabulary and the word 'community' used in its place, because, according to him, the first was connected with aggressive associations in people's minds and the second not. Now, if we interpret the paradox in terms of some such wish, we have an explanation of what has happened, an explanation, moreover, which relates the proof to the conclusion in a way that *makes sense.*

We cannot, with reason on our side, think that a person who maintains the impossibility of motion *believes* that a familiar word for a familiar phenomenon has no application. But no such difficulty stands in our way, if we interpret his statement in terms of an artificially gratified wish *to dispense with the word.* The word remains in actual use and no metaphysician gives it up in normal discourse. But this does not prevent him from composing an *artificial* language, not meant for use in workaday life, which, like a dream, will answer more nearly to his desires. If we suppose that in the metaphysical dictionary of some philosophers 'motion' has been deprived of its use, it then is easy to see what the sentence 'Motion is impossible' comes to. It expresses an *a priori* proposition, not in ordinary language, but in a special language of *metaphysical wish-fulfilment.*

The relevance of the proof to the conclusion becomes comprehensible in the light of the present hypothesis. The proof may be viewed as expressing a *linguistic grievance,* which is used to justify the artificial realization of a linguistic wish. It is a source of dissatisfaction to some people that the word 'instant', or the term 'the *now*', should be one thing and masquerade as another thing, that it should wear the outer cloak of a time-interval denoting substantive and not be one in fact. 'Instant', 'the *now*', 'moment' are counterfeit substantives. This is the 'fault' in language which disturbs; and the philosopher vents his grievance and soothes his feelings by composing a language which has no place for them.

In the language in which 'Motion is impossible' expresses a logical necessity, there is no room for 'instant', 'moment', and 'the *now*'. The proof calls attention to a linguistically unsatisfactory state of affairs, which is remedied by the conclusion.

It is no wonder, then, that no error of reasoning has been found in the proof, for there is none. One can accept the proof or reject it, which is to say one can feel disturbed by the facts it brings out about 'instant', etc., or one can be quite unmoved by them. And that is all there is to it. All this is effectively concealed by the grammar in which the paradox is phrased. Schopenhauer made the penetrating observation that our intellect is in the service of our emotional needs; and, indeed, it would hardly come as a surprise if the motivation for the paradox turned out to have deeper sources than the superficial one that meta-analysis discovers for us.

On the basis of our explanation of what the paradox comes to it is possible to give an account of the three points of view with regard to the proof. A person who holds that the proof contains a mistake and its conclusion says something false rejects both the grievance and the remedy, but uses the scientific style of discourse in which the paradox is stated to do this. What he does is to accept the grammar of logical demonstration, of argument and conclusion, and reject the content. We might, with hardly any exaggeration, say that it is characteristic of the philosophy of Common Sense to prefer the shadow of metaphysics to its substance, that it accepts the scientific façade and with linguistic conservatism, rejects its dramatic content. That is why it is felt by many people to be so disappointing.

The second point of view, which holds the proof to be correct and its conclusion true, accepts both the style and the content of the paradox. The third view, which makes the proof out to be the explanation of what motion really consists in, i.e., the scientific explanation of a phenomenon, also accepts the language of demonstration, but uses the demonstration to retain and *redefine* the word 'motion', rather than to cast it out. The proof is a way of giving to 'motion' the new definition 'occupation of different positions at different times'. It is plain that metaphysical mathematicians who give this definition to 'motion' wish to make *more pronounced* the syntactically name-like use of 'instant', which appeals to them rather than repels them.

I wish to conclude with some general comments on all four of Zeno's paradoxes of motion. The four paradoxes actually reduce to two: The dichotomy and the Achilles and the tortoise are substantially the same; and the stadium and the flying arrow make the same point, though they make it differently. And, in fact, all four paradoxes have, so to speak, the same target.

The argument of the flying arrow expresses a semantic complaint against the mathematical use of the term 'instant of time', which differs radically from the ordinary use of 'instant' and 'moment'. In ordinary, everyday speech it makes perfectly good sense to say, 'Jones paused for an instant' and 'It took him only a moment to dash across the street'. But the mathematical use of 'instant' (*The Shorter Oxford English Dictionary* defines 'instant' as a *point* of time!) is such that it makes no sense whatever to say that anything happened in an instant of time: it makes no sense to say, e.g., 'Jones paused for a *mathematical* instant'. The complaint is about the name-like use of a word which, in fact, is not used as the name, either general or proper, of an interval of time. The word has the *grammatical* function of a substantive, and this creates the semantic illusion that the word denotes a minute interval of time. It is this semantic illusion against which the complaint is directed.

The stadium paradox, which purports to demonstrate that half of an instant of time is equal to the whole of the instant, expresses the same linquistic complaint against the mathematical use of 'instant'. It attempts, but in a linguistically concealed way, to expose the fact that the words 'instant' and 'moment' do not denote microscopically small time-intervals. And it does this by showing that the supposition that the words denote time-spans implies a contradiction. Drawing the contradictory consequence consists in doing no more than showing that *no* mathematically expressible interval of time is *brief enough* to be a *mathematical* instant or moment, which is the same thing as calling attention to the fact that 'instant' *denotes no time interval,* however short. But calling attention to this linguistic fact is the same as pointing out that 'instant' is a noun which has *zero naming function,* i.e., that it is a grammatical noun only, not also a semantic noun, and, thus, that it is a linguistic fraud.

It may be remarked here that the claim that a *physical* distance, say a physical line of a given length, does not consist of geometric points, makes the same complaint against the geometrical use of the word 'point'. A geometrical point is not a unit of length, however small; and this, expressed in the less misleading linguistic idiom, is to say that as it is used in geometry the noun 'point' is not the name of a spatial unit. Again, the dissatisfaction is directed against a name which is a semantic sham, against a word which has the formal, grammatical use in sentences of a name, but not the substantial use of one.

The dichotomy connects up directly with the instant of time, or point of time, paradoxes. The Achilles and the tortoise adds nothing new to the dichotomy; and I now wish to consider briefly a version of the dichotomy which does not refer to points. I do this in order to avoid getting involved in an extended discussion of the geometrical use of the word 'point'. The version I wish to discuss is as follows: In order to traverse a given distance, d, a moving body, a, must first traverse $\frac{d}{2}$, and in order to traverse $\frac{d}{2}$, a must first traverse $\frac{d}{4}$, etc., *ad infinitum*. That is, in order to traverse *any* distance, however short, a must finish traversing an infinite number of distances which decrease toward zero after the manner of an infinite geometric sequence. But since it is logically impossible to *finish* traversing a non-terminating number of distances, regardless of whether or not they decrease in length, motion is impossible and a is forever fixed to its place.

The conclusion of the argument, namely, that motion is impossible, is not about the physical phenomenon of motion nor about the word 'motion'. I think it is clear by now that the conclusion does not deny the existence or possibility of physical motion nor does it deny that the word 'motion' has application to actual or theoretically possible phenomena. The argument, then, is not to be interpreted as being an attempt to demonstrate either of these two things. What, then, are we to make of the argument? What does it try to show?

It must be quite plain that the argument tells us something about *infinite geometric series,* for it tells us that in order to traverse a given distance, d, a must first traverse $\frac{d}{2}, \frac{d}{4}, \frac{d}{8}, \frac{d}{16}$, etc., *ad infinitum*.

Amongst other things, it tells us something about the geometric series $1 + \frac{1}{2} + \frac{1}{4} + \frac{1}{8}$ . . . And what it tells us is the well-known fact that the series has no last member, that no value of $\frac{1}{2^{n-1}}$ is the smallest number derivable from $\frac{1}{2^{n-1}}$ by substituting numbers for n, however large. The sentence, 'It is impossible to finish traversing an infinite number of regularly decreasing distances', says that it is impossible to run through, or *add up and arrive at the sum of,* an infinite geometric series. In a paper to the *Aristotelian Society,* Bertrand Russell maintained that it is 'medically', not logically, impossible to write out the whole of an infinite series.[1] But this is simply ridiculous. The impossibility of running through the *whole* of an infinite series is logical, not physical, because the series is non-terminating; and running through an *entire* series entails counting its *last,* terminal member. No infinite series can be a *whole,* completed, series.

This is true. But what are we to make of having this pointed out to us *in connexion with the idea of motion?* It can easily be seen that the argument calls attention to a tremendous difference between finite series and infinite geometric series. An infinite geometric series has no last term and it has no sum, in the arithmetical sense of 'sum'; it has only a limit. In these respects it is entirely different from a finite series. And, in fact, an infinite geometric series is a *formula* for generating series, the so-called 'partial series'. The infinite series

$$1 + \tfrac{1}{2} + \tfrac{1}{4} + \tfrac{1}{8} + \; . \; . \; .$$

is the partial series $1 + \frac{1}{2} + \frac{1}{4} + \frac{1}{8}$, together with implicit instructions as to how *further* partial series are to be written; this it does by illustrating how the terms are related to each other. The dots '. . .' do not denote the *remainder* of the series, in the way in which the line '. . . $+30$' in the expression '$3 + 6 + 9 + 12 + $. . . $+30$' stands for the remainder of a series. It is *nothing more than* the instruction to go on in the same manner.

The argument of the dichotomy points out the great difference between an ordinary series and an infinite geometric series, and the conclusion states a concealed alteration of terminology. The conclusion expresses the decision not to classify so-called 'infinite

[1] *Proc. Arist. Soc.,* Vol. XXXVI, p. 143.

series' with series, which is to say, it expresses the linguistic decision not to call an infinite series a 'series'. An American mathematician once did a similar thing and without concealment; he
refused to use the expression 'finite number' on the grounds that
infinite numbers are not numbers and, therefore, that the word
'finite' does not *distinguish* between numbers. Again, the argument
of the dichotomy is a linguistic complaint against lumping infinite and finite series together by calling both 'series', and the
conclusion corrects the situation by denying the name 'series' to
what are called 'infinite geometric series'.

But how is the idea that motion is impossible connected with
the refusal to call an infinite series a 'series'? Among other things,
it is a spectacular way of introducing a contracted use of the word
'series'. In connexion with the argument, viz., that a distance consists of an infinite geometric series of distances, the conclusion that
motion is impossible, or that *a distance cannot be traversed,* comes to
saying that since an infinite geometric series has no sum (or is not
a whole), it is not a series. Quite clearly it is a colourful way of
declaring that it is absurd to call an infinite series a 'series'.

To sum up. The first two paradoxes are semantic complaints
against calling an infinite geometric series a 'series'. The second
two paradoxes are, in effect, complaints against the same thing;
they reject the attempt to make an infinite series *look,* linguistically,
like an ordinary series, i.e., a finite series. The dichotomy constitutes an objection to applying the term 'series' to so-called infinite
series, because they have no last member and are therefore not
whole series. Russell speaks of 'the mistaken supposition that there
cannot be anything beyond the whole of an infinite series, which
can be seen to be false by observing that 1 is beyond the whole of
the infinite series $\frac{1}{2}, \frac{3}{4}, \frac{7}{8}, \frac{15}{16}$ . . .'[1]. But Russell is mistaken. There is
no *whole* series beyond which 1 lies; 1 is the *limit* of the series. And
the series is not a *whole* in the sense of a *completed* series, after the *last*
member of which 1 comes.

The flying arrow and the stadium paradoxes constitute objections
to the namelike use of 'point'—'point of time' or 'point of space', it
does not matter which. The terms 'mathematical instant', 'moment',
'infinitesimal' or, to use an expression of Anaxagoras', 'the least
of what is small', are syntactical, not semantic, names. But they

[1] *Our Knowledge of the External World,* (1929), p. 188.

have the formal, if not the actual, rôle of denoting the last member, the least of what is small, of an unending decreasing series. They are semantically spurious but are designed to make an infinite geometric series *look* like a *completed* series, by making it appear to have a *last* member, and therefore making it appear to have an arithmetical sum which cannot be arrived at arithmetically by adding the terms.

Weierstrass banished infinitesimals from the actual doing of mathematics, but Russell and others, who speak about the *whole* of an infinite series, provide excellent evidence for believing that Weierstrass did not banish infinitesimals from the *thinking* about mathematics. The formal, but otherwise spurious, substantives 'point' and 'instant' make it grammatically possible to speak about the *whole* of an *unending* series; that is, they make it possible to speak of a formula for generating 'partial series' as if the formula were the series it generates. Their use makes the infinite series

$$1 + \tfrac{1}{2} + \tfrac{1}{4} + \tfrac{1}{8} + \ldots$$

look, at least in formal respects, *like* the finite series

$$3 + 6 + 9 + 12 + \ldots + 30,$$

by enabling one to think of the infinite series *as if* it were terminating:

$$1 + \tfrac{1}{2} + \tfrac{1}{4} + \tfrac{1}{8} + \ldots + \textit{infinitesimal}$$

or

$$d + \frac{d}{2} + \frac{d}{4} + \frac{d}{8} + \ldots + \textit{point}.$$

The instant-of-time paradoxes are expressions of opposition to this verbal chicanery. The four paradoxes, taken together, constitute an attempt to expose the enormous difference between finite series and so-called infinite series; and they end with conclusions which refuse to recognize 'point' and 'instant' as being even the formal, make-believe names of the last members of unending geometrical series. They also refuse to classify infinite series with finite series under the common designation 'series'.

IX

NEGATIVE TERMS

I T is not uncommon for philosophers to take scornful attitudes toward each other's views and to dismiss them as ridiculous and an insult to our intelligence. Indeed, one is tempted to think that an important *technique of refutation* in philosophy is scorn and ridicule, a technique, that is to say, of intellectual intimidation. But it need hardly be remarked, or perhaps it *does* need pointing out, that such an emotive procedure leads to no insight into the theories dismissed. For it has to be realized that of all the disciplines which make use of proofs and refutations, philosophy stands alone in having no solidly established results.

In the present paper I wish mainly to consider a view which has been dismissed by many philosophers as scandalous nonsense and as being based on the grossest of mistakes. My purpose is to examine this view soberly and dispassionately and try to see what it comes to and also to discover whether it is based on the gross mistake some people think it is based on. The view I propose to examine has been expressed in sentences like the following: 'Anxiety reveals the nothing'; 'We know the nothing'; 'The nothing exists'.

What is to be made of these sentences; how are we to interpret them? And what sort of mistake, if any, is a person making who utters them with the assured air of stating propositions about the truth of which there can be no doubt? The sentences are strikingly unusual because, for one thing, they use the word 'nothing' in a grammatically strange way. In ordinary speech 'nothing' is not prefaced with the definite article; it is not grammatical English to speak of 'the nothing'. And for another thing, the word 'nothing', quite apart from the strangeness of its being combined with the definite article in the sentences, is being used in a queer way that eludes our understanding. It is hard for us to see what anyone, for example, the sophist Gorgias, wishes to convey with the words 'Nothing exists'.[1] Some philosophers have voiced the complaint that the sentence 'The nothing exists' does not have a translation into the common vernacular and have, on the basis of this fact, proceeded to the position that the sentence is literally without sense. Thus, the sentence, if it does have sense, presents us with two difficulties which stand in the way of our interpreting it: (1) the use of 'nothing' with the definite article, 'the nothing'; and (2) its use with 'exists', 'Nothing exists'. And before trying to interpret its use in 'The nothing exists' it will be helpful to divide our problem and first attempt to arrive at an understanding of what a philosopher is saying who declares that 'Nothing exists'.

Imagine someone saying in earnest: 'At this moment, for instance, I see nothing on the small table next to the armchair in my study, and I also see nobody in my armchair. I *see* nothing and nobody, so of course they exist. Unquestionably others too have also seen nothing and nobody in various places, so other people also know perfectly well that nothing and nobody exist. Many people, of course, deny that nothing and nobody exist, but it is not easy to understand the psychology of such sceptics'. Said in all seriousness by a person, these words produce a mystifying effect. For he uses language which is like the language of someone who is talking about extremely refined and subtle objects, ghost-like entities which those of us with less refined perception or those of us who lack the necessary rapport with the occult are not privileged to see.

His words suggest the occult; but, despite his talk, reason cannot permit its being supposed that he is seeing or claiming to see a very refined and subtle object. A person who truly says that he sees nothing on the table and nobody in the armchair does not see an object on the table nor does he see anybody in the chair. When two people inspect the same table and one declares that he sees nothing on it while the other declares that he does not see anything on it, it is not the case that one sees something which the other somehow fails to see: what is seen is the same for both.

[1]See John Burnet, *Greek Philosophy, Pt. I, Thales to Plato*, p. 120.

Only as a Lewis Carroll joke should we say to the second person, 'Rub your eyes and look harder'. Nor can it be supposed that the first person is suffering from some sort of hallucination, is stating the existence of something which he imagines he sees. His words do not, nor are they intended to, express an empirical belief about the existence of something he thinks he sees, a belief which could elicit from us the comment, 'He thinks he sees nothing, but he isn't really seeing it'. His mistake, if he is making one, is not a perceptual mistake with regard to a state of affairs. Apart from his words, his behaviour, it is to be noted, is in no way different from that of the person who says he does not see anything on the table. It is not like that of a person who is suffering from a hallucination. In the present context, the assertion that nothing exists quite plainly cannot be construed as an utterance which is intended to state an empirical fact about the existence of something. It cannot be construed as affirming the existence of a kind of thing, nor can it be construed as denying the existence of everything—as denying, e.g., that the table on which there is nothing exists. Philosophers are using the sentence to do a different kind of work.

More natural, perhaps, than the idea that the statement makes an empirical claim about a state of affairs is the idea that it constitutes an improper use of language or that it misdescribes the use of an ordinary word: more specifically, that the statement either uses the word 'nothing' in an improper, senseless way or is a misdescription of the use of the word. The latter idea is more natural, though by no means the more important one to examine. The notion that metaphysical propositions are empirical is too easily dismissed nowadays, with the result that what is dismissed without sufficient insight remains to trouble and make ambiguous the reasoning of philosophers who dismiss it. However that may be, the usual charge levelled against what we may call the Metaphysician of the Reality of Nothing is that he has committed the gross blunder of thinking that because 'nothing' is a substantive word it is the name of an object.

It is quite possible, to be sure, for a person to believe that the word 'nothing is the name of a thing. Imagine a newcomer to the English language being taught nouns like 'house', 'moon', 'Jones', and how to use them in simple sentences. Along with these words, which are classified for him as substantives under parts of speech, he is told that 'nothing' is a noun but is not taught its use. It could easily happen in such a case that he would think that 'nothing', like the other substantives he had been taught, is the name, either general or proper, of a thing. We can imagine, further, the sort of trick being played on him that the two rascally tailors in the fairy tale played on the gullible king. His teachers not only classify 'nothing' as a substantive, they also utter such sentences as 'Nothing is next to the chair', 'I see that nothing is now on the table', and behave as if they were talking about something. They carry their prank so far as to act amazed and become somewhat condescending when he conveys to them that he does not see anything. Finally, to cover his embarrassment over his inferred optical inferiority, he starts talking and behaving like his teachers. Such a person would have a false notion about the actual use of 'nothing'.

The case of the metaphysician who gives the impression of believing that 'nothing' is the name of a thing is entirely different. He has *complete* information about the use of the word and no verbal prank has been played on him. He was taught not only its grammatical classification but also its actual use and knows it perfectly well. And if, in spite of this, he nevertheless does in fact believe that it is the name of a thing, then he is indeed *grossly* mistaken. But this precisely is the trouble with the idea that he has a mistaken belief about the ordinary use of the word: the mistake is *too gross* for him to have made it. If it is hard for us to conceive of anyone who has been properly instructed in the use of words like 'chair' and 'coat' and uses them correctly every day as well as responds appropriately to their use by others *believing* that the words are *not* names of articles of furniture and clothing, it should, if we stop to think of it, be equally hard to think of anyone who has been properly trained in the correct use of 'nothing' actually believing that it is the name of an object. It should be hard to think this of anyone, despite his *philosophical talk,* which, it has to be admitted, lends superficial plausibility to the charge. To be sure, it is psychologically possible to have a belief which conflicts with what we know perfectly well; when the *need* to believe is great enough, we believe, in spite of what we know. But it would be foolish to suppose that a metaphysician's need to believe that 'nothing' is the name of an entity is so great as to blind him completely to the crudity of his blunder, and so great, moreover, as to prevent his seeing his blunder when it is pointed out to him. For it is completely safe to bet that if it were patiently explained to him that the word is not used in ordinary language as a name he would be quite unmoved. For some mysterious reason, he does not accept ordinary usage as in any way showing the incorrectness or impropriety of his *philosophical* sentences, though he does accept common usage as a corrective to any linguistic mistakes he may make in *non-philosophical* conversations. It is this mystifyingly stubborn refusal to accept correction that needs to be explained and remains unexplained on the view that he has made a linguistic blunder.

It may be said that a philosophical belief is entirely different from an ordinary, everyday belief. Philosophical beliefs are one thing and ordinary beliefs and doubts are quite a different thing, it may be contended, and we must not expect from the former what we expect from the latter. A philosopher once gave me an argument which he said was a conclusive refutation of a current view about the nature of ethical statements. I asked him whether the most important advocate of this view, a philosopher with whom he had discussed the view on a number of occasions, would accept his refutation and give up his view, and was told in a voice which reprimanded me for being so naïve, 'No, of course not'. But our not expecting from a philosophical belief and argument what we expect from an ordinary belief is in need of explanation, and it is not explained in the least by saying that philosophical propositions are believed *philosophically*. To call a belief 'philosophical' is only to give a name to something we do not understand. What we want to understand is the supposedly mistaken belief that 'nothing' is the name of an object; and it is of no help to say that the person who believes it cannot see his mistake because his belief is philosophical and quite different from the belief a well-known philosopher humorously confessed he had until recently, that 'longitude' was pronounced with a hard 'g'. It is no help whatever to distinguish between the metaphysician and a stranger to the English language who has a wrong ordinary belief about the use of a word by saying that the former's wrong belief is philosophical.

If we think objectively and with detachment on the subject it becomes clearly unplausible to suppose a philosopher believes that 'nothing' is commonly used as the name of an entity, while at the same time not denying that he knows its actual use. The impulse to *refute* plays a considerable part in the barrier we erect against our seeing this and against our understanding the nature of the theories we 'refute'. But over-easy Sir Lanceloting is little more than Don Quixote charging a windmill; it slays no metaphysical monsters.

Philosophers who place no weight on the consideration that it is unplausible to suppose that a metaphysician can continue to believe, in the face of criticism, that 'nothing' is the name of an object give two main reasons for not thinking the supposition unplausible. For one thing, it is maintained that it is quite possible to know how to *use* a word correctly and nevertheless misdescribe its use. And for another thing, it is maintained that the force of an argument for a philosophical view can be so persuasive as to convince a philosopher of the truth of his view, despite his knowing on other grounds that it is false, that he can be *swept away* by his argument into holding his view. Let us examine these reasons separately.

The point that knowing how to use a term correctly is different from knowing how to *explain* its use, so that it is possible for a person to misdescribe its use while being able to use it perfectly well, is not to be disputed. This point reminds us of the distinction G. E. Moore has made between knowing the meaning of a word and knowing the analysis of its meaning. Just as a person may be able to walk unerringly from Victoria Station to Piccadilly Circus but misdescribe the route to others, or even be at a loss altogether to describe it, so it is possible for us to be able to use a word properly but, nevertheless, give a wrong explanation of its use. In order to be able to use words like 'nothing' and 'yesterday' it is not necessary to be able to describe or explain *in other words* their use. But anyone who is able to use a word correctly is able to *show* how it is used; for all that is required to show how a word is used is to *use* it.

And not only this. A person who knows the use of a word but misdescribes it will *give up* his description if his attention is called to an instance of actual usage with which his description does not square. If, for example, someone who knows how to use 'chair' tells us that it *means* any object which is used by people to sit on, and is really trying to explain in other words what the word means, then, if it is pointed out to him that people sometimes sit on tables, tree stumps, and even floors, and that tables, tree stumps, and floors are not chairs, he will admit that his explanation is wrong and give it up. He will admit it is wrong, just as a person who mis-describes the way to Piccadilly Circus will admit his directions are wrong if we take him with us and, following his directions, end up in Chelsea. But the case is different with the metaphysician: facing him with evidence of actual usage does not make him give up his apparently false description. The distinction between use of a word and description of its use explains how it is possible to have mistaken ideas about words we know how to use perfectly well, but it does not explain why, in the case of a philosophical misdescription of a word, bringing instances of actual usage to bear against the misdescription does not result in its being given up. It does not explain the remarkable difference between a meta-physical mistake and an ordinary linguistic error. It throws no light on the question as to why a metaphysician who believes that 'nothing' is the name of a thing fails to give up his belief when it is pointed out to him that, unlike saying that a book is on the table, saying that nothing is on the table is the same as saying there is not anything on the table.

It can be seen that the second reason, namely, that a meta-physician is able to hold his view despite what he knows because he is convinced by the argument which backs it also fails to clear up this mystery. There is no question but that, quite in general, we are frequently led to hold false views by fallacious arguments which seem sound to us. But it is as plain as anything can be that no reasoning, regardless of how sound it may seem, can stand up against known fact, and that no argument, however impeccable it may seem, can prevent us from rejecting a proposition which we know to be false. And it is just as plain, with regard to an ordinary case of someone having been misled by an argument into accepting a false proposition, that if he is presented with undeni-able fact which goes against the proposition, he will accept the fact and reject the proposition and its proof. He would not insist in the face of fact that the argument *is* sound and that therefore the proposition it backs *is* true. But precisely the opposite happens time and again in metaphysics. Calling a metaphysician's attention to actual usage, to instances of the way he uses an expression and to the way he responds to its use by other people in everyday discourse, does not discourage him about the validity of his argument and the truth of his view. Instead of discarding his argument as certainly containing a fallacy, even though he cannot discover the fallacy, he resists the idea that the facts conclusively show that the argument must be fallacious. It is this resistance against admitting that the facts invalidate the argument and show his proposition to be false that is not accounted for by those who maintain that he holds his view because he is taken in by its demonstration. An argument can sometimes beguile us into accepting a proposition which we should otherwise reject as false, but to imagine that it can continue to do its magic work in the face of presented and undeniable fact is to indulge in unrealistic thinking. Indeed, it seems more plausible to think that metaphysicians become ingenious in behalf of the views they are determined to hold than to think that they become convinced of the views by arguments.

The mystery increases when we consider the purported reason on which the view that nothing exists is based; for taken as an *argument*, it is so transparently false that we do not understand how anyone could be taken in by it, nor why the mistake is not recognized immediately on its being pointed out. The supposed argument for the view, i.e., the reasoning which leads to holding the view, is that 'nothing' must be the name of an object because it is a substantive word. But this argument is so transparently fallacious that we are puzzled to think that anyone could be deceived by it. We can hardly imagine anyone seriously arguing that 'chair' and 'coat' are not names of things because 'nothing' is a noun which is not the name of anything. We should find it equally hard to imagine anyone seriously arguing that because 'coat' and 'chair' are names of things, the substantive 'nothing' must also be a name. And supposing that by a miracle the term did mislead someone, we are at a complete loss to understand what could have happened to prevent his seeing the mistake once it is pointed out to him that not all substantives are names, and that from the fact that 'nothing' is a substantive it does not follow that it is a name.

It seems plain that if we go on the assumption that the metaphysician is either misdescribing the use of 'nothing' or has been led into talking nonsense because of a misconception of its use we can give no reasonable account of his resistance to correction. There can be no hope of understanding why he does not *feel* corrected. There is, however, another possible hypothesis left to consider. This is not that the metaphysician has made a blunder and for some unaccountable reason resists correction but that he has not made any sort of mistake. This hypothesis does not come naturally to us; it is entirely foreign to our way of looking at metaphysics. But it will not seem as strange and unplausible as it does at first sight if in conjunction with the fact that the metaphysician knows the ordinary use of 'nothing' we take seriously his resistance to correction of *his* idea of the use of the word. It is, after all, possible that he knows better than we do what *he* is doing with the word and does not accept correction because he is not using or describing the word mistakenly. This is a hypothesis which a genuine desire to understand what has happened should lead us to investigate.

Now, if unlike 'Existence exists', which either misdescribes the use of 'existence' or uses it mistakenly, the sentence 'Nothing exists' neither uses 'nothing' in a senseless way nor misdescribes its actual use in ordinary language, what does the sentence come to, what is its interpretation? What is being done with the word 'nothing'?

Suppose a physicist at a party where couples are waltzing were to say, 'Those people are working only moderately hard'. We should be rather shocked to hear him speak in this way and protest that they were not *working,* that they were *waltzing* and entertaining themselves. If he went on to say that he could see they were waltzing but that none the less they were working, that waltzing is a form of work, we might naturally think he had a wrong notion of the use of 'work' and was applying it improperly to the dancing couples. We should then feel inclined to correct his language. But if he went on to explain that he was quite familiar with the ordinary, vulgar use of 'work' but in the present situation was using it in its technical physical sense of *expenditure of energy,* then we should no longer feel shocked or think he was using the word in an improper, mistaken way. We should no longer be tempted to correct him, though we might well think that he was using an ordinary term in a special technical sense which in the given situation would mislead people.

In the same way, a metaphysician who uses the word 'nothing' in a way which surprises and baffles us is using it in a special, philosophical way, which a little ingenuity suffices to penetrate. If, like the physicist, the metaphysician were in a position to explain how he is using 'nothing', what he is doing with the word, we should be pacified and no longer try to correct him, though our interest in his utterance might vanish with our puzzlement. Unfortunately, he cannot explain what he is doing with the word in the statement 'Nothing exists'; he can only use it in a way which fascinates and satisfies him. There is nothing cryptic in this remark once it is realized that we use language in unconscious ways as well as in conscious way. And what we have to try to do is to understand the unconscious thing he is doing with the word. There is a strong and understandable temptation to think that a metaphysician who uses a familiar word in a way we do not understand and, furthermore, can give no explanation of his usage, is talking nonsense, is using the word senselessly. But it has to be realized that it is psychologically possible to use language in unusual ways and, without being able to explain our use, still make sense, though not obviously so. Like the artist who paints his pictures without being able to explain their underlying meanings, the metaphysical artist creates with words but cannot explain his creations. The hidden things he does we have to discover for ourselves.

Consider the following sentences taken from *Alice Through the Looking Glass*:—

'I see nobody on the road,' said Alice.

'I only wish I had such eyes', the King remarked in a fretful tone. 'To be able to see Nobody. And at that distance too! Why it's as much as I can do to see real people in this light!'

.   .   .

'Who did you pass on the road?' the King went on, holding out his hand to the Messenger for some hay.

'Nobody,' said the Messenger.

'Quite right,' said the King, 'this lady saw him too. So of course Nobody walks slower than you'.

'I do my best,' the Messenger said in a sullen tone. 'I'm sure nobody walks much faster than I do!'

'He can't do that,' said the King, 'or else he'd have been here first!'

This is delightful linguistic whimsy which we can enjoy and understand. A humorous *game* is being played with the word 'nobody', and what makes it possible to play this game with a semblance of linguistic realism is the fact that the word grammatically lends itself to the verbal game. The word 'nobody' is quite plainly being used, in pretence, *as if* it were the name of a person, an unrealish and more subtle and difficult person to see than an ordinary, substantial, everyday person like John Smith. What makes this engaging, make-believe use of 'nobody' possible is that it is a grammatical substantive. The word 'nobody' is, of course, *only a grammatical substantive*; it is not, to invent an expression, a *semantic substantive*, that is to say, a substantive which, like 'Massachusetts' or 'moon', is a general or proper name of an object. But the fact that 'nobody' functions grammatically like a semantic noun creates the whimsical possibility of pretending that it also *is* a semantic noun. Lewis Carroll has not written literally nonsensical sentences, sentences which are verbal jingles devoid of any sense. We can quite well understand what he is doing with the word 'nobody', the language game he plays with it, and we can enter into his game with enjoyment of the comical uses the word lends itself to.

We now have a clue to the metaphysical use of 'nothing', a clue which if taken together with Plato's profound observation that the genius of comedy is the same with that of tragedy[1] can lead to considerable insight. Like Carroll, the Metaphysician of the Reality of Nothing knows the linguistic facts, grammatical and semantic, about the use of 'nothing' and 'nobody', and we may well conjecture that he too is playing a verbal game. But he plays his game with 'nothing' with a different attitude. He takes it seriously, without his tongue in his cheek.

For some reason, which may go quite deep psychologically,[2] the metaphysician is seriously dissatisfied with the fact that the word 'nothing' has the grammatical function of a substantive but does not, so to speak, get enough linguistic credit for its

[1] *Symposium*, 223.
[2] The assertion that *anxiety* reveals the nothing suggests this.

grammatical work. He is discontented with its being *merely* a grammatical noun and sees the possibility of assimilating it into the class of semantic nouns, without making it the name of anything. What he does to correct the unsatisfactory linguistic state of affairs is to make more pronounced the similarity between the functioning of 'nothing' and that of words like 'moon' and 'ghost'. He gratifies his wish to have 'nothing' as a thing-denoting substantive, instead of as a noun which does not name, by *creating* a bit of language in which 'nothing' is used *as if* it were a name. The sentence 'Nothing is on the table' is like the sentence 'The inkwell is on the table', but not like enough for him; for 'Nothing is on the table' has, in ordinary English, the translation 'There is not anything on the table'. And what he does to make the sentences more alike, make the function of 'nothing' more like that of 'inkwell', is to preface 'nothing' with the definite article. Instead of saying, 'Nothing is on the table', he says, 'The nothing is on the table', and so prevents the translation of 'nothing' into 'not anything'. The metaphysical statement 'The nothing exists' informs us that 'nothing' is being treated as a semantic substantive in the private grammar book of the metaphysician. The word has not actually been changed into a thing-denoting substantive. It has become a name with *zero naming function*, a name by grammatical courtesy only. The statements 'The nothing exists' and 'we know the nothing' simply realize the metaphysician's wish, not in fact to use 'nothing' as the name of a thing, but to use it in such a way in sentences as to make it *look* as if 'nothing' is the name of a thing. And he realizes his wish by *exaggerating* a grammatical similarity at the expense of a semantic difference.

It is easy to see now what has been done with the adverbial particle 'not' in the queer sentence 'The nothing nots'. 'Not' has been changed into a grammatical verb and formally classified with verbs denoting an action. But like 'nothing' which names no thing, 'nots' names no action. The sentence 'The nothing nots' produces the eerie illusion of stating the existence of a mysterious something which does a mysterious act, and perhaps the grammatically curious things done with 'nothing' and 'not' have been done with the purpose of producing this illusion. In any case, it is possible to make sense of what has been done with language. In the ordinary sentence 'The rabbit runs', 'rabbit' is the general name of an animal and 'runs' is a verb which denotes an action. In the metaphysical sentence 'The nothing nots' the words 'nothing' and 'nots' are only linguistically make-believe name and verb. But just as we can understand ordinary make-believe, so we can also understand the more subtle linguistic make-believe of a metaphysician.

The present reconstruction of what has happened makes intelligible the metaphysician's resistance to the usual criticisms directed against his view. He is not talking nonsense, and so remains unmoved by the charge that he is. Nor is he misdescribing the ordinary uses of 'nothing' and 'not'. For his use of these terms is a *changed* use. It is a new grammatical use which we can understand and either accept or reject, depending on whether it appeals to us or repels us.

The explanation we have arrived at throws light on the further and more sophisticated metaphysical theory that 'the real is the positive',[1] the theory, in other words that there are no negative facts, e.g., that 'there is not a fact "sun-not-shining" which is affirmed by the true statement "The sun is not shining"'.[2] Consider the following:—

> Let us take some very simple negation, such as 'this is not white'. You say this, we will suppose, in the course of a discussion with the laundry. The phrase 'this is white' is in your mind, *this* is before your eyes, and 'this is grey' is a sentence describing your experience. But 'this is not white' is not a sentence describing what you see, and yet, on the basis of what you see, you are sure that it is true, in other words, that 'this is white' is false.[3]

And also the following:—

> Suppose you are told 'there is butter in the larder, but no cheese'. Although they seem equally based upon sensible experience in the larder, the two statements 'there is butter' and 'there is not cheese' are really on a very different level. There is a definite occurrence which was seeing butter, and which might have put the word 'butter' into your mind even if you had not been thinking of butter. But there was no occurrence

[1] H. W. B. Joseph, *An Introduction to Logic*, p. 171.
[2] B. Russell, *Human Knowledge* (1948), p. 500.
[3] B. Russell, *Inquiry into Meaning and Truth*, p. 99.

which could be described as 'not seeing cheese' or as 'seeing the absence of cheese'. You must have looked at everything in the larder, and judged, in each case, 'this is not cheese'. You *judged* this, you did not see it; you saw what each thing was, not what it was not.[1]

To many readers, and in particular to philosophical defenders of ordinary language, these quotations will seem to contain downright mistakes about ordinary language. If we interpret the statement that ' "this is not white" is not a sentence describing what you see' as making a factual linguistic claim about 'this is not white' (and a whole host of similar negative sentences), it is obviously false. For interpreted as making such a claim, the statement declares that the words 'I see that this is not white' are devoid of intelligibility. Just as 'I hear the sweetness of honey' makes no literal, descriptive sense in English because the phrase 'the sweetness of honey' does not describe anything which we could with sense be said to hear, so, according to the interpreted claim, 'I see that this book cover is not white' makes no descriptive sense because 'This book cover is not white' does not describe anything which we could with intelligibility be said to see. But, of course, 'I see that this is not white' is a perfectly intelligible sentence in ordinary English and frequently expresses what is true. And this could hardly be unknown to a metaphysician who seems, on the surface, to deny it; and it certainly could not be denied by him once his attention is called to it.

Or, again, take the words 'There was no occurrence which could be described as "not seeing cheese" or as "seeing the absence of cheese" '. These words appear to express the claim that the ordinary phrase 'seeing the absence of cheese' describes no conceivable occurrence; and if this is in fact the claim that is being made, then it amounts to stating that 'seeing the absence of cheese' is an empty phrase, syntactically correct, but otherwise devoid of sense. For if the phrase had a meaning, it would describe an occurrence, actual or theoretically imaginable; and if it describes nothing, it is meaningless. If this is the claim made by a philosopher who says that 'There was no occurrence which could be described as "seeing the absence of cheese" ', then there can be no real question as to whether he is mistaken. For it is an easy

[1] B. Russell, *Inquiry into Meaning and Truth*, pp. 89–90.

matter to think of any number of occurrences which would properly and correctly be described by phrases of the form 'sees the absence of *x*', 'sees no *x*', 'sees that there is no *x*', 'notices the absence of *x*', etc. If, for example, you go to a party hoping to see your friend Jones there, you could, after having looked at all the guests present and not seen him, truthfully and certainly with literal sense say to your host, 'I see that Jones is not here'. A school teacher on frequent occasions can be described as 'seeing the absence of one of his students'. And it is sometimes true and properly describes an occurrence to say, 'To his annoyance he saw that the dictionary was not in its accustomed place on the table'. Without going into tedious repetition, it cannot with any sort of plausibility be thought that a philosopher who *seems* to be claiming that such expressions are senseless is actually claiming this.

Consider, further, the word 'judge'. In ever so many cases of a person not seeing a thing, for example, in the case of your failing to find a collar stud for which you are looking in a cluttered drawer, it would be a proper way to describe the situation to say, 'I have looked long enough; I judge that it isn't here'. The sentence 'Jones did not see his coat in the cloakroom and inferred it was not there' describes what happened, even if it were true that Jones's coat was concealed by other coats and his inference was false. In other cases, however, it would be linguistic tomfoolery to use 'judge' and 'infer'. Suppose you wanted your dictionary, went to the small stand on which you usually kept it, and found it was not there. In such a case it would be incorrect English, a misuse of 'judge', to say, while looking at the bare stand, 'I *judge* that the dictionary is not on the stand'. This would be as much an absurdity of language as it would be for you to say at a time when you are in your study, 'I judge that there is no elephant in my study'. And it would also be improper English, in the circumstance of your looking at the bare stand, to say, 'I do *not see* that the dictionary is not on the stand', while it would be a proper way of describing the situation to say, 'I *see* that the dictionary is not on the stand'.

But we miss entirely the point of what the metaphysician is doing if we think he is making mistakes about ordinary language. The fact that the putative mistakes which dupe a metaphysician are so very obvious and glaring to *others* should warn us that there is much more than appears on the surface.

A philosopher who tells us that 'the statements 'there is butter' and 'there is no cheese' are really on a very different level' is in an obscure way calling attention to an actual linguistic difference between the statements. And it is not difficult to discover what the difference in 'level' is. When we truly assert that we see butter, there is *something* which we are seeing. But when we truly assert that we see no cheese, or that we notice the absence of cheese, there is not a thing that we are seeing. The nouns 'butter' and 'cheese' are names of articles of diet, but the terms 'no butter' and 'absence of cheese' are not names of anything. The words 'white' and 'grey' are adjectives which name colours, but the terms 'not white' and 'not grey' are not names of colours. The difference in 'level' between 'there is butter' and 'there is no cheese' and between 'this is grey' and 'this is not white' lies in the difference between the functioning of 'butter' and 'no cheese' and in the difference between the functioning of 'grey' and 'not white'.

Consider what has been said about the conjunction 'or': 'But how about "or"? You cannot show a child examples of it in the sensible world. You can say: "Will you have pudding or pie?" but if the child says yes, you cannot find a nutriment which is "pudding-or-pie"'.[1] Children are, of course, successfully taught the use of 'or', but they are not taught it by being shown 'examples of it in the sensible world'. The use of 'or' is not taught in the way 'cow' and 'pudding' are taught. We teach a child the word 'cow' by applying it to some things and withholding its application to other things: we point to cows, each time pronouncing the word 'cow', and correct the child when it calls the wrong things 'cow'. But we don't teach it 'or' in this way, i.e., by showing it examples in the 'sensible world'. The reason why we cannot find examples of 'or' in the sensible world is not that there is some sort of practical difficulty which stands in the way of our finding them, or that, like centaurs, none happen to exist; we cannot find examples because no value of 'x or y' is the name of a thing. Unlike 'pie' and 'pudding' and 'man' and 'mouse', 'pudding or pie' is not the name of a nutriment and 'man or mouse' is not the name of an animal. The impossibility of finding an article of diet answering to

[1] *Inquiry into Meaning and Truth*, p. 89.

'pudding or pie' is an impossibility which is created by a linguistic fact of usage. A philosopher who remarks that you *cannot* find a nutriment which is *pudding or pie* or an animal which is *man or mouse* is in an unclear form of speech pointing out that it *makes no sense* to speak of finding any objects answering to these terms because they are not names of a nutriment or of an animal. What he is concerned to do is to point out the semantic difference between the names 'pudding' and 'pie' and the expression 'pudding or pie'.

Similarly, a philosopher who states that 'there is butter' and 'there is no cheese' are on a different level is referring to the semantic difference between the terms 'butter' and 'no cheese', 'grey' and 'not white', the difference, namely, that 'butter' is the name of an article of diet and 'no butter' is not, and that 'white' is the name of a colour and 'not white' is not. By permitting such sentences as 'I see no cheese in the larder' and 'It is plain to see that this shirt is not white', ordinary language tends to conceal the semantic difference between negative and positive terms and, furthermore, creates the temptation, to which some metaphysicians succumb, to assimilate negative terms into the class of positive terms, i.e., to treat 'no butter' *as if* it named a thing and 'not white' *as if* it denoted a colour. In other words, by grammatically minimizing the difference between negative and positive terms, ordinary language creates in some thinkers the temptation to conceal the difference even more, to play the same game with negative terms that the existentialist metaphysician plays with the word 'nothing'. And what a philosopher does, who is impressed by the semantic difference between negative and positive terms and is *opposed* to any attempts to conceal the difference, is to *change the use of* 'see' and 'judge' in such a way as to make more pronounced than it is in ordinary language the difference between negative and positive terms. He *alters language* for the purpose of making a linguistic difference more conspicuous.

In his new, philosophical way of speaking, it will make descriptive sense to say 'I see butter' and 'I see that the rose is red', but it will make no descriptive sense to say 'I see no cheese', or 'I see the absence of cheese', and 'I see that the lily is not red'. The expressions 'no cheese' and 'not red' are not to count as describing what we *see*, and this comes to *contracting* the use of 'see', *restricting* the word to its use with positive terms. In place of using 'see', and in general 'perceive', with negative terms he uses 'judge', which is verbally *stretched* for the purpose of doing this new work, work it does not do in ordinary language. In his metaphysical language he replaces the ordinary sentences 'I see that there is no cheese on the table' and 'I see that the rose is not blue' by the philosophical sentences 'I *judge* that there is no cheese on the table' and 'I *judge* that the rose is not blue'. In this way, with the help of a contracted use of 'see' and a stretched use of 'judge' he is able to make more pronounced the semantic difference between negative and positive terms. The statement, 'You see what each thing is, not what it is not', informs us that in the *made-up* language of some metaphysicians the word 'see' has only *part* of its ordinary use, its use with positive terms.

X

APPEARANCE AND REALITY

'SENTIENT experience, in short, is reality, and what is not this is not real. We may say, in other words, that there is no being or fact outside of that which is commonly called psychical existence. Feeling, thought, and volition (any groups under which we class psychical phenomena) are all the material of existence, and there is no other material, actual or even possible'.[1] These words excite our interest at several different levels. They affect us emotionally, evoke ghosts of former feelings, while they arouse scepticism with the extravagance of their apparent claim; and at the same time they leave us with a vague and uneasy sense that we have not rightly understood them. The related sentence which I propose to examine here, namely, 'things are but appearances',[2] affects us in the same way. These words produce an emotional effect which haunts us because we cannot relate it to our conscious thoughts; the claim they apparently are used to make is altogether too extravagant to maintain in the face of fact; and

[1] F. H. Bradley, *Appearance and Reality,* 8th Impression, p. 144.
[2] *Ibid.,* p. 71. This occurs in the following context: '. . . the results, which we have reached, really seem to have destroyed things from without and from within. If the connexions of substantive and adjective, and of quality and relation, have been shown not to be defensible; if the forms of space and of time have turned out to be full of contradictions; if, lastly, causation and activity have succeeded merely in adding inconsistency to inconsistency—if, in a word, nothing of all this can, as such, be predicated of reality—what is it that is left? *If things are to exist,* then where and how? But if these two questions are unanswerable, then we seem driven to the conclusion that *things are but appearances*'. My italics. It is quite clear from this that Bradley holds that 'things do not exist' and, therefore, that whatever it is he expresses by the words 'things are but appearances' can also be expressed by 'there only appear to be things'.

although what these words express seems clear, we are left with a dissatisfied feeling that perhaps we have misread them, that perhaps their real import somehow has eluded us.

The metaphysical position that 'things are but appearances' or, to put it differently, the position that there only appear to be things, seems to make an astonishing factual claim which, if true, exposes the world of supposedly solid, substantial things as being no more than an illusion of the senses. Things dissipate into insubstantial phantoms, books into the appearances of there being books, the sun into the appearance of there being a sun; and depending on what our deeper needs are and how they connect with the view, it induces anxiety or reassures. For some people the view destroys a world and replaces it with a nightmare world of shadows; for others it destroys an unwelcome reality and replaces it with a reassuring dream; and for some people it does both things. Whether we believe the view to be true or think it to be too obviously false to merit serious consideration, we do naturally take it to be about things, to the effect that there are none although it does appear that there are. A philosopher who puts forward this theory and supports it with arguments looks to be doing what a scientist does who tells us that the stars do not have the orbits they appear to have in the night sky or that they are moving away from the earth with a tremendous velocity. But comparing the philosopher with a scientist produces a vague feeling of uneasiness and makes us unsure as to whether we have properly understood his words, although their literal import seems plain enough.

To be made aware of the vast and mysterious gulf between the practice of science and the practice of philosophy no more is needed than to notice a few things which are directly before our eyes and demanding attention, e.g., the inconsistent ways in which a philosopher speaks and behaves in relation to the position he advocates and how philosophers divide and debate over his view. We have only to open our eyes to doubt seriously that the scientist and the philosopher are concerned with the same 'universe of discourse' and to doubt that the words 'things are but appearances' are intended to convey information about things. In fact a careful examination of the philosopher's words in relation to his behaviour makes the conclusion both clear and certain that, unlike the sentence "The so-called canals on Mars are just an optical illusion', they do not express a proposition about the apparent existence of things, but only imitate sentences which do express such propositions.

It cannot have escaped attention altogether that a philosopher has not come to this view, which if taken at its face value must impress itself with staggering force, as the result of an inspection of things that is more subtle and careful than we ordinarily make of them, or as the result of experiment. For although he makes his statement with the confidence of a scientist who has at his disposal evidence which, once produced, would make a disconcerting theory irrefutable, he reports no special, out-of-the-ordinary observations and mentions no experiments. He does not call our attention to peculiarities in the behaviour of things, somehow overlooked by us, which expose their lack of substance and, so to speak, show that there is no face behind the mask. Everyone immediately and without the slightest hesitation or doubt would recognize the impropriety of saying: 'Close and careful scrutiny of what everyone naturally takes to be massive, enduring pyramids, or solid bricks, or apples which we not only see and feel but smell, taste, and eat, reveals that they are no more than the stuff of dreams, mere appearances'. A philosopher who with conscious sincerity and conviction holds that the appearances of there being things are all delusive sees no better (nor less well), hears no better, feels with no greater sensitivity than ordinary people or than the philosophers who disagree with him. And a philosopher who is won over to the view after having rejected it is not won over to it as a consequence of perceiving things differently; or if he abandons the view he does not do so because he has been convinced by *experience* that what he had been so sure was an illusion is, after all, real. Puzzling as it may be, recourse to observation or to any sort of empirical investigation is not considered necessary in order to hold the view or to give it up.

It has to be admitted that a straightforward reading of the metaphysical sentence 'things are but appearances' makes it seem unquestionable that the philosopher is denying the existence of physical things and that in doing this he is making a factual claim with regard to them. But accepting this reading creates the problem of squaring it with the philosopher's behaviour, the problem of explaining his curious disregard for procedures which alone could justify his holding the view imputed to him by our reading of his words. He is pictured as making a stupendous factual claim about things, a claim which science certainly cannot match, and he gives no indication of feeling the slightest need to produce or even to look for evidence. But how is this to be explained? To suppose his psychology is unusual won't do. For the best experimental scientist, on being confronted with the philosophical utterance and invited to give his considered judgement, will react in one or other of the expected ways in which *philosophers* react: he will judge it to be false on the basis of evidence which he knows is in the possession of a philosopher who accepts it or judge it to be true regardless of the testimony of his senses.

The proposition (whatever that may be) which his sentence is used to denote does have his conviction and, furthermore, he feels no need to base his conviction on experiential evidence. This much, it seems to me, is too plain to be open to question. The proposition which the popular and immediate reading of his words identifies as the proposition which has won his conviction is one which requires an absolutely fantastic state of mind to believe without evidence, but apart from the construction placed on his words there is no reason whatever for thinking that he suffers from an unusual condition of mind. If we insist that the proposition imputed to him is the proposition of which he is convinced, we cannot, without making an unwarranted assumption about his psychology, give a reasonable explanation of how it is that he is convinced. And because of his lack of concern to produce evidence we are driven to the conclusion that his conviction is pretended. If, on the other hand, we insist that he is convinced, and that his unconcern as regards evidence is not to be taken as indicating an unusual state of mind, then we are forced to conclude that the popular reading, though natural, is mistaken.

We have to choose between the literal reading of his words and his behaviour, for the two will not unite into anything which gives us an intelligible, realistic picture of the situation. And since it is our interpretation of his words which makes his behaviour seem unaccountable, the obvious thing to do is to give it up and try to discover an interpretation which is consonant with his behaviour. Fortunately there exists an independent consideration which makes it certain that the proposition imputed to the philosopher is not the proposition which is expressed by his words *as he uses them*. This is the following.

It is clear that a claim is factual only if it is such that in the case in which nothing exists which goes against it there could, as a matter of theoretical possibility, exist instances counter to it, and in the case in which there exist instances counter to it, such instances could, as a matter of theoretical possibility, fail to exist. It is equally clear that a person who makes a factual claim knows what it would be like for there to be a situation which, if he were confronted with it, would make him give up his claim, even though he dismisses every actual situation to which his attention is drawn in refutation of it. Hence, if the words 'things are but appearances' were being used to express a factual proposition about things, if they are being used to make the claim that human bodies, Tower Bridge, the earth underneath us, the moon, or the many other things which we perceive daily do not in fact exist, the philosopher would know and be able to say what it would be like for there really to be things, as against there only appearing to be. But this he cannot do; he cannot describe any circumstance given which he would be compelled to abandon his words and admit that the claim they made no longer held good. His being unable to do this shows us as clearly as anything can be shown that his use of the words, whatever it may be, is not to make a factual claim about things. The popular reading of his words unwittingly depicts the philosopher as being in the position of a person who confidently asserts that there only appear to be jabberwocks but who cannot say what it would be like for there to be a jabberwock or recognize one if he encountered it.

To see this better let us consider an ordinary, non-metaphysical case of someone declaring that what appears to exist does not actually exist, for example, the case of a desert companion assuring us that what looks to be a lake in the distance is only a mirage. He can, of course, elaborate on his statement by going on to describe in what ways we should be disappointed if we made our way toward the mirage expecting it to be a lake. This he can do only if he can describe in what ways a lake is different from a mirage. He cannot warn us against what we mistakenly take to be a lake in the distance without being able to tell us what we can expect if there is a lake which we cannot expect if there is only a mirage, i.e., what we can expect to see, feel, taste, etc., if there is a lake and what we cannot expect to see, feel, taste, etc., if there is only a mirage of a lake. We may say that a mirage, unlike the real thing, fails us at certain points. If what we have been assured is a mirage fails us in none of the respects in which the real thing satisfies us—if on our going up to it it does not vanish, if we slake our thirst at it, cool our faces in it, hear the splashing sound of water—we should say that what we were told was a mirage is, after all, a lake; and our companion would agree with us and admit he had been mistaken. In short, in making the factual statement that there is a mirage of a lake, not a lake, he is able to explain what it would be like for there to be a lake and not a mirage.

The metaphysical case differs radically from the ordinary case. Suppose our desert companion behaves differently. As in the case above, he assures us that there only appears to be a lake in the distance and that what we are seeing is a mirage. However, the 'mirage' does not vanish when we go up to it, drink from it, walk around it, wade in its shallows. But when we twit our companion about the assurance with which he had expressed himself, instead of hearing the expected confession to having been mistaken, to our astonishment we hear him insisting in earnest and with his first assurance that it is a mirage, even as he enjoys the coolness of the water as much as we do. In answer to our objections that unlike a mirage it has not vanished on our going up to it and that it meets expectations which mirages cannot meet, he says, 'This mirage is not an ordinary, run-of-the-mill mirage; this is a *complete* mirage. Ordinary mirages, which fail us in certain respects, are incomplete, whereas the one we are enjoying fails us in no respect because it is complete; but both kinds alike are only mirages, both alike are delusive appearances'. This answer, taken together with his behaviour, makes it plain that our desert companion has become a metaphysician: he cannot, if asked to explain in what way the complete mirage of a lake is different from a lake, mention a particular in which one differs from the other, and so cannot say what it would be like for there to be a lake.

Similarly, a philosopher who denies the reality of the physical world finds himself in the strange predicament of being unable to give an account of what it would be like for the physical world to be real. He rules himself out from being able with literal sense to mark a point of difference between there being a physical world and its only looking as if there is one and thus rules himself out from being able to tell us what it is the existence of which he is denying. The words 'things are but appearances' may be replaced by the words 'There appear to be things but in reality there are none',[1] in which the expression 'in reality there are none', or what is equivalent to it, the expression 'there are no things' seems, like 'There are no canals on Mars', to be used to put forward a factual claim. But its looking to be used in this way is a verbal deception. For since the user of the expression cannot depict a situation given which he would say, 'Now there are things, and not just appearances', he cannot be using the expression to deny that there are things.

To put the matter somewhat differently, whatever it is that the words 'There are no things' are made to mean, they are being so used that nothing actual is allowed to count against what they say, and, moreover, nothing describable is allowed to constitute a theoretical case against what they say. Consequently, they are being so used that what they say is not open to theoretical falsification. They do not, therefore, express an empirical proposition, and so do not express a proposition about the existence or non-existence of physical things. The sentence 'There are no pink elephants' puts forward a factual claim because the sentence 'There are pink elephants' expresses a proposition which could, theoretically, be true. But the philosophical sentence 'There are no things' makes no factual claim because the sentence 'There are things' is not allowed to express a proposition which could conceivably be true. Seeing this enables us to understand the philosopher's remarkable oversight in the matter of producing experiential evidence for the position popularly attributed to him, an oversight which would be possible only in the land of the lotus-eaters. Since his words, as he is using them, do not express a theoretically falsifiable proposition, they do not express a proposition of the sort to which experiential evidence is relevant.

How then, if we reject the interpretation of his words which comes first to mind, are we to understand them? Several features connected with the utterance of the words make it now seem plausible to think that one of the conjunction of propositions

[1]The justification for this is given in footnote 2, p. 199.

which they are used to denote is *a priori,* the proposition, namely, which is separately expressed by 'There are no things'. For one thing, the assurance with which the proposition is stated together with the now understandable disregard for evidence is *appropriate* to a logically necessary proposition. It is like the assurance with which we say that the successor of a prime number greater than 2 is not itself a prime number. For another thing, the claim that it is true is based on *arguments,* which substitute for evidence; and this again is appropriate to a proposition the truth-value of which is necessary. One writer has voiced against Parmenides the complaint that 'he had an argument, but no evidence'[1] for the position that motion and change do not exist. This charge holds good in the case of the modern counterpart of Parmenides, who also has arguments but no evidence for the proposition denoted by 'There are no physical things'. This is bewildering if the sentence is construed as making a factual claim, but not if it is taken to express an *a priori* proposition. Further evidence for thinking that the proposition which has won the philosopher's conviction is *a priori* is his maintaining that the arguments adduced show that the proposition denoted by 'There are physical things' is *self-contradictory.* He maintains that '. . . the results, which we have reached, really seem to have destroyed things from without and from within',[2] and the context makes it quite clear that results which are purported to have done this flow from considerations which, it is claimed, demonstrate contradictions. All in all, the external evidence points to the conclusion that the metaphysical position is *a priori,* and that like a mathematician who establishes the *a priori* truth that there is no greatest prime number by demonstrating a contradiction in the hypothesis that there is a greatest prime, the philosopher establishes by a *reductio ad absurdum* form of argument the proposition denoted by the sentence 'There are no physical things'.

This sentence gives, of course, only part of the metaphysical view, the other part of which is given by 'There appear to be physical things'. What kind of proposition it is, *a priori* or empirical, which is expressed by the second sentence is not certain; but it does look as if it is empirical and that it is the proposition which the natural reading of the sentence would identify as being

[1]Benjamin Farrington, *Greek Science,* Vol. I, Pelican Books, p. 53.
[2]F. H. Bradley, *op. cit.,* p. 71.

its meaning. It looks as if the words 'things are but appearances' express a position which is partly *a priori* and partly factual, a position, that is, which consists of a combination of propositions one of which is expressible by the sentence 'It is logically impossible for physical things to exist' and the other by the sentence 'There exist, as a matter of fact, appearances of there being things'. More concretely, a philosopher, who with conviction based on the findings of logic and the testimony of the senses says, 'things are but appearances', implies that it is, for example, logically impossible for there to be loaves of bread and bodies which take nourishment from them but that there seem to be loaves of bread and human bodies. Logic elicits a self-contradiction from the proposition given by 'Physical things exist', and so establishes the logical impossibility of its being true; and our senses present us with data which make true the factual proposition given by 'Physical things appear to exist.'

The present construction, it can be said, is much more circumspect intellectually than the first construction, which made out the philosopher to be stating an empirical proposition about the existence of things. The first now seems based on no more than the most superficial verbal impressions, which can survive inspection no more than a Potemkin village. The present construction placed on the words 'things are but appearances' appeals to us because it takes into account the non-empirical procedure used in arriving at the proposition they express and seems to square the proposition with the procedure. Nevertheless, important objections stand in the way of accepting it, objections which show that accepting the construction requires our believing what, if we preserve our sense of reality, we must reject as being too unlikely to be taken seriously. For one thing, to accept the interpretation of 'Things do not exist', according to which the sentence expresses the proposition which is less ambiguously expressed by 'It is logically impossible for there to be things', is to be committed to the opinion that the philosopher supposes the general term 'physical thing' and the more specific words 'penny', 'chair', 'bread', etc., to be literally senseless. For another thing, it is to be committed to the opinion, which needs aggressive arrogance to blind one to its flimsiness, that the philosopher suffers from a curious intellectual myopia which prevents him from seeing a self-contradiction which clamours for attention and which he fails to recognize as a contradiction when his notice is called to it. Further difficulties can be brought to light; but these two objections, if they can be sustained, are sufficiently grave to warrant our abandoning the interpretation.

Consider first the contradiction which immediately develops in the position that things are only appearances if it is identified with the conjunction of propositions that it is logically impossible for there to be things and that things appear to exist. It needs no intellectual acumen to see that whatever appears to us to be the case could conceivably be the case, and that its looking or seeming to us as if a certain state of affairs obtains implies that we know what it would be like for there to be that state of affairs. A sensible appearance is an appearance of an actual or a hypothetical reality, i.e., it is an appearance of a state of affairs which exists or an appearance of there being a state of affairs which does not exist. And with regard to *any* appearance[1], however unusual or odd, circumstances can be imagined in which the appearance could be mistaken for the reality. Clearly, it is possible to imagine this only because reality could, theoretically, be as odd as the appearance represents it. Thus, for example, it is possible to imagine miracles appearing to occur—the sun standing still for days or a river being turned into blood—and being taken for the realities; and an appearance could be taken for the reality only if the reality could conceivably be as it appears. We might say the delusive appearance a of there being a state of affairs ϕ *represents,* or, to stretch a word, *pictures* what would, if it existed, falsify a proposition to the effect that a is 'mere' appearance; i.e., a pictures a state of affairs which would constitute a falsifying instance of the proposition that it only looks as if ϕ exists and, thus, pictures what would make true the proposition that ϕ exists. A proposition stating the existence of what appears or could appear to exist, i.e., a proposition of the form *There is a ϕ* to which there corresponds a true or possibly true proposition of the form *There appears to be a ϕ*, is such that it could itself theoretically be true. Hence, by holding the view attributed to him the philosopher would commit himself to the idea that the existence of things is theoretically possible and that we

[1]Throughout this paper 'appearance' is used in the sense of 'sensible appearance'.

know what it would be like for there to be a state of affairs verifying the proposition that things exist and also to the idea that the existence of things is logically impossible, that the proposition that things exist is necessarily false. To hold that there appear to be things the existence of which is logically impossible is to embrace the immediate self-contradictory consequence that we can imagine a situation which would upset an *a priori* truth, or the consequence that at least some propositions are both true *a priori* and such that they could conceivably be false.

The two assertions, the assertion that it is logically impossible for physical objects to exist and the assertion that there appear to be physical objects, form a patently self-contradictory conjunction. If we accept the second assertion the first becomes false: it becomes false to say that it is *logically* impossible for physical objects to exist. If we accept the first assertion the second becomes false: it becomes false to say that there appear to be, or even that there could appear to be, physical objects. This consequence hardly needs elaborating. No one in ordinary life would, without realizing that he was contradicting himself, say in the same breath that it is logically impossible for a heavy downfall of rain to occur in which not a single drop of rain falls and also that it could, possibly, look to anyone as if a rainless rain were falling, or say that it is logically impossible for a triangle to have two sides and also maintain that he was perceiving the appearance of there being a two-sided triangle or even that there could be such an appearance. It will, I think, be granted without hesitation that no one using language as it is commonly used would say such a thing as that there appears to be a two-sided triangle or that it seems that a rainless rain is falling, or that he is imagining a triangle with only two sides or a rainless rain. Quite in general, a statement which makes a logical claim that ϕ is impossible implies that the corresponding statement that ϕ exists in appearance is self-contradictory. What cannot exist, because its existence would imply a contradiction, cannot exist as 'mere appearance', because the existence of the appearance would also imply a contradiction. What is self-contradictory not only cannot exist but cannot appear to exist; and there can no more be self-contradictory appearances than there can be self-contradictory realities.

This is too plain for anyone to deny, and I think that we are

justified in believing that anyone whose language suggests that
he does deny this only appears to do so and is in fact denying
something else. I think we are justified in believing that in holding
the metaphysical view that the physical world is just an illusion
the philosopher does not wish to deny this. He does not, in other
words, hold that there appear to be self-contradictory situations
or that there exist appearances which are internally inconsistent.
It may be observed, parenthetically, that it is usual in philosophy
to count an opponent refuted when we remark a contradiction in
a view attributed to him; and we rarely, if ever, think of the
possibility that *the presence of a contradiction indicates that the view is
not the one held by the philosopher*. To see that this possibility is less
remote than it must at first seem we have only to observe how
little moved philosophers are by the contradictions other philosophers discover in their views, or if made uneasy how momen-
tary their uneasiness is and how quickly they forget that their
positions contain contradictions. Philosophers fancy themselves
bulls in each other's intellectual china closets; but no philosopher
sees, although not because he suffers from defective vision, that his
own crockery is broken.

The other serious objection which stands in the way of our
accepting the notion that the view that there are, in reality, no
physical things is an *a priori* true proposition and also, that the
sentence which expresses it uses words as they are ordinarily used,
is that we should have to think a metaphysician who holds the
view to be believing that the term 'physical thing' and words like
'watch', 'stone', 'mountain' have no literal sense, that they are,
descriptively, in a class with nonsense syllables. For anyone who
understands the phrase 'There are no' and actually *thinks* that the
sentence 'There are no physical things, no watches, stones, mountains, human bodies' expresses a logically necessary proposition
would be believing that 'physical thing', 'stone', 'mountain',
'watch' had no application, either actual or theoretical. He would
be believing that general names of things have no actual or hypothetical denotation. To see this does not require our having esoteric information about the nature of logically necessary propositions. It only requires our grasping the difference between sentences which express empirical propositions and sentences which
express *a priori* propositions.

It can easily be seen that a fundamental difference between a sentence stating a physical impossibility,[1] e.g., the sentence 'It is impossible to sink a battleship with a pea-shooter', and one which states a logical impossibility,[1] e.g., the sentence 'It is impossible to sink five out of four ships', is that what a sentence of the first kind declares to be impossible is conceivable, while what is declared by a sentence of the second kind is inconceivable. That is, in understanding the sentence 'It is impossible to sink a battleship with a pea-shooter' we know what it would be like for there to be an occurrence answering to the phrase 'sinks a battleship with a pea-shooter', whereas in understanding the sentence 'It is impossible to sink five out of four ships' we do not know what it would be like for there to be an occurrence answering to the phrase 'sinks five out of four ships'. And we know what it would be like for there to be an occurrence answering to the first phrase and do not know what it would be like for there to be an occurrence answering to the second phrase because the first phrase has a descriptive use, describes a hypothetical occurrence, and the second has no descriptive use whatever. The sentence 'It is impossible to sink a battleship with a pea-shooter' describes a situation or occurrence which it declares to be impossible, while the sentence 'It is impossible to sink five out of four ships' describes no situation or occurrence which it declares to be impossible. In general, sentences which express what is *logically* impossible differ from sentences which express what is *physically* impossible in the respect that sentences of the first kind do not describe or denote occurrences or states of affairs the existence of which is declared impossible and sentences of the second kind do describe or denote occurrences or states of affairs the existence of which is declared impossible.

It will no doubt seem to be flouting what is clear and undeniable to say that a sentence which expresses a logical impossibility does not, as does a sentence which expresses a physical impossibility, describe what it declares to be impossible. It will seem patently absurd to maintain that, e.g., the sentence 'It is impossible to sink

[1]For convenience 'physical impossibility' is used as short for 'true empirical proposition to the effect that something is impossible' and 'logical impossibility' as short for 'true *a priori* proposition to the effect that something is impossible'.

five out of four ships' does not declare the impossibility of what is denoted by 'sinks five out of four ships', or that the sentence 'It is impossible for anyone to run while remaining motionless' does not deny the possible existence of what is denoted by 'runs while remaining motionless'. For if such a sentence does not describe or name or denote a hypothetical situation which it declares to be impossible, it does not declare anything whatever to be impossible, which is absurd. The sentence 'It is impossible for anyone to run while remaining motionless' certainly does, it might be argued, state the impossibility of *something,* in contradistinction to a nonsense sentence like 'It is impossible for toves to brillig without grolling', which does not describe anything it states to be impossible. In this respect it is like the sentence 'It is impossible for Blenheim Castle to float in the air' or like the sentence 'It is impossible to sink a battleship with a pea-shooter'. Like the latter two sentences it must, if it is not to count as literal nonsense, say *what it is* which it declares to be impossible. A sentence which states something to be logically impossible is not, of course, a piece of literal nonsense; hence, it will be urged, it must be false to say that sentences which express logical impossibilities fail to describe or name or denote occurrences or situations the existence of which they declare to be impossible. In respect of describing hypothetical occurrences or situations they cannot be different from sentences denoting physical impossibilities.

To answer this objection it first has to be admitted that a sentence like 'It is impossible to sink five out of four ships' differs from the sentence 'It is impossible for toves to brillig without grolling' in not being literally nonsensical, and that it is like the sentence 'It is impossible for Blenheim Castle to float in the air' in having an intelligible meaning. But to argue from this likeness and difference that the sentence describes an occurrence the possibility of which it denies is to exaggerate an outward similarity between sentences denoting physical impossibilities and sentences denoting logical impossibilities. This is not the place to make a detailed examination of the nature of *a priori* propositions or to try to explain what it comes to to say that anything is logically impossible. Undoubtedly there is a strong temptation to say that a sentence which expresses a logical impossibility does declare *something* to be impossible and thus, unlike the nonsense sentence and like a sentence which expresses a physical impossibility, it describes or names a situation or an occurrence the existence of which it denies to be possible. Attention to matter of linguistic fact, however, compels us to the conclusion that it differs from a sentence which expresses a physical impossibility precisely in the respect of *not* describing what it is which is declared impossible. The following consideration will make this clear.

The term '*a priori* proposition' is so used that it makes no literal sense to say '*p* is an *a priori* proposition which could conceivably have a truth-value other than the one it has'; and the term 'empirical proposition' is so used that it is literal nonsense, an absurdity of language, to say '*p* is an empirical proposition which could not conceivably have a truth-value other than the one it has'. In contrast to the term 'empirical truth', which applies to propositions that are open to possible falsification, the term '*a priori* truth' applies to propositions which are not open to possible falsification. This means that with regard to an *a priori* true proposition no theoretical situation or occurrence can be envisaged which, if it obtained, would make the proposition false, since if, as in the case of a true empirical proposition, such a situation or occurrence could be envisaged, an *a priori* true proposition would have to be open to conceivable falsification. Thus, for example, the proposition that it is impossible to flatten an anvil with a soap-bubble is such that it could, theoretically, be false, and seeing that it could, theoretically, be false *consists* in knowing what it would be like for there to be an occurrence which would make it false. If, then, with regard to the necessarily true proposition that it is impossible for an anvil to be heavier than itself it were possible to conceive of a state of affairs which would make it false, conceiving such a state of affairs would be the same as *seeing* that it could, possibly, be false. There is, of course, no seeing that a necessarily true statement is not necessarily true; hence there is no conceiving a state of affairs which would make it false. And there is no conceiving a state of affairs which would make an *a priori* true proposition false, because it makes no literal sense to say that such a state of affairs is being conceived. It makes perfectly good sense to say 'S is conceiving an anvil being flattened by a soap bubble coming down on it' or 'S imagines himself sinking a battleship with his pea-shooter', but it makes no sense to say 'S knows what it would be like for an anvil to be heavier than itself' or 'S imagines himself sinking five out of four ships'.

The fact that it makes no sense to speak of one's conceiving a circumstance, however fanciful, which would upset an *a priori* truth sheds light on the great difference between sentences expressing physical impossibilities and sentences expressing logical impossibilities, and it shows how very different the use of the word 'impossible' is in sentences which denote logical impossibilities from its use in sentences which denote physical impossibilities. The sentence 'It is impossible to flatten an anvil with a soap-bubble' expresses an empirical proposition; and it can now be clearly seen that it would not express a proposition which is open to conceivable falsification if it did not describe an occurrence which would falsify it. The sentence describes what it declares to be impossible and what it describes with the phrase 'flattens an anvil with a soap-bubble' is what would make false the proposition it denotes. Understanding the sentence entails knowing what it would be like for what is declared to be impossible to happen; understanding the sentence therefore entails knowing the descriptive use of 'flattens an anvil with a soap-bubble'. The sentence 'It is impossible for an anvil to be heavier than itself', despite its outer verbal likeness to the preceding example, can be seen now to be vastly different from it. The fact that the sentence expresses an *a priori* true proposition entails that no circumstance can be described which would count against it. Thus, it fails to describe anything which it declares to be impossible, since if it did it would describe what would make it false. The phrase 'anvil which is heavier than itself' does not function descriptively in the sentence, so that understanding the sentence does not, as in the case of the empirical sentence, entail knowing what it would be like for there to be a situation which answers to what for convenience may be called its 'descriptive part', i.e., the phrase 'anvil which is heavier than itself'. Instead, *it entails knowing that the phrase has no descriptive sense*. A sentence of the form 'It is impossible . . .' which expresses an *a priori* truth, or any sentence which is equivalent to such a sentence, declares an impossibility without saying what it is that is declared impossible. It thus is like the sentence 'It is impossible for toves to brillig without grolling' in not saying what it is that is stated to be impossible and unlike it and like the sentence 'It is impossible to sink a battleship with a pea-shooter' in having literal meaning.

This is not the place to do more than point out that unlike the descriptive part of 'It is impossible for toves to brillig without grolling' the descriptive part of 'It is impossible for an anvil to be heavier than itself' contains no nonsense words, and, of course, it has syntax, and in these respects is like the descriptive part of 'It is impossible to flatten an anvil with a soap-bubble'. But it nevertheless differs from 'sinks a battleship with a pea-shooter' and is like 'toves brillig without grolling' in this respect: it has no descriptive sense. A person who understands the sentence 'It is impossible for an anvil to be heavier than itself' knows the constituent words of its descriptive part, knows that they are put together syntactically, and knows that their combination has no literal descriptive sense.

To come back to the philosopher who, with the assured confidence of one who knows, asserts that 'things are but appearances' and is taken to be maintaining that it is *logically* impossible for physical things—trees, books, and the like—to exist. If the sentence 'It is impossible for physical things to exist' expressed an *a priori* proposition, the term 'physical thing' and such words as 'tree' and 'book' which are general names of physical things would have no application whatever. They would have no actual or hypothetical denotation. To say 'There is a bird in the tree' or 'There is a book on the chair' would be as descriptively senseless as to say 'The integer between 8 and 9 is a prime number' or 'The anvil on the scales registers more than it registers'.

But the term 'physical thing' and general substantives like 'book' and 'anvil' have in everyday speech perfectly intelligible meanings. The sentence 'It is impossible for there to be physical things' cannot both express a logically necessary proposition and be using 'physical thing' as it is ordinarily used. And for us to suppose that the philosopher claims to know that his sentence both expresses a necessarily true proposition and that it uses 'physical thing' as it is commonly used is tantamount to thinking that he claims to know that the term 'physical thing' and such familiar substantives as 'chair' and 'shoe' have no literal sense. But this idea does not deserve serious consideration. It cannot with the slightest semblance of reason be thought that he knows the use of 'physical thing' and the use of a great number of other words but, strangely and unaccountably, believes that they are literally meaningless.

It may be worth while to look again at the supposed contradiction in the view that there only appear to be physical things, that is, the contradiction which emerges in the view when it is understood as a conjunction of two propositions one of which is *a priori*. It will be recalled that the contradiction implied by the position that it is logically impossible for things to exist and that appearances of there being things do exist is that the existence of things is both logically possible and logically impossible, or, what is equivalent to this consequence, that the existence of appearances of there being physical things both is and is not logically possible. Seen in the semantic light of what has been shown about the descriptive parts of *a priori* sentences of the form 'It is impossible . . .' this consequence has, in the language in which it is expressed, the verbal correlate that every word of a fundamentally important class of words in everyday use in that language is literally meaningless. It should be noticed that this inconsistency is not the same as the inconsistency which arises from supposing a philosopher who knows ordinary usage to be maintaining that it is logically impossible for there to be things. It is instead an inconsistency between two ideas which enter into the position which has this consequence. The inconsistency pointed out earlier is between what the philosopher says and what, apart from this, he unquestionably knows, and is not one which is internal to his philosophical view. The present inconsistency is internal to his philosophical view; it is an incompatibility between two philosophical propositions he asserts.

It need hardly be remarked that a term ϕ is so related to the word 'appears' that if ϕ is senseless or has no actual or hypothetical application, the sentence 'There appears to be a ϕ' is devoid of literal significance, and if 'There appears to be a ϕ' has literal significance ϕ is not a nonsense term: 'appearance of there being a ϕ' applies to an appearance, in fact or in conception, only if ϕ names a possible reality. Thus, if ϕ is the nonsense syllable 'rujb' the sentence has no sense, and it also lacks sense if ϕ is the term 'four-sided triangle'; 'appearance of there being a four-sided triangle' is no more used to describe an appearance than is 'appearance of there being a rujb'. Now in subscribing, as the philosopher is supposed by us, to the proposition which is expressed by the words 'It is logically impossible for there to be physical things', he must have the idea that substantives which are used as general names of things are lacking in sense. No one who understood the use of 'logical impossibility' or 'self-contradictory' would knowingly say 'It is logically impossible for there to be a four-sided triangle' or say that the conception expressed by the phrase 'four-sided triangle' is self-contradictory and not think that the words 'four-sided triangle' lacked application. It is plain, thus, if we take at their face value the words of a philosopher who in quite straightforward language says that the conception of a physical thing is self-contradictory or that it is logically impossible for there to be things, we have to think that the philosopher has the idea that 'physical thing' lacks application. It is equally plain that no one would say, with understanding of what he was saying, 'There appear to be physical things', without thinking that 'physical thing' has application, actual or imaginable. In short, to take the words 'things are but appearances' to be declaring the apparent existence of what they state to be logically impossible is to impute to the metaphysician two conflicting things, that he thinks every word of a fundamentally important class of words is senseless and has been given no use and also that he thinks they have application. It is, in other words, to imply that he thinks certain words are senseless while thinking that phrases of the form 'appearance of there being a ϕ' in which they occur apply to actual or possible appearances. And not only is it to be supposed that he thinks these things, but it also has to be supposed that he thinks them simultaneously and gives hidden expression to both of them in the same short utterance.

Now, apart from his philosophical talk, there is no evidence whatever for believing that he has the queer idea that the general names of things, e.g., the nouns 'tree' and 'shilling', are verbal fakes, words which only imitate those which have an honest use. In no behaviouristic respect does he give us the slightest reason for believing this. If he had *both* ideas, both the idea that words which in ordinary conversation function as general names of things are nonsense terms and the idea that they are real verbal currency, his

behaviour would be in some ways affected; his idea, it is reasonable to expect, would have consequences on his behaviour. When
a person has conflicting beliefs he is made to some degree ambivalent; each belief will be an inner obstacle to his acting on the
other belief, and this will manifest itself in his conduct. But no
one is so naïve as to entertain for a moment the notion that the
Metaphysician of the Unreality of Things is a verbal Hamlet who,
at least at times, cannot make up his mind as to whether any of
the familiar names of things used in everyday discourse are or are
not literally nonsensical. Everything goes against our accepting
the notion that he has the utterly grotesque idea that the familiar
names of things have no application, or that lacking application
they nevertheless have intelligible use in expressions of the form
'There appears to be a ϕ', *except his philosophical words*. But his
philosophical words are just not good enough evidence. Rather,
the unplausibility of this conclusion is a good reason for rejecting
it and thus for abandoning the construction placed on his utterance 'things are but appearances', a construction according to
which he pronounces to be logically impossible what he says
appears to exist. It is far less extravagant and unrealistic to reject
the conclusion and with it the interpretation placed on his words
(even if this is the interpretation placed on them by the philosopher himself) than it is to insist on the interpretation and accept
the conclusion.

What then is to be made of his metaphysical pronouncement?
How is it to be understood, if it is not to be understood in either
of the ways already suggested? Obviously we shall be no better
off than philosophers are if we adopt any of the usual views as to
how, in general, philosophical utterances are to be understood.
To put the matter very shortly, we have to choose between the
universally held but insufficiently examined belief that philosophical statements mean what they are usually taken to mean and
a view according to which they are *utterly different* from this. It
will be recalled that Champollion was able to make progress in
the deciphering of the Rosetta Stone only after he had dissented
from the learned opinion of his day regarding the nature of hiero-
glyphs. And we too shall start making progress in our attempt to
understand the nature of philosophy only after rejecting the
standard views, none of which, it has to be realized, gives a satis-

factory explanation of the puzzling fact that philosophical disputes are interminable and philosophical 'mistakes' persistently go unrecognized by those who make them. To reject them requires an unusual effort of mind not only because doing this goes against general opinion but also because it goes against what seems so plain and undeniable that any other view about the nature of philosophy must appear strange and forced. But an opinion may be false even though universally received, and the strangeness of a new idea is not an infallible guarantee of its being false.

It will be helpful, in our attempt to arrive at a satisfactory explanation of what the view comes to, to consider again by itself part of the view that things are no more than appearances, the part expressed by the sentence 'It is impossible for there to be things'. To hold, as many idealistic metaphysicians seem to hold, that physical things are by their very nature self-contradictory, 'destroyed from without and from within', is to maintain, in an indirect mode of speech, that the term 'physical thing'[1] has a self-contradictory meaning, and hence that the term has no descriptive sense. Now two things have to be accepted and *reconciled*. We have to accept the fact, which it is possible to deny only in philosophy, that the philosopher knows perfectly well that 'physical thing' and general names of physical things have application, and therefore that he knows perfectly well that these terms do have descriptive use and do not have self-contradictory meanings. We also have to accept the fact that he maintains 'physical thing' and the many words which denote physical things to be self-contradictory. Furthermore, we have to reconcile what he knows with what he maintains, which is to say that we have to discover an interpretation of what he maintains which will not be inconsistent with what he knows. No other procedure is open to us, since, plainly, what he knows is not in doubt and not subject to interpretation. Now, in maintaining that what is 'generally understood when we use the word "thing" . . . seems now undermined and ruined',[2] which is a florid way of saying that 'thing' is a self-contradictory term, he cannot, despite his seeming to say so,

---

[1] Or the equivalent term in any other language in which the theory is formulated.

[2] *Appearance and Reality*, p. 71.

be maintaining that *as it is ordinarily used* it is self-contradictory, that its everyday literal meaning as well as the everyday literal meanings of 'chair', 'shoe', etc., are self-contradictory. Hence, the only possible way of construing his claim that they *are* self-contradictory terms is to suppose that he has *made* them self-contradictory and in this way has *deprived* them of their ordinary literal meanings. So to speak, these words now lead a double life: *academically,* they are verbal mutes, stripped of their everyday use; *practically,* they continue to speak their everyday message.

It becomes evident now that there is no actual conflict between what the philosopher 'holds' about the academically changed term 'physical thing' and what he knows about everyday language. The sentence 'It is impossible for physical things to exist' would express a logically necessary proposition if 'physical thing' were self-contradictory, and the philosopher is able to maintain that it does express a logically necessary proposition by making 'physical thing' self-contradictory. The sentence is made to stand for an *a priori* proposition by linguistic fiat, by an act of linguistic creation or destruction, depending on how it is looked at. And he is able to hold his view in the face of what he knows and against *all* arguments,[1] because what he holds is in conflict with no sort of fact. Like Humpty Dumpty the philosopher is master and cannot be refuted. His arguments, whatever they may come to, do not demonstrate contradictions in the term 'physical thing' or in such everyday substantives as 'brick', 'chair', 'hat'; nor is their work to do what they cannot do, demonstrate contradictions where none exist. Their work, rather, is to *import* contradictions into the terms.

This much may, I think, be fairly concluded about what a metaphysician is doing who holds that it is logically impossible for physical things, objects like watches, balls, and shoes, to exist, namely, that he alters ordinary usage but does this unconsciously and in a form of speech which effectively keeps hidden what he is doing from others as well as from himself. But this conclusion could be maintained with regard to the claim that the existence of phycical things is impossible only if that claim were made without its also being held that there appear to be things. If we consider the claim in conjunction with the statement that there exist

[1] He can, of course, be intimidated.

appearances of there being things, i.e., if we consider it in the context of the view that 'things are but appearances', our conclusion stands in need of modification. For in holding that things have 'turned out to be merely appearances' the philosopher allows the term 'thing' and general names of physical things to have their use in phrases describing appearances. This shows that he does not wish to make them descriptively senseless, even in academic fantasy. If, then, we try to understand the hidden things a philosopher does with language, instead of conceiving our task to be that of scoring against an intellectual opponent and crying contradiction at every turn, how are we to read the statement that it is impossible for things to exist?

It has to be supposed, for one thing, that importing a contradiction into the term 'physical thing' is not intended to have the effect of destroying the possibility of its being applied: the case of a philosopher importing a contradiction into a term which has a literal use is very different from the normal case of someone demonstrating a contradiction in a term, e.g., 'greatest prime number'. The metaphysician is master of his contradictions and makes them do the work he wants them to do. In the present case the contradictions supposedly discovered in the meaning of 'thing' are intended to show that things *do not exist* or that they *are unreal,* and not to show that appearances of there being things do not exist. Unlike a person who on being told about an unusual mirage of a dark blue lake which was uniformly light green dismisses the narrative as descriptive nonsense, the metaphysician insists that 'rejecting the inconsistent as appearance'[1] is not to deny that appearances exist[2]: self-contradictory appearance is a 'beggarly show', but 'there is no possibility of conjuring its existence away from it'.[3]

In the normal case, an argument which shows or is taken to show a term *t* to be self-contradictory shows or is taken to show not only that the statement '*t* exists' is self-contradictory but also that '*t* appears to exist' is self-contradictory. It shows or is taken to show that not only is it logically impossible for *t* to exist but also that it is logically impossible for there to be an appearance of *t* existing. To put the matter somewhat differently, in the non-philosophical case, showing that *t* has no theoretical denotation,

---

[1] *Appearance and Reality*, p. 136.   [2] *Ibid.*, pp. 131–2.   [3] *Ibid.*, p. 132.

i.e., that nothing can be imagined such that if it did exist *t* would apply to it. But if *t* has no theoretical denotation, it has none when it is used in an expression of the form 'appearance of there being a *t*', which is to say that the expression describes no appearance.

The philosopher, however, makes an unorthodox claim as to what the contradiction he produces in the meaning of 'thing' shows, namely, the logical impossibility of there being things but not the logical impossibility of there appearing to be things. But to think that he is guilty of the obvious inconsistency of which he appears to be and that this is all there is to it, is to be duped by the obvious. If we try to force the philosophical case into the mould of the ordinary case of a contradiction being established in the meaning of a term, we shall flatter ourselves with the 'discovery' of inconsistencies in the position of a philosopher but we shall not succeed in understanding him. The self-contradiction which the philosopher gives the impression of eliciting from the notion of a physical thing is allowed to count against the existence of things but is not allowed to count against the existence of appearances of there being things. It is to be gathered, thus, that importing a contradiction into the word 'thing' is not intended to have the effect of depriving the word of both its actual and conceptual denotation, contrary to what was argued earlier when the statement 'It is impossible for there to be physical things' was considered by itself, apart from the connected statement 'There appear to be physical things'. Curious as it may seem, the contradiction does only part of its expected work. It eliminates the actual application of words like 'stone' and 'shoe' but leaves them hypothetical denotation: it allows them no descriptive use in sentences which declare the existence of objects answering to their descriptive parts but allows them their descriptive use in sentences which declare the existence of appearances of there being such objects.

It is important to see that the claim that this is what the contradiction does is no more a mistake than is the claim that the meaning of 'physical thing' is self-contradictory. The contradiction, it has to be remembered, is metaphysical, which is to say manufactured, and the point of manufacturing it is to make it do special work. In the present case its work, plainly, is not to justify discontinuing the use of a large class of words; it is, rather, to justify *restricting* their use to occurrences in phrases denoting appearances and to sentences using such phrases. The contradiction is used as a linguistic rationalization for making a syntactical, not a semantic, change. That is, it constitutes a pretext for discontinuing their use in sentences of the form 'There are ϕ's' or in sentences which entail sentences of this form,[1] and therefore for limiting their use, syntactically, to sentences of the form 'There appear to be ϕ's'.

This is the only credible construction to be placed on what a philosopher is doing who is not ignorant of the use of the term 'self-contradictory' and maintains that being self-contradictory makes impossible the existence of a state of affairs but does not make impossible the existence of an appearance; which, to express the matter verbally, is to say he maintains that 'inconsistent reality' describes no theoretical reality but 'inconsistent appearance' describes not only conceivable but actual appearance. This is the only reasonable explanation of what a philosopher does who in so many words maintains that such a sentence as 'There is a butter dish with butter on it' expresses a logically impossible proposition, but when it occurs as part of the sentence 'It looks as if there is a butter dish with butter on it' does not express anything which prevents, logically, the proposition expressed by that sentence from being true.

A philosopher who holds that 'things are but appearances', that the physical world is a cosmic mirage, is not, as it may seem to some people, making a pronouncement about the world, nor is he, as it may seem to other people, making a pronouncement about the intelligible use of words in everyday discourse. He professes to discover contradictions in the meanings of everyday words, to lay bare internal inconsistencies in familiar concepts, and creates the illusion of demonstrating or attempting to demonstrate the non-existence of the universe. What he actually does, behind the impressive but delusive verbal screen of eliciting contradictions and establishing propositions of fundamental importance, is to alter the structure of language. In the changed language there is no place for sentences which state or imply the existence of things, but there is place for sentences, using general names of things,

[1]Expressed awkwardly but more accurately by the words '. . . or in sentences expressing propositions which entail propositions expressed by sentences of this form.'

which declare the existence (or non-existence) of appearances. All sentences of the form 'There are ϕ's' (where the values of ϕ are substantives like 'book', 'shoe', and 'cow') as well as sentences which imply them are academically shelved, while sentences of the form 'There appear to be ϕ's', and equivalent forms of sentences, are retained. But this is hidden by the philosopher's way of stating himself, a way of stating himself which gives some people the idea that he is a remarkable scientist who by the unaided power of his mind is able to wrest from nature her deepest secrets, which gives to other people the idea that he is a Logician of Language who corrects our language map for us, and which gives to other people still the idea that he is a blunderer who misrepresents language and myopically remains attached to his misrepresentations. Instead of saying that in the language *as reconstructed by him* there is no place for sentences stating the existence of things, he says that 'things are but appearances'. And regardless of whether we reject his position, are uncertain about it, or accept it, he succeeds in making us dupes to his verbal game.

If we are curious to know why anyone should wish to change language in the way just described, what the *point* of exorcising a great class of useful sentences from our language could possibly be, we need to have a firm grasp of the fact that the alteration is not intended for everyday use. The point of the reconstructed language, which is not meant to supplant ordinary language, is not practical; rather, the function of the reconstructed language is like that of a work of art, to give a special kind of satisfaction. One thing which shows clearly that the alteration announced by the words 'things are but appearances' is academic or fantasied is the fact that no attempt is made to satisfy an obvious requirement for the practical use of the revised language, a requirement which if left unsatisfied would prevent sentences of the form which the philosopher is concerned to retain from doing their work. The sentences he is concerned to retain, i.e., sentences which state the existence of appearances of there being things, can do their usual work, say what such sentences say in the language of everyday discourse, only if it is possible in the reconstructed language to formulate sentences which carry on the work done by the deleted sentences. If the owner of a boat decided, for whatever reasons, that the tiller was unsatisfactory, removed it and left the rudder intact, but neglected to replace the tiller by something to take over its function, he would be doing something comparable to what the philosopher is doing. Or to conjure up a further analogous case, a person would be doing what the philosopher is doing if he removed the hands from his watch and without replacing them or in any way changing the fixed position of the face in relation to the works kept the watch wound. Without something to do the work of the tiller the rudder becomes useless, and without something to take over the job of the hands the face loses its function, because of the way tillers are related to rudders and watch hands to watch faces. Similarly, sentences stating the apparent existence of things are so related to the corresponding sentences stating the existence of things that if sentences of the second class are removed from the language and no provision is made for formulating sentences which will do what they now do in the language, sentences of the first class will automatically lose their present descriptive function. For instance, the literal meaning of the sentence 'There appears (or looks or seems) to be a castle in the air' is so bound up with the literal meaning of the sentence 'There is a castle in the air' that 'There appears to be a castle . . .' would cease saying what it now says, lose its present descriptive function, if language were so altered that there was no possible way of expressing what 'There is a castle in the air' now expresses. Clearly if the point of eliminating one class of sentences while retaining the other class were practical, e.g., to facilitate communication, remove verbal awkwardness, or effect greater precision of expression, the metaphysician would make linguistic restitution of some sort in order to prevent sentences of the other class from passing out of currency. The fact that he does not do this shows that the remodelling of language is not motivated by a dissatisfaction with the actual use of language or by the practical wish to reform it.

The inescapable conclusion is that the fantasied remodelled language is *intentionally left unfinished,* though the intention is undoubtedly not conscious. The utterance 'things are but appearances' covertly and indirectly describes a prosaic alteration of language but produces the illusion of making a colossal claim about reality; and it cannot in earnest be doubted that the production of this illusion is of importance to the philosopher. The point, or part of the point, of effecting the incompletely worked out language change now comes to light: the utterance has both to create the illusion of making a factual claim of fundamental importance and to carry with it the irrefutability of an *a priori* statement, from which the metaphysician derives his confidence. And the utterance can satisfy both conditions only if sentences stating the existence of things are deleted without being replaced by sentences which do their work, while sentences stating the appearance of there being things are retained. The claim made by the words 'things are but appearances' would not, of course, be compatible with the completely worked out language change, and a metaphysician who completed the change would have to give up saying 'things are but appearances'. He is able to make his pronouncement and in doing this create the illusion of expressing an unassailable theory about the world only by failing to satisfy the requirement of his linguistic deletion.

The hypothesis, or perhaps it would be better to say the meta-hypothesis, developed in these pages about the philosophical view that what we take to be the physical world is only a delusive appearance cannot but arouse scepticism and may even provoke considerable resentment. For it must be plain that the application of the meta-hypothesis, if correct, is not limited to the view considered here, and it can hardly be said that the meta-hypothesis puts what the philosopher does in a light which he could find gratifying. In a famous passage Freud describes three great 'outrages upon its naïve self-love' which cultured mankind has had to endure in the last few hundred years. And if the present hypothesis is correct in its general outline, a special group of intellectuals must endure still a further blow to their ego: it exposes these intellectuals, who have prided themselves on being impersonal seekers after truth, as the dupes of games they unconsciously play with language.

It would indeed be surprising if the meta-hypothesis brought forward to explain the view did not seem fantastic, certainly more fantastic than the view it seeks to explain. Nevertheless, when looked at with emotional detachment we must grant that the words 'things are but appearances' cannot be about things and appearances nor yet can they be construed as purporting to convey information about the actual, established use of language. It must be admitted that a not inconsiderable merit of the meta-hypothesis is that it does give an explanation of how these words can be uttered soberly and with assurance, words which on one interpretation can only be looked on as the product of a delirium and which on another interpretation must be taken to indicate a strange case of linguistic amnesia which comfortably lives side by side with the unforgotten use of language.

The result arrived at so far is that a philosopher who holds that a world of physical things only appears to exist is describing an incompletely remodelled version of ordinary language. The philosopher unquestionably feels his statement to be of great importance, but it would be unrealistic to imagine him to be a linguistic reformer. Instead, it has to be realized that his statement is, so to speak, an exotic plant and requires a special atmosphere in which to live and flourish. In this respect it is like a dream, which requires special conditions, e.g., a temporarily weakened sense of reality, in order to play its rôle effectively in the mind of the dreamer. The great importance of the utterance to the philosopher makes it safe to compare it with a dream in still another respect: like a dream it is fundamentally a wish-fulfilment which can make its appearance against resistances only by presenting itself in a disguised form. It cannot be denied that part of the importance of the words 'things are mere appearance' lies in their being able to produce a dramatic intellectual illusion, an illusion which gives its metaphysical *entrepreneur,* and also those who identify themselves with him, a feeling of power, the power to destroy a world or to recreate a world by doing magical things with words. Behind the metaphysical pronouncement we can detect unconscious self-aggrandizement, we can glimpse the Wizard of Oz who justified the grandiose image he secretly had of himself by staging awesome effects. But the fascination and importance this view has for a philosopher who holds it is not wholly explained by the fact that the delusive idea to which it gives rise, of his laying bare the insubstantiality of the world, enables the philosopher to give subjective gratification to his wish for 'omnipotence of thought'. It must in addition to doing this have one or more special meanings which he unconsciously understands and which he puts into the service of his unconscious needs. The well-known phenomenon of psychological over-determination makes us expect this, and our expectation in the present case is strengthened by the fact that the philosophical rejection equally with the acceptance, the 'disproving' equally with the 'proving', of the metaphysical view about things and appearances heightens one's inner sense of power. It is not a *psychological* exaggeration to say that debates between metaphysicians are conflicts between titans whose weapons are thoughts; but it would be a psychological exaggeration to suppose that the wish for mental omnipotence could be the only determinant of the metaphysical view.

It is, as a matter of fact, possible to glimpse a number of ideas which the words 'things are but appearances' are unconsciously made to stand for. One of these, which is unequivocally suggested by the words, lies so near to consciousness that bringing it to light is not likely to arouse the emotional scepticism which mention of unconscious ideas usually calls forth. It may therefore be of some point to discuss it briefly. It is a well-established fact that many people experience to a greater or lesser degree a 'turning away from reality'. Disappointing experiences will cause one person to seek the asylum of a monastery, another to live the lonely life of a recluse, and a third to find the scholar's ivory tower a place of peace, to mention only a few out of the innumerable possibilities. All of these represent to some degree a 'flight from reality'. The disappointments which the world inflicts on everyone, the frustrations which everyone has to endure, automatically cause more or less withdrawal of love from objective reality; and the more his love is withdrawn from the world the less interest the individual finds in it. He then comes to depend on introversion for emotional satisfaction. His attention shifts from the world around him to inner fantasies. Interest and curiosity follow the path of libido; and when the world is invested with libido it is vivid, felt to be charged with 'meaning', and arouses the liveliest interest and delight. When libido is withdrawn, the world loses its vividness and colour, life is felt to be 'meaningless' or is felt to be sufficiently unsatisfactory to raise the question as to what its 'meaning' is. Interest in the world, which has become a Platonic cave and a 'beggarly show', goes into a decline, and absorption with private fantasies replaces it: 'the reality threatens to migrate to another world than ours'.[1]

Op. cit., p. 121. This is out of context, but its meaning is unmistakable in its

It can hardly seem strained to conclude with regard to a thinker who condemns the world as being a beggarly show and who feels reality threatening to migrate to another world that he has in some measure turned away from the world and is using the words 'things are but appearances' to voice his low opinion of it. It is pertinent to note that the sense of *important* is one of the obsolete meanings of the word 'real'; and the word still carries with it emotive overtones of approval. It continues to have a persuasive use, even though it no longer is used as a synonym for the word 'important' or for the word 'valuable'. The terms 'unreal', 'mere appearance', and the like, also, in addition to their literal meaning, carry with them emotively derogatory connotations which are associated with such terms as 'non-genuine' and 'worthless'. Thus it would hardly stretch present usage if the Metaphysician of the Unreality of the Physical World unconsciously used the terms 'real' and 'mere appearance' in their obsolete senses of important and worthless. It seems plain that for him, as well as for others who have his needs and are able to make his associations to the words 'things are but appearances', these words express the belief,

Things are meaningless and without worth.

This belief he needs to have both in order to justify his turning away from the objective world and in order to reassure himself that he loses nothing by doing so. The philosophical words express, not a conscious belief about things and appearances, but an unconscious devaluation of things. Behind the verbal appearance of making a stupendous factual claim about the physical world,

All is illusion, insubstantial appearance,

the philosopher is an Ecclesiastes who says

All is vanity, this world is devoid of merit.

The philosophical view that things are mere appearance may

context. To quote more fully: 'Our attempts, so far, to reduce the world's diverse contents to unity have ended in failure. Any sort of group which we could find, whether a thing or a self, proved unable to stand criticism. And, since it seems that what appears must somewhere certainly be one, and since this unity is not to be discovered in phenomena, the reality threatens to migrate to another world than ours. We have been driven near to the separation of appearance and reality; we already contemplate their localization in two different hemispheres—the one unknown to us and real, and the other known and mere appearance'.

now be described as an intellectual structure which consists of three main interconnected strata: a linguistically produced illusion that a theory about the world is being announced; a concealed description of an academic and incompletely worked out re-editing of language which requires the preservation of ordinary language as a backdrop against which the philosophical sentence produces its dramatic effect; and, finally, one or more unconscious ideas the philosophical statement is made to denote. This is a remarkable and subtly integrated structure the greater part of which, like that of an iceberg, is invisible, concealed by an illusion which gives its creator the status of a special kind of scientist, the status of scientist of the suprasensible.

XI

ARE SELF-CONTRADICTORY
EXPRESSIONS MEANINGLESS?[1]

IT is the purpose of this study to examine several theories which have at times been held, either explicitly or by implication, and perhaps unconsciously, in answer to the philosophical question 'Do self-contradictory expressions have meaning?' I wish to state at the outset that it is no part of my purpose to attempt in the course of the discussion to judge in favour of any one of the existing views: no attempt will be made to strengthen any view by adducing further considerations in its favour or to weaken the credibility of competing views by further criticism. Instead, my object is to analyse the nature of the question and of the various theories and supporting arguments, and in this way to try to arrive at an explanation of what the question asks and of what the theories and arguments come to.

The prevailing, and entirely natural, idea of the dispute with regard to self-contradictory expressions is that philosophers who engage in it have a clear idea of the nature of the problem and of their various theories about its solution, and are disagreeing amongst themselves over which theory is true. Nevertheless, the suspicion strikes one and becomes strengthened that the philosophical dispute is *intrinsically* irresolvable, i.e., is such that no conceivable further fact of any sort would resolve it, would make any philosopher see that his theory was false. This suggests the possibility that what seems obviously to be in question, namely, the truth-values of the competing theories, is not actually in question,

---

[1]Discussions with my student, Miss Barbara Caldwell, helped clarify a number of points in this study.

but that the difference of opinion concerns something else, something, furthermore, that is effectively hidden from the awareness of the philosophers themselves. However far-fetched it may seem, the idea to be pursued here, for whatever understanding it may lead to, is that what philosophers are doing when they state their theories and support them with relevant arguments, is utterly different from what they give the plain appearance of doing.

Prof. G. E. Moore has stated a striking and important paradox, the investigation of which seems to me to give insight into the nature of many philosophical problems and theories. He has claimed[1] that many philosophers have been able to hold 'as part of their philosophical creed' propositions inconsistent with what they knew to be true; and it must be admitted as a plain fact that his claim is not without foundation. Some philosophers *have,* in the presence of what they knew, been able to hold that a table is an attribute or that propositions about the past are predictions. The phenomenon to which Moore calls our attention, when considered with emotional detachment, is so strange that one cannot help wondering what magic powers exist in a 'philosophical creed' to produce such a remarkable effect on the minds of philosophers. And one cannot help but suspect that at least many, if not all, philosophical propositions are of a different species from the familiar ones we have commerce with in everyday discourse. The strangeness of the phenomenon lends some justification to this suspicion, and it clearly deserves investigation. In the case of the present problem about self-contradictions I wish to pursue this suspicion with the help of a direct consequence of Moore's paradox: namely, the equally paradoxical corollary that some philosophers have been able to disagree with each other while knowing everything necessary in order to know which of the various theories are false and which true, so that if some of these philosophers are right and the others are wrong, those who are wrong know that they are wrong and the others are right, and those who are right know that they are right and the others wrong.

The expression 'Are self-contradictory expressions meaningless?' has the form of a question which is a request for factual information. It has the structure of questions like 'Do the sentences of "Finnegan's Wake" have literal meaning?' and 'Does this

[1] 'A Defence of Common Sense', *Contemporary British Philosophy,* Vol. II, 203.

undeciphered enemy document actually have a meaning, or is it meaningless and just a diversionary trick?', the answer to which is arrived at, either conclusively or with some degree of plausibility, by some sort of examination or an experiment. Philosophers who have set themselves the task of answering this question have given the impression of thinking it to be with regard to matter of fact about self-contradictory expressions; for they have arrived at their theories by what evidently seems to be a sort of experiment conducted on such expressions.

Prof. C. H. Langford holds that self-contradictory statements are meaningless and tells us, in support of his view, that 'when we try to envisage the unitary meaning of a statement of this kind ["Men exist and men do not exist"] we find that this is quite impossible, and that therefore it has no single meaning, but rather one meaning corresponding to one part of the verbal expression and another to another'.[1] On the other hand, Prof. Donald C. Williams maintains that self-contradictions are 'just as intelligible' as expressions for contingent and necessary propositions: 'If ∼N is to be called "absurd", "nonsense", "inconceivable", these words must therefore be taken in their workaday sense to mean impossible or incredible, not actually meaningless. Strictly, impossible statements are not even incredible, in the literal sense that they cannot be believed . . . Some very thoughtful persons have . . devoutly believed self-contradictory propositions: that the circle can be squared, for instance, or the doctrine of transubstantiation'.[2] Although Williams holds a different theory from that held by Langford, he arrives at it, in part, as the result of a similar experiment. According to him some sort of 'introspection' shows that self-contradictory expressions have meaning: 'The theoretical analysis of meaning convinces me that ∼N should be just as intelligible as N or C, and empirical introspection indicates that it is'.[3]

Langford gives the reader the impression of basing his theory on some sort of *Gedankenexperiment*, which he describes as consisting of the attempt 'to envisage the unitary meaning' of a self-contradictory sentence, and which Dr. A. C. Ewing describes as

---

[1]Lewis and Langford, *Symbolic Logic,* pp. 476–7. See also G. F. Stout's *Studies in Philosophy and Psychology,* pp. 314–15.

[2]'The Nature and Variety of the *A Priori*', *Analysis,* Vol. V, No. 6, p. 90.

[3]*Ibid.,* pp. 89–90.

an attempt 'to think out'[1] what it means. In the case of Williams also the idea is created that a process of mental looking is resorted to, but this time with an opposite result. From the language these philosophers have used to describe the procedure by which they were led to their views one would quite naturally gather that they had arrived at them inductively, by subjecting a number of expressions to a mental examination upon the results of which they framed a theory about *all* self-contradictions. Langford furthers the impression that the examination is an empirical process of looking for the accompaniment of a sentence, by virtue of the existence of which the sentence is meaningful and otherwise not, when he writes: 'Take, for example, the sentence "Ghosts *could* not exist". Here the separate words are meaningful enough; but when we try to apprehend what the sentence as a whole stands for, and try to envisage the situation, not verbally but in terms of genuine ideas, the only entity we come upon is the fact that ghosts *could* exist, for which, of course, the words "Ghosts could not exist" are not a proper expression'.[2] Williams, of course, explicitly states part of his procedure to be 'empirical introspection'.

What these philosophers do, at least in appearance, is analogous to what people normally do when they are in doubt as to whether a canvas has a painting on it: they get closer and look more carefully. The puzzling thing about the case of the philosophers is not their procedure, which seems appropriate and should lead to a conclusion, but the fact that they come away from their examination with opposite opinions. It is as though after both had examined the canvas carefully, one were to say there was no picture, while the other were to insist there was a picture, that he could see it quite plainly. An interested observer of their disagreement who had not himself examined the canvas would hardly know what to think: whether one philosopher suffered from an unusual optical defect or whether the other was given to vivid and convincing hallucinations.

The view that self-contradictory expressions have meaning has led philosophers to still further theories. Williams, for instance, by his insistence that 'inconceivable' when used in connexion with self-contradictions has the 'workaday sense' of impossible or incredible gives us some reason for supposing him to be holding, at

[1]'Meaninglessness', *Mind*, July, 1937, p. 363.   [2]*Op. cit.,* p. 475.

least by implication, that propositions commonly classified as necessary are really empirical. According to his view, 'It is inconceivable that the hour hand of my clock should point to two different hour numerals at one time' says the same as 'It is incredible that the hour hand of my clock should point to two different hour numerals at one time', where 'incredible', it would seem, has the sense it has in 'It is altogether incredible, I'll admit, but the cow *did* jump over the moon'. Williams does not himself derive from his words the consequence that necessary propositions are empirical. C. W. Whiteley, who also holds that self-contradictory expressions have meaning, goes on to assert outright that necessary propositions are empirical.[1]

Still other philosophers, who hold the same view about self-contradictions but are impressed by the *a priori,* unempirical character of such a proposition as is expressed by the sentence 'It is inconceivable that seven out of the enemy's flotilla of six ships should have been sunk in the engagement' have held self-contradictions to express what is *logically* inconceivable. Thus, in one place Prof. C. I. Lewis states that 'round square' has a meaning and 'represents something inconceivable'.[2] Elsewhere he writes, 'Plainly, it is incorrect to say that terms like "round square" have no connotation, or that they are meaningless. This term is distinguished from a nonsense-locution like "zuke" by definitely implying the properties of roundness and squareness. And it is only by reason of this meaning—this connotation which it has, that one determines its inapplicability to anything consistently thinkable'.[3] H. W. B. Joseph distinguishes between propositions and sentences —'A proposition is a sentence, but not merely a sentence: it is a sentence expressing or meaning a judgement'[4]—and also maintains, '*We cannot think* contradictory propositions'.[5] These and other things they say lend colour to the idea, though they do not make it certain, that both Lewis and Joseph hold, by implication and perhaps unconsciously, that self-contradictory sentences express propositions or have meanings that are unthinkable. Indeed,

---

[1]'Truth by Convention', *Analysis,* Vol. IV, Nos. 2 & 3, pp. 25–7.
[2]Lewis and Langford, *op. cit.,* p. 68; see also what precedes and follows this.
[3]'The Modes of Meaning', *Philosophy and Phenomenological Research,* Vol. IV, No. 2, p. 241.
[4]*An Introduction to Logic,* p. 18.
[5]*Ibid.,* p. 13.

Lewis explicitly defines 'logical inconceivability' to mean 'self-contradictory', so that it would seem that *all* he is saying when he states that 'a round square which is not round is inconceivable'[1] is 'a round square which is not round is self-contradictory'. But like Joseph, he distinguishes between sentences and propositions,[2] and so holds that self-contradictory sentences express or 'represent' *meanings* that are inconceivable. Moreover, the *overtone* of the choice of language, which cannot be dismissed as altogether irrelevant and as giving us no clue to the thoughts of these philosophers, is that the meaning of a self-contradictory expression, as 'something represented' by the expression, is beyond our powers to comprehend or envisage, something we are unable to think or conceive—just as it is out of the question for us to see microbes with the naked eye. It is not certain that either Lewis or Joseph wish to hold any such view, but neither is it clear that they do not actually hold it. In any case, it is a theory which very likely has been held at some time, and ought to be considered. Thus, again, Hume *seems* to have held it: 'That the cube root of 64 is equal to the half of 10, is a false proposition, and can never be distinctly conceived. But that Caesar, or the Angel Gabriel, or any being never existed, may be a false proposition, but still is perfectly conceivable, and implies no contradiction'.[3]

It has been seen, so far, that there are three different theories in answer to the question, 'Are self-contradictory expressions meaningless?' Langford holds that they are meaningless, Williams maintains that they have meaning, and still other philosophers seem to believe that they have inconceivable meanings. To revert to our analogy: it is as if three people, who were concerned over whether there was a painting on the canvas, got close to the canvas and carefully examined it, and came to different conclusions. One insisted there was no picture, that the canvas was bare; another claimed there was a picture; and the third asserted that the canvas had an invisible picture. One cannot help being reminded of the fairy tale about the emperor's new clothes which were visible only to the pure of soul. The idea one gets of what is

[1] Lewis and Langford, *op. cit.*, p. 67.
[2] *Ibid.*, p. 49. 'Propositions are not strings of marks, or series of sounds, except incidentally; in essence, a proposition expresses an asserted meaning'.
[3] Hume's *Enquiries*, Ed. L. A. Selby-Bigge (2nd ed.), p. 164.

happening is that different people are making different claims on the basis of some sort of process of mental looking for the meanings of sentences, on the basis of 'empirical introspection'. The impression gained is that knowledge of the meanings of the constituent words of a self-contradictory expression, and of their syntactical connexions, is not enough for knowing whether it has a meaning, and that further looking of some sort is necessary. Langford seems to imply this when he describes himself trying 'to envisage the situation, not verbally, but in terms of genuine ideas'.

The peculiarity of the situation, which makes it unlike an ordinary disagreement to the settling of which looking is relevant, is that their eyes, to continue the analogy, are equally good. With regard to a sentence which all would agree was self-contradictory, e.g., 'Some yellow things are colourless', neither will know more, nor for that matter would claim to know more, about the ordinary meanings of its constituent words or about their syntactical relations than the others. We can easily imagine these philosophers explicitly agreeing among themselves, and in conformity with ordinary usage and accepted grammatical conventions about the actual meanings of 'yellow' and 'colourless', etc., agreeing also that 'being yellow' is incompatible with 'being colourless', and nevertheless maintaining their divergent opinions. No one knows nor claims to know any linguistic facts about the statement that the others do not know, so that the disagreement is not caused by any difference in their linguistic information; they are all equally well informed. Nor is it caused by any such fact as that the sentence is difficult to grasp because of its extreme length and involved structure. What is even more striking about the controversy and makes it even more unlike an ordinary verbal dispute is that their linguistic information is *complete*. Each of them knows everything it is necessary linguistically to know in order to know whether 'Some yellow things are colourless' has a meaning, lacks it, or has a meaning which no human being is capable of conceiving.

The manner in which philosophers have discussed this problem creates the notion that the meaning of an expression is, in the words of Prof. Moritz Schlick, 'a kind of entity inherent in a sentence, and hidden in it like a nut in a shell—where it might be discovered'.[1] The controversy seems to be one in which the contestants

[1]'Meaning and Verification', *Philos. Rev.*, Vol. XLV (1936), p. 348.

know the syntax and constituent words of a given self-contra-dictory expression and know that it is self-contradictory, that is, they know the linguistic facts determining its use or its lack of use in the language and are attempting by a process over and above the process of learning such facts to ascertain the further fact as to whether it has a meaning. They have thus made it appear, in general, as though knowing the meaning of an expression is some-thing in addition to knowing its constituent words and syntax, so that one might know the latter and not know what it meant or whether it had a meaning. They thus create the notion that ex-pressions can have meanings over and above the use made of those expressions in the language, that they have meanings which are not determined by their use and have not been bestowed upon them by the way people have used them. This is a notion that sug-gests itself naturally to many people. Thus Heinrich Hertz has said: 'One cannot escape the feeling that these mathematical formulas have an independent existence and an intelligence of their own, that they are wiser than we are, wiser even than their discoverers, that we get more out of them than was originally put into them'.[1]

The source of this idea is obscure; one may guess that it perhaps goes back to the primitive belief in magic words and formulas, and that psychological remnants of this superstition continue to exist in the minds of even the most advanced thinkers. However that may be, this idea of the meaning of an expression is one which it is hard to think any philosopher would consciously and seriously entertain. It must be plain to everyone that nothing in our lan-guage means anything which it is not and never has been used to mean or means more than it is or ever has been used to mean. It is true to say that a metal, e.g., gold, is something over and above the use made of it; but it must be plain to everyone that the meaning of an expression is not something in addition to the way the ex-pression is used, something which has to be discovered in addi-tion to what we learn when we are taught the constituent words and the rules governing their combination.

For suppose an expression had a meaning not determined by its use, past or present, how should we go about trying to discover its meaning, and what would be a test for establishing that it had

[1] Quoted by E. T. Bell in *Men of Mathematics,* p. 16.

that meaning? Consider what we should do if someone assured us that we could not possibly learn all the separate rules of a certain game, e.g., chess, by consulting a rules book or by observing how it is played by experts. We might think in such a case that there were more rules than were given in the usual books, more rules than even experts, for the most part, used. But what should we think if in answer to our question, 'What further rules are there?' we were told that *nobody* knows, that the game had more separate rules than were framed for it by those who invented the game or by those who later in any way altered or added to it? We should, of course, not take such an answer seriously, or rather we should take it as a humorous way of saying that the game had no further rules and give up looking for any. In the same way, if in answer to our question, 'What, in addition to the linguistic facts determining the use or lack of use of E, must be known in order to know whether it has a meaning and what it is?' we were told that nobody knows because its meaning was not to be got at by learning the constituent words and syntax of E, we should conclude E had none in the language. There are not two distinct processes, one of learning the constituent words of E and the manner in which they are put together and the other of learning its meaning,[1] because there are not two distinct sets of facts, one, facts with regard to its use, the other, facts with regard to its literal meaning.

It can now be seen that if the dispute is a disagreement over whether, in fact, self-contradictions have or lack meanings, then it is a clear instance of Moore's corollary paradox. The linguistic information is the same for all the disputants. No one knows any more about the constituent words or the grammar of their combinations than the others; all know equally well that, e.g., 'round square' is 'distinguished from a nonsense-locution like "zuke" by definitely implying the properties roundness and squareness'. Their linguistic information is also complete; there is nothing, no further fact, they have to know in order to know that it has a meaning, if it has one, or that it lacks a meaning, if it does not have one. Hence if the problem with regard to self-contradictions is like a problem of decoding an intercepted enemy document, they all know the correct answer: they have the linguistic key. We are

[1]Idiomatic phrases are, of course, an exception to this.

thus faced with the paradox of philosophers disagreeing with each other while, at the same time, knowing everything necessary in order to know which of their theories is true and which false, so that if some of the philosophers are right and the others are wrong, those who are wrong know that they are wrong and the others are right, and those who are right know that they are right and the others wrong.

Once we come to this result, it is natural for us to seek for an explanation of what makes it possible for philosophers to continue to disagree in face of the facts which should completely resolve their differences. To have to accept their disagreement as just a strange fact about philosophers is unsatisfactory. It is hard to believe that philosophers are as abnormal as Moore's paradox implies. A detective who was certain he had caught a thief red-handed just as he was leaving the Louvre with a missing canvas under his coat and was later told that one art expert claimed the canvas was just a bare canvas, that another expert pronounced it a valuable Van Gogh from the Louvre collection, while still a third maintained the painting on the canvas was invisible, could hardly be expected to remain satisfied with the explanation 'Strange, but that is the way art experts are'. He has to know whether to arrest the man or let him go. We feel the same way about the explanation 'Strange, but that is the way philosophers are', especially if we have noticed that ordinary, nonphilosophical people when asked the question 'Do self-contradictory expressions have meaning?' divide on it exactly in the same way philosophers divide on it. The fact that ordinary people talk the way philosophers do, that they *become* philosophers, when presented with the problem, puts the thought into our minds that perhaps there is something unusual, and not as yet understood, about the philosophical canvas, about the problem itself, rather than about the philosophers who express their theories on its solution. And only after having investigated the problem with this idea in mind and convinced ourselves that it is like any ordinary problem to the settling of which an examination of words and syntax is relevant should we finally be willing to come back to the first explanation and admit that that is the way philosophers are.

Fortunately, a further explanation presents itself to us, though we are not yet in a position to predict its outcome. It has the merit of being possible while *avoiding* Moore's paradox; this much is in its favour. Whether it turns out to be the true explanation will depend, so far as I can see, not only on whether it applies to other philosophical problems,[1] but also on whether philosophers come in time to recognize it as the explanation of what their problem is and of what their theories come to, on whether it 'clicks' with them. I cannot think of anything except the latter that would be *conclusive*.

What puzzles and mystifies us is to think that people could disagree while fully aware of the facts that are sufficient to prevent their disagreeing. Their information should preclude a difference of opinion of the sort they appear to have; it would as the normal thing leave no room for it. One may therefore justifiably permit oneself the conjecture that the disagreement is not about what we imagine it to be and that the theories are not actually in conflict with the facts they know and are agreed upon. It *may* be the case that the theories we tend naturally to associate with the words and the form of language philosophers have used are not actually what the words are intended to express. There is no other way, besides supposing this, of avoiding Moore's paradox, as anyone who thinks closely on the matter can see. Their information *should* preclude a factual linguistic difference of opinion. This makes it at least conceivable, if no more than as an outside possibility, that it is actually a feature of their dispute that no point of linguistic fact is in question. This is a possible avenue of investigation open to us, and the one I propose to follow.

The assumption that no point of linguistic fact is in dispute between philosophers who intelligibly divide on the question requires us to suppose that their contrary assertions are not statements of fact. Further, we have to think that the question to which their theories are *relevant* answers, that is, the question *philosophers* express by the words 'Do self-contradictory expressions have meaning?' is not a request for factual linguistic information about self-contradictions, to the effect that they lack meaning, have meanings, or have inconceivable meanings. The absence of any point of fact over which the dispute could conceivably be conducted makes us think the divergent views are not of a kind to

---

[1] See for example, John Wisdom's 'Philosophical Perplexity', *Proc. Arist. Soc.*, Vol. XXXVII, and Norman Malcolm's 'The Nature of Entailment', *Mind*, July, 1940.

which the concepts 'true' and 'false' are applicable and also that the question which is under *philosophical* consideration is somehow different from the factual request expressed by the same words, 'Do self-contradictions have meaning?' Unlike the latter, the answer to which (if it had one) would be a statement of fact about the correctness of applying 'meaning' to self-contradictions, the former question has to be construed as a request to which a true proposition about current usage would not be a relevant answer. How, then, are we to understand the views?

In the case of our present problem we get further insight if we withdraw our attention from the philosophical controversy with its tendency to stimulate us into taking sides and fix attention instead on the everyday use of 'meaning' in English. It happens to be the case that the ordinary use of the word tells us nothing about whether it is correct English to apply the word to expressions classified as self-contradictions or whether it is incorrect English to do this. Its ordinary use gives us no definite information to the effect that 'self-contradictions have meaning' constitutes an improper use of 'meaning' or a proper one. It leaves us, so to speak, with a blank on this point. To put the matter in another way, there exists no generally accepted criterion or rule for the use of 'meaning' which makes valid either ' " E is a self-contradictory expression" implies "E has meaning" ' or ' " E is a self-contradictory expression" implies "E is meaningless" '. We are left unprovided for in the case of self-contradictions.[1]

This throws light on our problem. If there exists no established, conventional rule according to which the application of 'meaning' is either correct or incorrect, we can readily see both how it is that no point of linguistic fact is at issue between philosophers who answer differently the query about self-contradictions, and what their assertions as well as the question come to. The *factual* question 'Are self-contradictions meaningless?' has no straightforward yes or no answer, or rather we might say, it has the straightforward answer that it is neither correct nor incorrect English to say 'Self-contradictions have meaning'. But the factual question is not the one philosophers are directly concerned with, nor are they, as they seem to be, trying to discover its answer. What its answer is, or

[1] See Alice Ambrose's 'Self-contradictory Suppositions', *Mind*, Oct., 1944, for a similar point about the use of 'meaning' in mathematics.

the fact that it has no straightforward yes or no answer, they know as well as anyone who knows the actual use of 'meaning'. Thus, when Williams says, 'The theoretical analysis of meaning convinces me that ~N should be just as intelligible as N or C', we can detect his awareness of this behind the words 'should be'. Otherwise why the uncertainty of 'should be' rather than the conclusiveness of 'is'? The fact is that neither analysis nor consulting a linguistic Solomon will, as 'meaning' is currently used, establish the existence of a rule which makes it definitely correct to apply the word to self-contradictions.

It is not difficult, however, to see how dissatisfaction might easily arise over the lack of definite rules with regard to the application or non-application of 'meaning' to self-contradictions. It requires little imagination to realize that people who are concerned with 'the problem of meaning' would become dissatisfied with the ordinary, inexact use of 'meaning', which fails to take into account a whole class of expressions, and would *wish* to remedy the situation. 'Meaning' is an untidy, inexact word, which is a source of dissatisfaction to many people, particularly to those with a liking for exact classifications or to those with a deep-seated intolerance of situations for which there exist no rules to guide them. And it seems to me our credulity is not stretched too much, certainly no more so than it is by Moore's paradox, if we understand the philosophical views in terms of the wish, not to discover the answer to 'Are self-contradictions meaningless?' but to *make,* by an act of linguistic creation, a correct answer. So construed, the views represent linguistic decisions to use 'meaning' in a definite way with respect to self-contradictions: the philosopher who asserts 'Self-contradictions are without meaning' has decided to regularize the word by definitely withholding it from self-contradictions; the philosopher who tells us that self-contradictions have meaning has also decided to regularize the word, but he accomplishes this by applying it to them.

In a different connexion, a mathematician has remarked: 'The idea of a sum of an infinite series has caused endless confusion among philosophers. This is because they have failed to adopt a clear cut definition of the sum of such a series and then to adhere strictly to the definition'.[1] We might say of the present problem

[1] N. J. Lennes, *College Algebra* (1st ed.), p. 113.

that philosophers have decided to *make* clear-cut the use of 'meaning' in ordinary English. Their philosophical statements are not *answers* to a question about established linguistic usage, which, as it turns out, has as yet no definite answer of the sort they want it to have; either of their statements would become the correct answer only if it became the conventional answer. The question to which their statements *are* relevant answers is a request for a linguistic decision with regard to a type of case which is not provided for by conventional language. Roughly, the philosophical question, misleadingly expressed by the words, '*Are* self-contradictory expressions meaningless?' is 'How *should* self-contradictions be classified with respect to the linguistic category "meaning"?'

To sum up the conclusions we have been led to in our attempt to avoid Moore's paradox: The philosophical question 'Are self-contradictions meaningless?' is a verbally concealed request for a decision with regard to an application of 'meaning' for which conventional use has made no stipulation. The views in answer to it state the as yet nonconventional classifications of self-contradictory expressions with respect to the category 'meaning'. These views are expressed in a form of language appropriate to statements of fact, in part, probably, to win assent to a linguistic *fait accompli*. We can now see what the controversy comes to and how it can continue without resolution. Each disputant urges the general acceptance of his own use of 'meaning'. When one philosopher *asserts* 'Self-contradictions *are* meaningless', not only is it the case that he tells us how he is going to use the word, but he also urges others to adopt his usage. And when another philosopher asserts 'Self-contradictions *have* meaning', he too does not merely inform us about the way he wishes to use it but urges its adoption on others. The controversy is thus a contest between philosophers over the adoption of their usage. And the continuation of the dispute without resolution is explained by the circumstance that no philosopher succeeds in winning over enough other philosophers, who prefer their own classifications, to his usage.

Consider a nonphilosophical problem about which people who are confronted with it express different opinions and remain unshakably divided. Stuart wants to sell a section of land which he thinks is utterly worthless. He finds a customer and assures him that the land is rich in oil, but that for urgent financial reasons he must sell it for much less than it is worth. The gullible man buys the land, drills for oil, and finds it. Now, did Stuart lie? Most people after having this case described to them will say Stuart lied. Their reason for saying this invariably is that he intended to deceive. Others will insist he did not lie; and their reason is that he said what was true.

Now it is clear that the dispute about this problem does not result from a lack of information about what happened, about the facts of the case. Nor is the division over whether the definition of 'lie' makes it correct or incorrect to apply 'lie' to what Stuart said; the people who give different answers know perfectly well its conventional use. Unlike the situation with regard to 'meaning', the dictionary provides us with a definition of 'lie', according to which it is incorrect to say Stuart lied. Bringing this definition into the dispute fails, however, to produce the expected result of resolving it. Instead, those who insist that Stuart lied behave as though the dictionary definition is *irrelevant* to what *they* are saying, to the problem they are concerned with. It becomes clear, thus, in the present case, that the question is really a request for a decision about the application of 'lie' in a type of situation which, though provided for by definition, is unusual enough to merit reconsideration. It is a request for a linguistic redecision.[1]

We can see also what the 'reasons' given for the answers come to. They are nothing more than descriptions of the features present in the situation which incline some people to answer in one way and other people to answer in a different way. That is to say, they simply express the criteria for the use of 'lie' which the situation satisfies or fails to satisfy. Thus, a person who holds that Stuart lied and supports his position with the argument, 'He intended to deceive', is actually pointing out that the situation answers to one of the rules for the application of 'lie'. Concentration on this feature, which seems to impress many people as being of utmost importance, inclines him to brand as a lie what Stuart said; he has, in other words, decided to make 'intention to deceive' the sole criterion for the application of 'lie'. This quite plainly is what Bertrand Russell decided to do when he wrote: 'It would seem that,

[1] For a fuller discussion of a similar problem see John Wisdom's 'Metaphysics and Verification', *Mind*, Oct. 1938, pp. 493–4.

when a man lies, the falsehood is in the expression. A lie is still a lie if it happens to be objectively true, provided the speaker believes it to be false'.[1] Russell's observation, 'It would seem that, when a man lies, the falsehood is in the expression', shows his recognition of the ordinary definition of 'lie', and by his following words he makes plain the small value he places on one of the conditions it imposes on the use of the word and his decision to dispense with it: 'A lie is still a lie if it happens to be objectively true . . .' On the other hand, a person who denies that Stuart lied, and bases his denial on the fact that Stuart said what was true, 'objectively true', is pointing out that the situation fails to satisfy one of the conventional defining criteria for the use of 'lie'. It fails to answer to, and goes against, a part of the ordinary definition of 'lie', which this person is unwilling to give up. This is the import of his argument, 'Stuart didn't lie, because he said what was true'. His decision is to retain, unaltered, the ordinary use of the word. Sometimes people will reconcile their differences by agreeing that 'subjectively' Stuart did lie but that 'objectively' he did not. What they are doing is to making new language which will permit them both to be right.

To come back to the problem about self-contradictions. The reasons, or arguments, philosophers state in demonstration of their theories should also be amenable to explanation in this way. They should, if our interpretation of the question and theories is correct or near-correct, lend themselves to an explanation which makes them out to be linguistic justifications for the various uses of 'meaning' decided on, despite their appearance of being arguments for the correctness of statements of fact. Thus, for example, when one philosopher asserts that self-contradictory statements are meaningless and bases his view on the argument that we cannot 'envisage the unitary meaning of a statement of this kind', these words must lend themselves naturally, and without serious distortion, to construction as a justification for a use of 'meaning' not dictated by conventional rules. And the same for the other arguments. If this turns out to be the case, the plausibility of the explanation of the nature of the dispute will, to a considerable degree, be increased.

Consider the argument for the view that self-contradictory sen-

[1] *An Inquiry into Meaning and Truth,* p. 267.

tences 'as wholes, do not stand for anything at all',[1] namely, 'When we try to envisage the unitary meaning of a statement of this kind, we find that this is quite impossible, and that therefore . . .' This way of putting the matter is extremely misleading. For it gives rise to the idea that we discover whether a sentence, e.g., 'The door was open at the time it was shut', has a meaning or lacks one by a process of looking for something which is the accompaniment of a sentence when it has a meaning, something which it 'stands for', so that if after sufficient looking we find no appropriate accompaniment we are justified in concluding the sentence is meaningless. The words do, however, suggest a feature by virtue of which 'meaning' correctly applies to expressions, a feature self-contradictory expressions do not have. Schlick, who joins Langford in holding that self-contradictions are meaningless, tells us in a less misleading way what this feature is:

> The height of a tower cannot be 100 feet and 150 feet at the same time; a child cannot be naked and dressed at the same time—not because we are unable to imagine it, but because our definitions of 'height', of the numerals, of the terms 'naked' and 'dressed', are not compatible with the particular combinations of those words in our examples. 'They are not compatible with such combinations' means that the rules of our language have not provided any use for such combinations.[2]

These words state quite unambiguously the reason why some philosophers have decided so to use 'meaning' as to exclude self-contradictions from the class of meaningful expressions. This is that in our language they have been given no *descriptive use*. They describe no situation whatever, actual or theoretically conceivable, because 'the rules of our language have not provided any use for such combinations'. Thus sentences like 'Smith has a painless feeling of pain', 'The iron anvil is not made of metal', are of such a sort that if they had a function in the language they would, like 'Smith has a sharp pain' and 'The iron anvil is surprisingly light', truly or falsely tell us something, inform or misinform us, about a state of affairs, or a situation, or an occurrence, etc. But they do nothing of the sort. 'The iron anvil is not made of metal' neither

[1] Lewis and Langford, *op. cit.*, p. 475.
[1] *Op. cit.*, p. 350.

informs nor misinforms us about anything. It says nothing about what anything is or theoretically might be. The reason for this is the linguistic fact that unlike 'iron anvil' and 'metal but not iron', for which applications have been provided, 'iron object not made of metal' has in our language been given no descriptive use. It is not used in sentences to tell us about what anything is, in the way in which non-contradictory noun phrases or adjective phrases normally are used. Lewis seems to recognize that self-contradictory phrases have been provided with no descriptive use when he speaks of their 'inapplicability to anything consistently thinkable'. It may be observed that if a self-contradictory phrase were provided with an application, if for any reason we gave 'painless feeling of pain' or 'naked but dressed' a descriptive use, we should no longer count it as *self-contradictory*. And when a philosopher says, 'We cannot think what it would be like for quadratic equations to go to race meetings or for squares to be round',[1] or says we cannot 'form an image of quadruplicity drinking procrastination',[2] what, in a misleading way, he is pointing out, is not that 'round square' or 'quadruplicity drinking procrastination' offers insurmountable obstacles to our thinking or imagination but that it 'expresses no thought',[3] it presents us with no sort of situation or circumstance whatever to think about or imagine. 'We cannot think what it would be like . . .', 'we cannot envisage . . .', 'we cannot combine the subject and predicate in thought'[4]; but what stands in the way of our doing this is the linguistic fact that self-contradictory expressions have been given no use. The self-contradictory phrase which 'combines the subject and predicate' has been provided with no application to anything whatever.

Concern over, and the wish to emphasize, the fact that self-contradictions lack descriptive use, which is a feature they have in common with expressions like 'Slithy toves did gyre and gimble in the wabe' and 'feels nonsense pink', to which 'meaningless' does correctly apply, inclines some philosophers to group them together under the linguistic category 'meaningless'. In effect their argument amounts to saying: 'Self-contradictions are

[1]A. C. Ewing, *Op. cit.*, p. 363.
[2]Bertrand Russell, *An Inquiry into Meaning and Truth*, p. 222.
[3]G. F. Stout, *Studies in Philosophy and Psychology*, p. 314.
[4]A. C. Ewing, *op. cit.*, p. 363.

similar in an important respect to strings of words which are properly called "meaningless", the respect, namely, of lacking use. By reckoning them among literally meaningful expressions we should *conceal* this important feature they share with meaningless strings of words. But by classifying them as being meaningless we, instead, bring out and emphasize this feature. This justifies the decision to deny the application of "meaning" to self-contradictions'.

Self-contradictory expressions, however, also possess other features, in respect of which they are different from meaningless combinations of words and are like expressions to which 'meaning' is correctly applicable. These features impress other philosophers and make them hold an opposite view. Thus, in addition to basing his view on what 'empirical introspection indicates', Williams gives the following argument: 'An impossible proposition is self-contradictory, not in that it needs itself be of the form $p.\sim p$, but in that it entails a proposition of that form; but a muddle of marks without meaning could neither contradict itself nor entail anything. The meaning is what is contradictory and impossible'.[1] And Ewing argues in the same vein: 'For after all—quadratic equations do not go to race meetings—is entailed by—quadratic equations do not move in space, and entails—quadratic equations do not watch the Newmarket horse-races; but, if it is capable of entailing and being entailed, surely it must be a proposition and not a mere meaningless set of words'.[2] These arguments bring out several features of self-contradictions which lead many people to say they have meaning.

It is, in the first place, clear that a self-contradictory sentence is different from a meaningless muddle of marks. 'The tower is 100 feet and also 150 feet high' is not a jumble of words like 'Up the cat mouse the ate'; it has syntax. Nor is it like 'slithy toves gimbled in the wabe'; none of its constituent words lacks use. These features—of having syntax and having no constituent words which lack literal meaning—sharply distinguish self-contradictory sentences and phrases from senseless strings of words. They are criteria the absence of which makes it incorrect to apply 'self-contradictory' to expressions, but makes the application of 'meaningless' to them proper. Thus, for example, though 'x is both

[1] *Op. cit.*, p. 90.   [2] *Op. cit.*, p. 360.

zuke and not zuke' has the *form* of a contradiction, it would not quite be proper English to characterize it as a self-contradictory sentence; and the same for, 'It is true and at the same time false that up the cat mouse the ate'. A still further property of self-contradictions, which differentiates them from a muddle of marks, is that they have implications. This is a property they have by virtue both of possessing syntax and of having no words without literal significance. Thus, 'The diameter of square x is longer than any other chord' can be deduced from 'x is a square circle' because of the meaning of 'square', of 'circle', etc., together with the form of combination of these words.

The fact that the phrase 'both dressed and naked' has no descriptive use, so that the sentence, 'The king is both naked and dressed', expresses no condition of anything and itself fails to be descriptive, is a point of similarity between muddles of marks and self-contradictions. But other of their features constitute both points of difference from muddles of marks and points of likeness to strings of words to which 'meaning' correctly applies. Philosophers who are strongly impressed by these latter features will be led into classifying self-contradictions with meaningful expressions. They will 'hold' that they have meaning, and in this way succeed in emphasizing important likenesses and unlikenesses slurred over by the counter-classification. 'Call self-contradictions "meaningless" ', we can imagine these philosophers thinking, 'and lump them together with mere muddles of marks or jumbles of words, from which they are so very different! That would be an intolerable linguistic injustice'. And they try to prevent this injustice by their classification. As is known, other philosophers remain unimpressed by their arguments, which signifies that they are more impressed by the likeness between self-contradictions and meaningless strings of words than by the likeness between self-contradictions and meaningful strings.

A further type of consideration is frequently brought up. It is pointed out that on the view that self-contradictory sentences are without meaning we should in many cases have to say: the negation of a meaningful sentence is a meaningless one, the negation of a meaningless sentence is a meaningful one, and the conjunction of two meaningful sentences is itself a meaningless sentence. We should of course have to say these things. But what of it; what sort

of *arguments* are these? The point of remarking on these consequences, which are not unknown to those who advocate calling
self-contradictions 'meaningless', is obscure, until we realize that
many philosophers feel them to be linguistically objectionable
consequences of an *irregular* classification. The import of these
complaints is that, for aesthetic reasons or for purposes of notational convenience, we ought to apply 'meaningful' to the negation of a meaningful sentence, etc.

The view that self-contradictions have meaning tends to
make some philosophers who adopt it *exaggerate* the similarity self-
contradictory statements bear to ordinary descriptive ones to the
point of holding them to be descriptive statements. Thus,
Whiteley explicitly commits himself to the theory that the sentence, 'I cannot be in London and Birmingham at the same time,'
'states a matter of fact about the world, about me and London and
Birmingham'.[1] In conjunction with this he holds the view that the
self-contradictory sentence, 'I am both in London and in Birmingham', is 'factual and not linguistic' and makes an 'assertion about
my situation in space'.[2] He thus commits himself by implication
to the view that the sentence describes a circumstance with regard
to a person, that it is a *descriptive* statement which says what is
false. A philosopher will hold this in disregard of the fact that he
knows perfectly well self-contradictions have no descriptive use.

As our language is at present used it is *false* to assert that self-
contradictions are descriptive. A person who knows the language
and nevertheless claims, directly or otherwise, that they are descriptions must, we submit, be understood to have decided to
adopt a revised use of 'description', so that in his usage the word
becomes applicable to self-contradictions. What he does may
be compared to what a mathematician does when he defines
'point' as 'circle with zero radius'. For as in the case of 'point', no
new property of self-contradictions has been discovered; only a
new classification has been made. They may now be *called* 'descriptions', without the fact of their having no descriptive function being in any way altered. They become, in this mode of
speech, descriptive statements with zero descriptiveness.

It is not difficult to see now what is at the bottom of the view that
self-contradictions have *inconceivable* meanings. It has been seen

[1]*Op. cit.,* p. 27. [2]*Op. cit.,* p. 25.

that the wish to make more conspicuous the feature which statements like '*a* is yellow but not coloured' and 'Not a drop of water fell in the downpour of rain' have in common with senseless series of words leads some philosophers to hold they are meaningless. It is also the case that they possess certain features which incline other philosophers to maintain they do have meaning and, furthermore, tempts some of them to exaggerate this claim into counting them among descriptive sentences. Self-contradictions do not thereby acquire a descriptive function. A person who holds that 'I am now both in London and Birmingham' would in certain circumstances describe a state of affairs does not give 'being in two different places at once' a use. He is satisfied merely with *calling* it a 'factual assertion' about his situation in space and indirectly, therefore, a 'descriptive sentence'. Other philosophers, however, are not altogether satisfied with this. They, in turn, are impressed by the difference between an expression which is descriptive *in name only* and an expression which is descriptive *in use* as well. This difference, which the present classification slides over, they wish in some manner to mark. They will not give up the exaggerated claim that self-contradictions are descriptive; instead, they *modify* the claim by asserting self-contradictions describe what is *inconceivable*. In this way they mark the difference between ordinary descriptive sentences and self-contradictory ones. By contrast with ordinary descriptive phrases, 'round square' becomes a descriptive phrase which is inapplicable 'to anything *consistently* thinkable'.

This is a highly misleading and mystifying way of marking the difference and of speaking about self-contradictions. It makes people imagine that sentences like 'The tower is both 150 feet and only 100 feet high', 'The church bell is now both ringing and not ringing' have mysterious sorts of meanings beyond our intellectual powers to grasp. And we may permit ourselves the speculation that perhaps this form of speech, with its misleading associations, is unconsciously motivated by the wish to use language which naturally gives rise to such associations. It is a well-known psychological fact that many people have a strong craving for the mystical and incomprehensible, for what is beyond their powers to frame in imagination. Literature, religion, and much of philosophy are full of references to enigmas that human understanding cannot penetrate. It would therefore come as no surprise if this craving, which is perhaps universal in mankind, found an attenuated gratification, subtly veiled from the intelligence, in the philosophical theory that self-contradictions have inconceivable meanings:—

I have been obliged to speak of philosophy as a satisfaction of what may be called the mystical side of our nature—a satisfaction which, by certain persons, cannot be as well procured otherwise.[1]

[1]F. H. Bradley, *Appearance and Reality*, p. 6.

XII

LOGICAL NECESSITY

M Y purpose in this essay is to try to get clear about the notion of logical necessity. To begin with, it would seem that we already know perfectly well how to answer the question 'What is logical necessity?' and that therefore there is no problem. For one thing, all of us are able to recognize propositions which have the character of being true by logical necessity, or of being true *a priori,* as opposed to propositions the truth of which is contingent. From the following set of propositions we are all able, in some cases immediately and without hesitation and in other cases after some deliberation, to distinguish between those which are necessarily true and those which are not:—

A flea is an insect.

Blue is a colour.

Friction generates heat.

$(p): p \supset \sim q. \ \ni. \ q \supset \sim p.$

Water must freeze at 32° F., regardless of altitude.

If all donkeys are capricious and some donkeys are not fleet, then some capricious animals are not fleet.

Only as a consequence of holding a *philosophical theory* would a person say that all six propositions are empirical; and if asked, away from the heat of metaphysical debate, to pick out those propositions in the set which are logically necessary, even he would be able to do so quite easily. All of us know quite well what logical necessity is, in the sense of being able to recognize logically necessary propositions. There can be no serious doubt about this.

For another thing, we all know the literal meaning of the term 'logically necessary'. It cannot be disputed that we know the use of the term, i.e., that we know to which propositions it is correct to apply it and to which not. And in knowing this, we know its literal sense. The meaning of a term is not something in addition to its use, nor is its use something in addition to its meaning. The two are one and the same. To deny this would amount to maintaining that a person who called the right animals 'cow' and never, except when perceptually mistaken, applied the word to the wrong thing, nevertheless failed to know the meaning of 'cow', or that he knew its meaning despite applying it indiscriminately to animals or despite being ignorant altogether of how to apply it. And this is absurd on the face of it.

If the question 'What is logical necessity?' is a request for examples of logically necessary propositions, we know how to satisfy it. And if it is a request for information regarding whether we know the meaning of the term 'logically necessary', we can satisfy the request simply by applying the term correctly to a number of propositions and withholding its application to others. Quite plainly, then, the *problem* about logical necessity is neither the problem of learning to recognize logically necessary truths nor the problem of discovering the meaning of 'logical necessity'. What then is it about? What does a person who knows the use of 'logically necessary' and asks the question 'What is logical necessity?' wish to discover?

One thing that will be said is that he seeks to discover the property or properties in virtue of the possession of which a proposition is logically necessary and in the absence of which it is not. This way of putting the matter, i.e., translating the question 'What is the nature of logical necessity?' into the question 'What are the properties in virtue of which a proposition is logically necessary?', makes it look as if he is trying to discover *hidden* properties of logically necessary propositions. It makes the philosophical question look like the physical question 'What tests must a mineral satisfy in order to count as platinum?' when asked by a person who does not know what the tests are. In a different connexion, G. E. Moore has asked 'What, after all, is it that we mean to say of an action when we say that it is right or ought to be done? And what is it that we mean to say of a state of things when we say that it is good or bad? Can we discover any general characteristic which belongs in common to absolutely *all* right actions, no matter how different they may be in other respects? And which do not belong to any actions except those which are right?"[1] It would seem that, according to Moore, ethical philosophers are trying to *discover* a hidden property of right actions, an unknown property in virtue of having which actions are morally right and in virtue of lacking which they are not. Is the problem about logical necessity also one of trying to discover a hidden property, or set of properties, of an entire class of propositions?

It requires no great amount of intellectual perspicacity to see that the problem cannot be this. For if a proposition were logically necessary in virtue of having properties which are hidden from us, we should not, prior to discovering them, be able to say which propositions were logically necessary and which not. We should be in the position of a person who could not distinguish between diamonds and diamond-shaped bits of glass; and we are not in that sort of position at all. No one would go to the fantastic extreme of thinking that there are as yet undiscovered properties which, so to speak, influence us magnetically and make us pick out logically necessary propositions without our knowing how it comes about that we pick them out. The question 'What is the nature of logical necessity?' cannot, quite plainly, be translated into the question 'What are the unknown properties which make a proposition logically necessary?'

The problem has sometimes been conceived as being one of arriving at the *correct analysis* of the meaning of the term 'logically necessary'. On this view of what the problem is, we can know the meaning of the term without knowing the analysis of its meaning. In general, we can know the meaning of a word like 'cow' or a term like 'logically necessary', know how to use it correctly, without knowing the analysis of its meaning. What a correct analysis is supposed to do for us is to make clear what we already know. Performing an analysis consists of listing criteria for the application of a term (decomposing a concept into its constituent concepts); and the result of a correct analysis is an explicit array of properties, the presence of which makes it correct to apply the term and their absence not. The correct analysis of the meaning of a term does not add to our knowledge; it does not give us new information about the meaning of a term whose use we know

[1] *Ethics* (Home University Library), pp. 8–9.

perfectly well. It only makes explicit the rules governing the use of the term. This is so because we cannot know the literal meaning of a term without knowing how to use the term, and we cannot know the use of the term without knowing the criteria for its application. We can, however, know the criteria for the application of a term without being able to *state* the criteria, just as a person can write correct English and not be able to state rules of grammar governing correct English.

It *may,* therefore, be the case that the question 'What is logical necessity?' is really the question 'What is the analysis of the meaning of the term "logical necessity"?' What makes this translation of the question doubtful, however, is the fact that so many very able logicians and philosophers have for a considerable number of years tried to analyse the notion of logical necessity without agreed success. No doubt the lack of agreement will be dismissed by all, or nearly all, philosophers as not tending in the least to show that their aim is not actually to analyse the notion. Nevertheless, the fact that what one group of philosophers puts forward as the correct analysis is challenged by another group which, in turn, puts forward a different analysis, is surprising and should give us pause. For the concepts of logical necessity, entailment, logical impossibility, and the like, are relatively simple by comparison with many concepts outside of philosophy which have, either partly or wholly, been successfully analysed. One may well wonder what it is that stands in the way of philosophers successfully analysing the meaning of the term 'logical necessity', if, indeed, this is their aim; and one may reasonably doubt that it *is* their aim.

Another thing which throws doubt on the claim that philosophers are concerned to discover the *actual* analysis of the notion is the curious fact that different philosophers have arrived at such widely different, and even *diametrically opposite,* results, which they hold with complete assurance to be correct. Some philosophers have taken the position that logically necessary propositions are really verbal, others that they are inductive generalizations, others that they can both be established analytically and also rendered probable inductively, by an examination of instances, and others still that they are non-empirical, non-inductive propositions about aspects of reality. This is an amazing divergence of results of analysis, which makes it not at all unreasonable to doubt that philosophers are actually doing what they think themselves to be doing. And at the end of this paper I shall formulate a hypothesis which places a different construction on what they are doing and on what their theories come to. I shall first argue against the views as if they are the false results of incorrect analyses of the concept of logical necessity, then proceed to an attempt to analyse the concept, and I shall conclude with a hypothesis according to which the philosophical theories are not theories in the usual sense, i.e., in the sense in which a theory explains a phenomenon and is either true or false.

Consider, first, Mill's view that propositions which are normally characterized as logically necessary are really empirical and are rendered probable or confuted inductively, by an examination of instances. On this view, the procedure for establishing or rendering probable the proposition that all fleas are insects is precisely the same as the procedure used to establish the proposition that all fleas jump. We examine many fleas, see that they all, without exception, jump, and proceed, with reasonable certainty, to the generalization that all fleas jump. In the same way, we examine many fleas, see that without exception they all are insects, and pass to the generalization that all fleas are insects. And the two propositions would be falsified in the same way, in the one case by discovering a flea which never and under no condition jumped, and in the other case by discovering a flea that was not an insect. The difference between the two propositions is that the first has been established with a greater degree of certainty than the second; and, in general, it is the very high degree of inductive certainty of some propositions which gives rise to the notion that they are logically necessary.

Taken as a claim to be the right explanation of logically necessary propositions, this view is simply ridiculous, so ridiculous, indeed, that it is hard to think how anyone could have come to hold it. For the claim implies that 'empirical' and 'logically necessary' are both meaningless terms, terms which have no application to any proposition whatever; and to see that it implies this requires no subtle reasoning. The view that propositions which are thought by everyone to be logically necessary, e.g., the propositions of logic and mathematics, are really empirical implies that there are no logically necessary propositions. A person who holds the view can cite no proposition to which he would say the term 'logically necessary' applies, and he holds, thus, that no proposition answers to the designation 'logically necessary' or, what comes to the same thing, that the term is meaningless. To put the matter in the verbal idiom, the sentence 'There are no logically necessary propositions' would say what is true only if the term 'logically necessary' lacked application to propositions and was literally without meaning. Unlike the sentence 'There are no centaurs', which denies the actual, but not theoretical, existence of animals to which the word 'centaur' is applicable, the sentence 'There are no logically necessary propositions' does not deny the existence of a species of propositions which, if they existed, would be denoted by the term 'logically necessary'. It denies, instead, that the term has even theoretical denotation. A philosopher who declares 'There are no logically necessary propositions' makes the *verbal* claim that 'logically necessary proposition' has no use. But this claim, if true, makes the meaning of 'empirical proposition' vanish into the meaning of 'proposition' and turns the sentence 'All propositions are empirical propositions' into the empty, uninformative sentence 'All propositions are propositions'. For if, in fact, 'logically necessary' has no use and fails to distinguish between propositions, 'empirical' also fails to distinguish between propositions and has no use. A philosopher who says 'All propositions are empirical; there are no logically necessary propositions' has not discovered a startling fact about propositions. He is making the absurd verbal claim that both 'logically necessary' and 'empirical' are meaningless terms.

A further theory which is in part like that of Mill and in part not, has been put forward by Professor C. I. Lewis. This theory does not state that all propositions are empirical, but it is like Mill's view in claiming that logically necessary propositions are open to confirmation by inductive procedures: logically necessary propositions can be established analytically, but also they could be rendered probable in the same way that empirical generalizations are rendered probable, i.e., by an examination of instances. Lewis writes: '. . . the statement that the class of (existent) cats is included in the class of animals is an implicitly analytic statement. It is genuinely analytic and what it affirms can be assured by reference to the meaning of "cat" and "animal" without recourse to further and empirical evidence. But also it might be established—as well established as most laws of science, for example—by generalization from observed instances of cats'.[1]

Like Mill's view, this view also seems to be false on the surface. For taken as an hypothesis about the nature of logically necessary propositions, it entails the self-contradictory consequence that necessarily true propositions are not necessarily true. It implies that the same proposition could be both true *a priori* and also possibly false, that its falsity is logically impossible and also logically possible. Any proposition which is open to being rendered probable or highly probable or even to being established conclusively by recourse to an empirical examination of cases is such that experience could, theoretically, show it to be false. Its falsity is a possibility which no amount of evidence for its truth could make *logically* impossible. Evidence, accumulated from the observation of instances, which renders a proposition p probable or highly probable, is also evidence which renders $\sim p$ improbable. But the fact that $\sim p$ could be rendered improbable on inductive grounds implies that it *could be true*; that is to say, it implies that a counter instance, which would upset p, could exist. And even in the case of a generalization which inductive procedure has established as certainly true, beyond the shadow of any reasonable doubt, the *logical* possibility of its being false remains; its denial remains *empirical*, the truth of which is ruled out by fact but not by logic. An examination of instances is relevant and possible only in the case of generalizations to which there could be *exceptions*, and it is, thus, relevant and possible only in the case of generalizations the denials of which could, logically, be true. But an *a priori* true proposition is one the denial of which could not, logically, be true. Hence, the view that the truth of a logically necessary proposition can be assured analytically, 'by reference to the meanings' of the words which express the proposition, and that it also might be established in the way in which a law of physics is established, by 'generalization from observed instances', entails the consequence that necessarily true propositions are not necessarily true. The view implies that the same proposition could

[1] *An Analysis of Knowledge and Valuation*, p. 91.

be true *a priori* and not open to theoretical falsification and also empirical and open to theoretical falsification.

As the word 'probable' is ordinarily used, it makes no literal sense to preface a sentence which expresses a logically necessary proposition with the phrase 'it is probable that'. And as the term 'improbable' is ordinarily used, it makes no literal sense to preface a sentence for a logical impossibility with the phrase 'it is improbable that'. In their ordinary senses these words are applicable only to empirical propositions. Anyone who understands the sentences 'All cats are animals' and 'There is a cat which is not an animal' and is using the words 'probable' and 'improbable' in their ordinary senses, knows that in saying. 'It is improbable that there is a cat which is not an animal' and 'It is probable that all cats are animals' he is committing an impropriety of language. How is his not *seeing* his mistake to be explained?

Mill's analysis of the meaning of the term 'logically necessary', and Lewis's also, implies that *a priori* propositions are about the world, that to establish them conclusively or render them probable is to establish or render probable propositions about the nature or existence of phenomena. Mill's view is explicit on this point; and Lewis's view, according to which logically necessary propositions can, in addition to being assured analytically, be established, 'as well established as most laws of science', by an examination of instances, also implies that they give us information about the nature or existence of things. There is still a third view which declares that some, if not all, logically necessary propositions are about the world. This is the theory that some *a priori* true propositions make factual claims about things without being inductive generalizations. The special class of logically necessary propositions which, supposedly, describe reality are called by Kant 'synthetic *a priori*'. The propositions to which 'logically necessary' applies, fall, on this theory, into either of two mutually exclusive classes, either into the class of analytic propositions, the denials of which are formal contradictions or formal inconsistencies, or into the class of propositions the denials of which are logical impossibilities but not formal inconsistencies. Propositions of the first class merely make explicit what we already know about things in knowing that their subject terms or antecedents denote the things. In this respect, propositions of the second class are different: in knowing that such propositions are true, our knowledge is extended beyond what we know about things in knowing that the subject terms of the propositions denote them. The predicate or consequent of a synthetic *a priori* proposition is not included in the conjunction of properties making up the subject or antecedent. Hence, it is like the synthetic, empirical proposition that, e.g., all gases heat when compressed, and unlike the analytic proposition that, e.g., all squares have four sides. But it is unlike an empirical proposition and like an analytic one in the respect that its predicate is connected by logical necessity to its subject: it has 'inward necessity'. Synthetic *a priori* propositions add to our knowledge of things and are, therefore, *descriptions* which can be known to be true descriptions without recourse to a series of observations. They inform us of logically necessary attributes of phenomena, attributes which cannot even in conception be *removed* from what they characterize. Hence, unlike empirical generalizations, the denials of which could be true, no series of observations could establish a synthetic *a priori* proposition, since no conceivable observation could show it to be false. Experience is necessary to make us aware of a synthetic *a priori* proposition, but experience cannot establish its truth.

As is well known, there is a division of opinion over whether any proposition can be both synthetic and *a priori*. Some philosophers maintain that the class of logically necessary propositions coincides precisely with the class of analytic propositions and that every proposition belongs to either of two mutually exclusive classes, either to the class of empirical propositions, which are all synthetic, or to the class of *a priori* propositions, which are all analytic. Furthermore, even amongst those philosophers who accept Kant's distinction there is no agreement over whether any given proposition is really synthetic *a priori* or merely analytic. Kant laid down a number of criteria for distinguishing between propositions of the two sorts, but philosophers have quarrelled endlessly over whether the examples he himself used to illustrate his distinction satisfy his criteria, and also over whether his criteria are consistent. Fortunately, for the limited purpose of this study it is not necesssary to enter into the usual debates centring on Kant's theory. As it turns out, only a single feature which synthetic *a priori* propositions have in common with analytic propositions will concern us; and this is a feature in respect of which both differ from empirical propositions. It alone needs to be examined in order to test whether *any a priori* propositions can be descriptive of the world.

Kant made clear what this feature is. He stated quite unambiguously that all *a priori* true propositions, whether analytic or not, 'bear the character of inward necessity', and no philosopher who accepts the usual distinction between *a priori* and empirical propositions would contest this. No *a priori* true statement is open to theoretical falsification. In this respect *a priori* true statements are all alike and they are also alike in respect of the way they differ from true empirical statements, which are open to theoretical falsification. The truth-value of an empirical statement is contingent and that of an *a priori* statement is not.

The interesting empirical propositions to consider in connexion with the question as to whether it is possible for a proposition to be both logically necessary and also descriptive of reality, or as to whether any proposition can give us 'theoretical *a priori* knowledge of objects', are those asserting physical necessities, e.g., the propositions that iron *must* melt at the temperature of $1,535°$ C., and that bodies in friction *must* generate heat. Such propositions inform us of the *irremovable* properties of things, which properties, although they can be thought away, are nevertheless such that we can with complete confidence expect them to repeat in things under similar conditions. They describe necessities in the world. To many philosophers, at least some *a priori* true propositions likewise seem to describe necessary aspects of reality, inflexibilities in nature. Thus, Bertrand Russell has written:—

> When Swift invites us to consider the race of Struldbugs who never die, we are able to acquiesce in our imagination. But a world where two plus two make five seems quite on a different level. We feel that such a world, if there were one, would upset the whole fabric of our knowledge and would reduce us to utter doubt.[1]

And also:—

> We do not know who will be the inhabitants of London a hundred years hence; but we know that any two of them and

[1] *The Problems of Philosophy*, pp. 122–3.

any other two of them will make four of them. This apparent power of being able to anticipate facts about things of which we have no experience is certainly surprising.[1]

Unquestionably, the unbreakable necessities with which nature presents us fill many people with surprise and awe. And unquestionably it would shake them profoundly and reduce them to 'utter doubt', if levers stopped behaving in the expected ways, if ice heated water, if bodies in friction cooled rather than heated, and iron melted at a temperature which softened butter just enough for spreading on bread. And Russell apparently has the idea that two plus two make four also describes a surprising necessity in the world, a necessity which enables us 'to anticipate facts about things'. His words give rise to the picture of people *imagining* a world in which two plus two make five and not acquiescing to it, finding such a world *even more disconcerting* than one in which levers, metals, gases, and astronomical bodies behaved in queer, unexpected ways. The language he uses makes it quite evident that he supposes that to assert that two people plus two more people make four people is to make a factual claim about things. It is easy to see that philosophers who think that at least some *a priori* truths are about physical phenomena are very likely to have the notion that they are about physical necessities which are *more* necessary and unbreakable than the common run of physical necessities, that they are the most necessary of them all.

Philosophers will, undoubtedly, disagree over whether 'Two plus two make four', 'A physical thing must be in one place only at any given time', 'Blue is a colour', are synthetic *a priori* or analytic. As it turns out, however, it is not necessary to come to a decision about them, since we shall be concerned only with the property which *a priori* true propositions all have in common, the property, namely, of not being open to theoretical falsification. I shall, therefore, treat them as if they are synthetic *a priori*. The important thing to show is that no proposition can be both logically necessary and also about aspects of reality; and showing this will be an important step toward clearing up the problem about the nature of logical necessity.

One argument against the notion that a necessary truth,

The Problems of Philosophy, p. 132.

whether analytic or synthetic *a priori,* can be informative about the nature or existence of anything is that, since its truth-value is intrinsic to it, it cannot be conditioned by the existence or nature of anything. No theoretical state of affairs could, if it existed, make an *a priori* true proposition false or an *a priori* false proposition true. The one is true unconditionally, regardless of what the world happens to be like, and the other is false unconditionally, regardless of what the world happens to be like. No matter how different the universe may become, a necessarily true proposition remains true. It therefore can say nothing about what the world is like and can give us no sort of information about the existence or non-existence of things nor about what their properties are.

This argument will be opposed with the contention that synthetic *a priori* truths *are* about the world but describe its necessary, essential features, features which *every* theoretical universe must have, as opposed to empirical generalizations which describe its accidental features, features which some theoretical universes lack. Thus, it will be maintained that the difference between the two assertions, 'Every buttercup is in one place only at any one time' and 'Every buttercup is yellow', is not that the first does not describe a condition of buttercups while the second does, but that the first informs us of a necessary, irremovable attribute of buttercups, and the second informs us of one of their accidental attributes. The necessary proposition, thus, is descriptive without being falsifiable by an imaginable reality, in contrast to the empirical proposition which is descriptive but theoretically falsifiable.

How is this argument to be met? I think that there is only one way of effectively meeting it, though this way of doing it seems to lead to the false conventionalist position that necessary propositions are really verbal. However that may be, instead of trying to get clear about the difference between empirical and logically necessary *propositions,* let us consider the *sentences* for such propositions. Furthermore, before considering these sentences, let us first examine equivalent sentences expressing logical impossibilities. More specifically, before considering such sentences as 'A thing must be in one place only at any one time', 'Two plus two make four', 'A blue thing must have colour', let us consider the equivalent sentences 'It is logically impossible for a thing to be in more than one place at a time', 'It is logically impossible for two things and two more things to fail to make four things', 'It is logically impossible for a thing to be blue and not have colour'. And let us compare these with sentences which express propositions about physical impossibilities, e.g., 'It is impossible for solid lead to float on water' and 'It is impossible for objects to be in friction and not generate heat.'

It is quite plain that the sentence 'It is impossible for solid lead to float on water' describes a state of affairs, the occurrence of solid lead floating on water, which it declares to be impossible. Our understanding the sentence implies that we know what it would be like for solid lead to float on water; and this means that we can conceive or picture ourselves encountering an occurrence which is described by the phrase 'Solid lead is floating on water'. Such an occurrence, if it took place, would make the proposition expressed by the sentence false. Otherwise, if the phrase did not describe a conceivable occurrence, which, if it happened, would falsify the proposition, the proposition would not be open to theoretical falsification; and the sentence would not express an empirical proposition. The sentence expresses an empirical proposition because it tells us what would falsify the proposition; and it tells us what would falsify the proposition by describing a *conceivable* impossibility.

The sentence 'It is logically impossible for a material body to be in two places at once' is entirely different, however much it looks like a sentence which expresses a proposition about a physical impossibility. What may be called the descriptive part of the sentence, in this case the phrase 'a material body which is in two places at once', cannot describe a state of affairs which the sentence declares to be impossible; it cannot have a descriptive function in the sentence. For if, like the descriptive part of 'It is impossible for solid lead to float on water', it functioned descriptively in the sentence, it would denote a state of affairs which would constitute a theoretical refutation of a logically necessary proposition, which is to say, it would describe what would make a theoretically unfalsifiable proposition false. The phrase cannot describe a conceivable impossibility without implying that the sentence expresses an empirical proposition, not one which is *a priori*. And it can only fail to describe a conceivable impossibility by failing to have descriptive sense, by lacking a descriptive use.

It won't do to say that the descriptive part of a sentence which expresses a logical impossibility *does* describe a state of affairs but describes one which is inconceivable to *us*, a state of affairs which *we* are unable to envisage, because of the way we are constrained to think. To say that we are prevented by the structure of our minds from being able to know what it would be like for there to be a situation which was actually described by the words 'is in two different places at once' or for there to be a situation which was actually described by the words 'is blue but has no colour' is to imply that a different type of mind could conceive what our limitations prevent us from conceiving. But this implies that a different type of mind would, in understanding the sentence 'It is logically impossible for a body to be in two different places at once', be conceiving a situation which would constitute a theoretical falsification of a logically necessary truth.

The descriptive part of a sentence which expresses a proposition of the form 'It is logically impossible that . . .' does not denote an inflexibly impossible state of affairs which we can conceive but to which we cannot 'acquiesce in our imagination'. Nor does it denote a state of affairs which is conceivable but which we are prevented from conceiving by our mental limitations. It can describe nothing which could, even theoretically, upset a logical impossibility. But this is to say it describes nothing whatever. The truth-value of the proposition expressed by the sentence is made impregnable by a *verbal fact,* the fact, namely, that the descriptive part of the sentence has no descriptive use. The sentence 'It is logically impossible for a particle of matter to be in two different places at the same time' expresses an *a priori* proposition only because the sentence ' "A material particle is in two different places at the same time" has no descriptive sense' expresses a true verbal proposition. In knowing to be true what, e.g., is said by 'It is impossible to boil water with ice', we know a fact about nature; in knowing to be true what is said by 'It is logically impossible for a particle of matter to be in several places at once', we know a fact about language.

This throws light on the nature of logical necessity. The sentence 'A thing must be in one place only at any one time' has the same meaning precisely as the sentence 'It is impossible for a thing

267

to be in more than one place at once'. Hence what we know in understanding the first is the same as what we know in understanding the second. And just as a fact about the way language is used protects against upset the claim made by a sentence whose descriptive part denotes a logical impossibility, so a fact about the way language is used protects a logical necessity against theoretical falsification. The sentence 'A thing (or the same thing) must be in just one place at a time' does not express a fact to the effect that things have an irremovable property; it does not describe an essential feature of reality. What we learn when we are made to understand the sentence 'The same thing must be in just one place at one time' is that if a thing, *x,* is in one place and a thing, *y,* is in another place, we do not *say* that *x* and *y* are the same thing. We learn a fact about linguistic usage, not an inflexible fact about things.

It is the same with the sentence 'Blue is a colour'. The equivalent sentence, 'A thing cannot be blue and lack colour', does not describe a situation which it rules out as impossible. The 'cannot' is logical and this means that 'is blue and lacks colour' has no use. What we know in understanding the sentence 'Blue is a colour' is the same thing. To bring out this point differently, consider how a person learns that 'Blue is a colour' says what is true. Does he learn this 'by an act of intuition or the perception of an aspect of reality'? Suppose someone were to say that blue is not a colour, while admitting that yellow, green, red, etc., are colours. Blue, we can imagine him maintaining, really belongs to a special category of its own, because blue things, and only they, give him a unique feeling. What could we do to show him that he is mistaken? We obviously cannot convince him by holding up blue things; for he would only say that in addition to seeing blue, he does not see the further property *colour.* Showing him that a blue thing is also coloured is not at all like showing him that in addition to being yellow, gold is also malleable. Nor can we convince him that he is mistaken by holding up blue things with red ones, etc., and in this way exhibiting the property they have in common, thus showing him that blue is a colour. For he maintains that blue does not have the property colour in common with red, green, etc. And we do not *see more than he sees*; we see exactly the same. It would be verbal whimsy to say, 'Well, it's your defective vision, a peculiarity of your eyes, which prevents you from seeing that red and blue do have the property *colour* in common'. We can convince him that blue is a colour only by getting him to accept the *linguistic* fact that blue is *called* a colour. We get him to accept a fact about verbal usage; we do not introduce him to a fact about things. The sentence 'Blue is a colour', or 'A blue thing *must* have colour', expresses a logically necessary proposition because, and only because, there is the verbal fact that the word 'colour' applies to everything to which the word 'blue' applies and that 'blue and not coloured' has no application, actual or theoretical.

The realization that what we know in understanding a sentence for a logically necessary proposition is a verbal fact and not a fact about the world has led some philosophers to take the position that a logically necessary proposition is verbal. Now, it *would* seem that if what we know in understanding a sentence for a logical necessity is a verbal fact and not a fact about things, then the proposition expressed by the sentence must be verbal. Thus, it has been argued:—

When we say that analytic propositions are devoid of factual content, and consequently that they say nothing, we are not suggesting that they are senseless in the way that metaphysical utterances are senseless. For although they give us no information about any empirical situation, they do enlighten us by illustrating the way in which we use certain symbols. Thus if I say, 'Nothing can be coloured in different ways at the same time with respect to the same part of itself', I am not saying anything about the properties of any actual thing; but I am not talking nonsense. I am expressing an analytic proposition which records our determination to call a colour expanse which differs in quality from a neighbouring colour expanse a different part of a thing. In other words, I am simply calling attention to the implications of a certain usage.[1]

This position implies that the sentence 'Blue is a colour' *expresses* the verbal proposition to the effect that the word 'colour' applies to everything to which the word 'blue' applies, and, thus, that the two sentences, 'Blue is a colour' and 'The word "colour" applies to whatever the word "blue" applies to', are translatable into each other. Hence, the logically necessary proposition expressed

[1] A. J. Ayer, *Language, Truth and Logic*, p. 79.

by 'Blue is a colour' is verbal. The various objections to this view are well known and hardly need detain us. An objection frequently made is that the denial of the verbal proposition is not a logical impossibility: it is not the case that it is logically impossible for the word 'colour' to fail to apply to whatever the word 'blue' applies to. A verbal proposition about usage is empirical. Usage could be other than it is. Hence, if the logically necessary proposition were verbal, it would be empirical: it would be logically necessary and also open to theoretical falsification. For another thing, the sentences, 'Blue is a colour' and '"Colour" applies to whatever "blue" applies to', are not translatable into each other. In the first sentence the words 'blue' and 'colour' occur but are not mentioned, whereas the second mentions them but does not use them. The first is about the words, the second not. Thus, with regard to someone who declared, 'Bleu est un couleur', it would be true to say, 'He said that blue is a colour' and false to say, 'He said that "colour" applies to whatever "blue" applies to'.

Taken as an explanation of the nature of logically necessary propositions, the theory that they are verbal is patently false. Nevertheless, the conclusion we reached about sentences for *a priori* propositions, analytic as well as synthetic, is not incorrect, and it does not entail the conventionalist position. It is natural to think that if what we know in undersanding the sentence 'Blue is a colour', or 'A blue thing necessarily is coloured', is a fact about verbal usage, then the sentence expresses that fact. But this does not follow. We have to distinguish between what we know in understanding a sentence for an *a priori* proposition and what the sentence *expresses,* what it *says.* 'Blue is a colour' does not express the verbal fact that 'colour' applies to whatever 'blue' applies to, although it is this fact that we know in understanding the sentence. The proposition expressed by the sentence, what it means, is not the verbal fact, although it is the verbal fact that *makes* the sentence express an *a priori* proposition and *justifies* our saying that blue is a colour.

Consider the difference between the sentences 'All fleas are insects' and 'All fleas jump'. To the first there corresponds the verbal sentence '"Insect" applies to everything to which "flea" applies'; and, similarly, to the second there corresponds the verbal sentence '"Jumps" applies to whatever "flea" applies to'. It is clear that in understanding the second verbal sentence and knowing that what it asserts is true, we know not only the use of 'flea' and 'jumps', but also a fact about the behaviour of fleas, a fact which observation alone can establish; for 'is a flea but does not jump' describes the possible behaviour of a flea. Thus, understanding the sentence 'All fleas jump' does not entail our knowing that what its verbal correlate asserts is true. And, of course, its verbal correlate is not about usage; non-linguistic fact, not usage, dictates the application of 'jumps' to whatever 'flea' applies to. Understanding 'All fleas are insects' does, however, entail knowing that what its verbal correlate says is true. We should say that a person did not know the meaning either of 'flea' or of 'insect' if he said that a flea was not an insect, and we should correct him by acquainting him with usage, by showing him that 'insect' and 'flea' are so used that the first applies to whatever the second applies to and that 'flea but not an insect' has no descriptive sense, is not used to describe an object, real or fantastic. In other words, understanding a sentence for an *a priori* proposition is equivalent to knowing facts of usage; but the sentence does not *express* the facts of usage. We might, if we stretch the word 'content', say that the sentence 'A flea is an insect' has the same content as the sentence '"Insect" applies to everything to which "flea" applies', but differs from the latter in the respect that it is in the *ontological idiom,* i.e., in the idiom in which words are *not mentioned*. What makes the non-verbal sentence 'A flea is an insect' express a logically necessary truth is the fact that the corresponding verbal sentence expresses a true proposition. The fact that 'A flea is an insect' expresses a logically necessary proposition entails and is entailed by the fact that 'As a matter of usage "insect" applies to whatever "flea" applies to' expresses a true empirical proposition. The likeness as well as the difference between the two sentences might perhaps be brought out by saying that they *come to* the same thing but *do not say* the same thing.

Let us now consider the four views about the nature of logically necessary propositions: (1) that they are nothing more than inductive generalizations with a high degree of probability, (2) that they are necessary truths which might be established by inductive procedures, (3) that some, if not all, of them are about reality, and (4) that they are all verbal.

It is natural for anyone who rejects these theories to think them the mistaken results of incorrect analyses. They have about them the *look* of explanatory theories about the nature of a special class of propositions. One thing, however, stands in the way of our taking them for what they seem to be, mistaken explanations of the nature of necessary truths. If we reflect with sober detachment on these views, we shall, I think, be struck by the unplausibility of supposing that people could have been taken in by them and have held them. It is altogether unplausible to imagine that an astute thinker like Mill, for example, had a queer intellectual blind-spot which prevented his seeing how linguistically absurd it is to say, 'It is highly probable that two people plus two more people always make four people'. But if, as it deserves, we dismiss the idea that he failed to see this absurd impropriety of language, then in supposing that he did see it, we are compelled to think, not that he embraced it, but that he did something else. We have to think that he was not using 'highly probable' and 'empirical generalization' improperly, but that he was using them in a *changed* way. And how he is using them is not hard to see.

There is a formal similarity between sentences for logically necessary propositions and sentences for empirical generalizations, between, e.g., 'All cats are animals' and 'All cats are mousers'. They both are of the form 'All – – – are . . .' And a philosopher who is impressed by this similarity and wishes to call special attention to it will *stretch* the terms 'highly probable' and 'empirical generalization' to cover logically necessary propositions. As applied to logically necessary propositions they have what may be called an *empty* use, a use just to heighten a formal similarity between sentences. In the sentence 'It is highly probable that all cats are mousers' the term 'highly probable' has its usual meaning, while in the sentence 'It is highly probable that all cats are animals' it has a stretched, empty use, the sole purpose of which is to make a linguistic likeness more conspicuous.

The other three theories can be explained in a similar way. A philosopher who wishes to emphasize the fact that sentences for *a priori* truths have their form in common with those for empirical generalizations, but is *equally impressed* by the difference between *a priori* truths and empirical generalizations, will stretch the term 'empirical generalization', or the phrase 'generalization from

observed instances', to cover, in an empty way, logically necessary propositions, *without giving up* the term '*a priori*' or its
equivalents. He thus brings out more sharply than ordinary language does a likeness between sentences without giving up
terminology which calls attention to the unlikeness between the
propositions they express. His view is not (as was argued earlier)
the self-contradictory one that logically necessary propositions
are also empirical, or that they might also be established by
generalization from observed instances, because he is doing something more with 'empirical generalization' and 'generalization
from observed instances' than using them in the ordinary way.
In addition to its ordinary use, the expression 'generalization
from observed instances' has been given a special task, and in its
special use it is not self-contradictory to say, '*p* is analytic and
might be established by generalization from observed instances'.

The Kantian theory is complicated by a number of factors, and
cannot be easily discussed. Here I shall limit myself to a brief
examination of one of its aspects and use examples which help
bring out only one point. According to one criterion for distinguishing between analytic and synthetic *a priori* propositions, the
proposition expressed by 'Blue is a colour' is synthetic *a priori*
because the meaning of 'colour' is not a conjunctive part of the
meaning of 'blue'. That is to say, *blue and not coloured* is not a value
of a logically inconsistent function of the form $F \sim f$ where f is a
conjunct in F; the concept *colour* is not 'covertly contained' in the
concept *blue*. The proposition stated by 'A spinster is unmarried',
however, is analytic, because the meaning of 'unmarried' is a conjunctive part of the meaning of 'spinster': the connexion of the
predicate with the subject is through identity'. In respect of the
fact that the meaning of its predicate-term is not part of the meaning of its subject-term, 'Blue is a colour' is like the sentence 'A cat
is a mouser'; for the meaning of 'mouser' is also not part of the
meaning of 'cat'. But it differs from 'A cat is a mouser' in that it
expresses a logically necessary proposition, in which respect is
like 'A spinster is unmarried'. The term 'synthetic *a priori*' was in
part invented to mark these similarities and differences between
sentences. And holding that synthetic *a priori* propositions are
about 'aspects of reality', i.e., holding the apparently self-contradictory view that some propositions are both logically necessary

and about the existence or properties of things, is only a verbal means of making prominent a linguistic likeness between sentences, namely, the similarity in the way in which their predicate-terms are connected with their subject-terms. This device consists in stretching the expression 'about reality', and its equivalents, to cover necessary truths which are stated by sentences which are such that the meanings of their predicate-terms are not parts of the meanings of their subject-terms. The phrase 'logically necessary and about reality' is not self-contradictory, because it does not use 'about reality' in its usual sense.

The conventionalist view that necessary propositions are really verbal is also not the self-contradictory position it appears to be. As the words 'verbal' and 'logically necessary' are *normally* used to distinguish between propositions, it is self-contradictory to say that a logically necessary proposition is verbal. Further, it is not the case that the sentences 'A cat is an animal' and 'As a matter of linguistic usage, "animal" applies to everything to which "cat" applies' express the same proposition; the first expresses a logically necessary truth, the second an empirical, verbal proposition. Nevertheless, it is the case that what we know in understanding the first sentence is the same as what we know in knowing that what the second says is true. The two sentences are not translatable into each other, but, to coin a new term, they are *convertible,* one into the other. The non-verbal sentence, 'A cat is an animal', would not express a necessary proposition if the verbal sentence, 'As a matter of linguistic usage, "animal" applies to whatever "cat" applies to', did not say what is true; and the verbal sentence would not say what is true if the non-verbal sentence did not express a logical necessity. We may say 'A cat is an animal' *converts,* in the verbal idiom, into 'As a matter of usage, "animal" applies to whatever "cat" applies to', and 'As a matter of usage, "animal" applies to whatever "cat" applies to' *converts,* on the ontological idiom, into 'A cat is an animal'.

It is to be noticed that although 'cat' and 'animal' are not mentioned in the non-verbal sentence, they are not *used*[1] there either. In this respect the non-verbal sentence is like the verbal sentence

[1]I.e., they are not used to denote or say something about an object, as for example, they are used in the sentences 'There is some sort of animal in the bushes' and 'Cats like catnip'. We might say that the words *occur* but are not used (descriptively) in the sentence.

and unlike other sentences in the ontological idiom, e.g., 'A cat is a mouser'. If, now, we ask what such a non-verbal sentence as 'A cat is an animal' is *about,* and what it says, we shall be tempted to give different answers, depending on which features of the sentence strike us as being important and which not. The sentence is not about cats nor yet about the use of the words 'cat' and 'animal', but neither is it literally meaningless. The answer to the question, 'What is the sentence "A cat is a mouser" about?' is that it is about cats; and the answer to the question, 'Are the sentences "A cat is an animal" and "A cat is a mouser" literally meaningful?' is that they are. Those philosophers who are impressed by the fact that the sentences are in the same idiom, which is a point of linguistic likeness between them, will try to bring out this likeness by holding the view that a sentence for a logically necessary proposition is also about something. Grammatical inventiveness shows them the way to the philosophical position that it is about a supra-sensible object: 'A cat is a mouser' is about cats and 'A cat is an animal' is about the universal *cat*, about supra-sensible catness.[1] They invent a pseudo object for such a statement to be about in order to enhance a similarity between classes of sentences, at the cost of minimizing the utterly different sorts of work the sentences do in the language.

Other philosophers, who are struck by the differences between *a priori* sentences and both non-verbal and verbal empirical sentences and wish to point up these differences, will maintain that *a priori* sentences are about nothing, that they 'say nothing' and are 'without sense'.[2] These philosophers use the expression 'without sense' in the made-up sense of 'says nothing', where 'says nothing' means 'is not about anything'. Their saying that a tautology is without sense in their way of speaking comes to saying that a tautology is not about anything. They invent this way of speaking in order to stress a linguistic dissimilarity between classes of sentences, between, for example, 'A cat is a mouser', which is about cats, and 'As a matter of usage "animal" applies to whatever "cat" applies to', which is about usage, and 'A cat is an animal', which is about neither. What prevents 'A cat is an animal' from being about anything is the idiom in which it is formulated.

[1]For a discussion of the theory of universals see Chapter III, 'The Existence of Universals'.   [2]L. Wittgenstein, *Tractatus Logico-Philosophicus,* 4:461.

It is a linguistic hybrid: it is in the non-linguistic idiom, yet is such that in understanding it what we know and all that we know is a fact of usage which it does not express. It differs from its parents in that it describes neither the world nor language. These points of difference some philosophers try to display more prominently by inventing a new way of speaking about *a priori* sentences: by saying that they are without sense, although not denying that they have literal sense or are literally meaningful.

If our concern is not the philosophical one of inventing new ways of speaking which will minimize or heighten points of similarity and dissimilarity between types of sentences but is the less spectacular concern of trying to see how our language works, then the explanation of the logical necessity of propositions is not hard to find. Philosophers commonly use the phrase 'expresses a proposition' to mean the same as 'is an indicative sentence which has literal meaning', so that to say that 'A cat is an animal' or that '$2 + 2 = 4$' has meaning is to say that it expresses a proposition. What it is for a sentence to express a logically necessary proposition will now be clear: it will express a logically necessary proposition if it converts (*not translates*) into a sentence which expresses a true proposition about usage. *A logically necessary proposition is the meaning of a sentence S in the ontological idiom, where S converts into a sentence about the use of expressions.*

To come back now to the conventionalist position, if a philosopher is sufficiently impressed by the fact of convertibility between sentences for necessary truths and their verbal correlates and thinks their difference of idiom trivial, he will wish to minimize the difference of idiom between them and bring out as sharply as possible the fact of their convertibility, which is a point of likeness between them. And he realizes his wish in one of the standard philosophical ways. He *adds* a use to the word 'verbal', gives it an extra, non-ordinary job. He applies the word to logically necessary truths just to mark more conspicuously the linguistic fact that sentences for necessary propositions and their verbal correlates are convertible, that, e.g., in understanding 'A cat is an animal' we know that 'As a matter of usage, "animal" applies to whatever "cat" applies to' says what is true, and conversely. Used to do its new work, it is not self-contradictory to say, 'Logically necessary propositions are really verbal'.

INDEX

The
International Library

OF

PSYCHOLOGY, PHILOSOPHY
AND SCIENTIFIC METHOD

Edited by

C. K. OGDEN, M.A.

Late Fellow of Magdalene College, Cambridge

The International Library, of which over one hundred and fifty volumes have been published, is both in quality and quantity a unique achievement in this department of publishing. Its purpose is to give expression, in a convenient form, to the remarkable developments which have recently occurred in Psychology and its allied sciences. The older philosophers were preoccupied by metaphysical interests which for the most part have ceased to attract the younger investigators, and their forbidding terminology too often acted as a deterrent for the general reader. The attempt to deal in clear language with current tendencies whether in England and America or on the Continent has met with a very encouraging reception, and not only have accepted authorities been invited to explain the newer theories, but it has been found possible to include a number of original contributions of high merit.

Published by

ROUTLEDGE & KEGAN PAUL LTD

BROADWAY HOUSE: 68-74 CARTER LANE, LONDON, E.C.4.

1959

INTERNATIONAL LIBRARY OF PSYCHOLOGY, PHILOSOPHY AND SCIENTIFIC METHOD

All prices are net

A. PSYCHOLOGY

GENERAL AND DESCRIPTIVE

The Mind and its Place in Nature. By C. D. Broad. £1 15s.

Thought and the Brain. By Henri Piéron. Trans. by C. K. Ogden. £1.

The Nature of Laughter. By J. C. Gregory. 18s.

The Gestalt Theory and the Problem of Configuration. By Bruno Petermann. Illustrated. £1 5s.

Principles of Gestalt Psychology. By K. Koffka. £2 2s.

Analysis of Perception. By J. R. Smythies. £1 1s.

PERSONALITY

The Psychology of Character: with a Survey of Personality in General. By A. A. Roback. *Revised Edition.* £2 5s.

Problems of Personality: a Volume of Essays in honour of Morton Prince. Edited by A. A. Roback. £1 8s.

Personality. By R. G. Gordon. £1 3s.

ANALYSIS

The Practice and Theory of Individual Psychology. By Alfred Adler £1 5s.

Psychological Types. By C. G. Jung. Translated with a Foreword by H. Godwin Baynes. £1 12s.

Character and the Unconscious: a Critical Exposition of the Psychology of Freud and Jung. By J. H. van der Hoop. £1.

The Development of the Sexual Impulses. By R. E. Money-Kyrle. £1.

The Psychology of Consciousness. By C. Daly King. Introduction by W. M. Marston. £1.

2

The Symbolic Process, and Its Integration in Children. By J. F. Markey. 14s.

The Meaning of Meaning: a Study of the Influence of Language upon Thought and of the Science of Symbolism. By C. K. Ogden and I. A. Richards. £1 8s.

Principles of Literary Criticism. By I. A. Richards. £1 5s.

The Spirit of Language in Civilization. By K. Vossler. £1.

CHILD PSYCHOLOGY, EDUCATION, ETC.

The Growth of the Mind: an Introduction to Child Psychology. By K. Koffka. Translated by R. M. Ogden. £1 12s.

The Language and Thought of the Child. By Jean Piaget. Preface by E. Claparéde. *Third Edition (revised and enlarged).* £1 5s.

The Child's Conception of Physical Causality. By Jean Piaget. £1 3s.

The Child's Conception of the World. By Jean Piaget. £1 5s.

The Child's Conception of Number. By Jean Piaget. £1 5s.

Judgment and Reasoning in the Child. By Jean Piaget. £1 1s.

The Origin of Intelligence in the Child. By Jean Piaget. £1 8s.

The Child's Conception of Space. By Jean Piaget. £2 2s.

The Child's Conception of Geometry. By Jean Piaget, Bärbel Inhelder and Alina Szeminska. *In preparation.*

Educational Psychology: its Problems and Methods. By Charles Fox. *Revised Edition.* £1 5s.

The Mental Development of the Child. By Karl Bühler. 15s.

The Psychology of Intelligence. By Jean Piaget. 18s.

The Psychology of Children's Drawings: From the First Stroke to the Coloured Drawing. By Helga Eng. *Second Edition.* £1 5s.

ANIMAL PSYCHOLOGY, BIOLOGY, ETC.

The Mentality of Apes, with an Appendix on the Psychology of Chimpanzees. By W. Koehler. With 9 plates and 19 figures. £1 5s.

The Psychology of Animals, in Relation to Human Psychology. By F. Alverdes. 15s.

The Social Insects: Their Origin and Evolution. By William Morton Wheeler. With 48 plates. £1 8s.

Theoretical Biology. By J. von Uexkuell. £1 4s.

The Individual and the Community: a Historical Analysis of the Motivating Factors of Social Conduct. By Wen Kwei Liao. £1 3s.

Crime and Custom in Savage Society. By B. Malinowski. With six plates. 16s.

Sex and Repression in Savage Society. By B. Malinowski. £1 1s.

B. PHILOSOPHY

Philosophical Studies. By G. E. Moore. £1 10s.

The Philosophy of " As If ": a System of the Theoretical, Practical, and Religious Fictions of Mankind. By H. Vaihinger. Translated by C. K. Ogden. £1 10s.

Five Types of Ethical Theory. By C. D. Broad. £1 8s.

Speculations: Essays on Humanism and the Philosophy of Art. By T. E. Hulme. Edited by Herbert Read. With a frontispiece and Foreword by Jacob Epstein. £1 1s.

The Metaphysical Foundations of Modern Physical Science, with special reference to Man's Relation to Nature. By E. A. Burtt. £1 8s.

Bentham's Theory of Fictions. Edited with an Introduction and Notes by C. K. Ogden. With three plates. £1 1s.

Ideology and Utopia: an Introduction to the Sociology of Knowledge. By Karl Mannheim. £1 8s.

The Philosophy of Peirce. Selected Writings. Edited by Justus Büchler. £1 15s.

Ethics and the History of Philosophy: Selected Essays. By C. D. Broad. £1 3s.

Sense-Perception and Matter : A Critical Analysis of C. D. Broad's Theory of Perception. By Martin E. Lean. £1 1s.

Religion, Philosophy and Psychical Research: Selected Essays. By C. D. Broad. £1 5s.

The Structure of Metaphysics. By Morris Lazerowitz. £1 5s.

Methods and Criteria of Reasoning. An inquiry into the structure of controversy. By Rupert Crawshay-Williams. £1 12s.

Reasons and Faiths. By Ninian Smart. £1 5s.

Tractatus Logico-Philosophicus. By L. Wittgenstein. German text, with an English Translation en regard, and an Introduction by Bertrand Russell, F.R.S. £1.

Foundations of Geometry and Induction. By Jean Nicod. With an Introduction by Bertrand Russell, F.R.S. £1 3s.

The Foundations of Mathematics, and other Logical Essays. By F. P. Ramsey. £1 3s.

The Nature of Mathematics: a Critical Survey. By Max Black. £1 4s.

Logical Syntax of Language. By Rudolf Carnap. £1 10s.

A Treatise on Induction and Probability. By G. H. von Wright. £1 10s.

Bertrand Russell's Construction of the External World. By Charles A. Fritz, Junr. £1 3s.

Logical Studies. By G. H. von Wright. £1 8s.

C. SCIENTIFIC METHOD

Scientific Thought: a Philosophical Analysis of some of its Fundamental Concepts in the light of Recent Physical Developments. By C. D. Broad. £1 12s.

Dynamic Social Research. By John T. Hader and E. C. Lindeman. 18s.

The Limits of Science: Outline of Logic and of the Methodology of the Exact Sciences. By Leon Chwistek. Introduction and Appendix by H. C. Brodie. £1 12s.

HISTORY, ETC.

An Historical Introduction to Modern Psychology. By Gardner Murphy. With a Supplement by H. Kluver. £2.

The History of Materialism and Criticism of its Present Importance. By F. A. Lange. Introduction by Bertrand Russell. £2 10s.

Philosophy of the Unconscious. By E. von Hartmann. £1 15s.

Outlines of the History of Greek Philosophy. By E. Zeller. £1 3s.

Psyche: the Cult of Souls and the Belief in Immortality among the Greeks. By Erwin Rohde. £1 15s.

Plato's Theory of Ethics: The Moral Criterion and the Highest Good. By R. C. Lodge. £1 12s.

Plato's Theory of Education. By R. C. Lodge, F.R.S. (Canada). £1 3s.

Plato's Theory of Art. By R. C. Lodge. £1 5s.

The Philosophy of Plato. By R. C. Lodge. £1 8s.

Plato's Phaedo. A translation with an Introduction, Notes and Appendices, by R. S. Bluck. £1 1s.

Plato's Theory of Knowledge. The Theaetetus and the Sophist of Plato. Translated, with a Running Commentary, by F. M. Cornford. £1 8s.

Plato's Cosmology: The Timaeus of Plato. Translated, with a Running Commentary, by F. M. Cornford. £1 12s.

Plato and Parmenides. Parmenides' "Way of Truth" and Plato's "Parmenides". Translated with an Introduction and Running Commentary, by F. M. Cornford. £1 4s.

Aristotle's Theory of Contrariety. By John P. Anton. £1 5s.

A LIST OF BOOKS PUBLISHED IN THE LIBRARY BUT AT PRESENT OUT OF PRINT

Analysis of Matter. By B. Russell.

Art of Interrogation. By E. R. Hamilton.

Biological Memory. By Eugenio Rignano.

Biological Principles. By J. H. Woodger.

Chance Love and Logic. By C. S. Peirce.

Charles Peirce's Empiricism. By Justus Büchler.

Child's Discovery of Death. By Sylvia Anthony.

Colour Blindness. By Mary Collins.

Colour and Colour Theories. By Christine Ladd-Franklin.

Communication. By K. Britton.

Comparative Philosophy. By P. Masson-Oursel.

Concentric Method. By M. Laignel-Lavastine.

Conditions of Knowing. By Angus Sinclair.

Conflict and Dream. By W. H. R. Rivers.

Conscious Orientation. By J. H. Van der Hoop.

Constitution-Types in Delinquency. By W. A. Willemse.

Contributions to Analytical Psychology. By C. G. Jung.

Creative Imagination. By June E. Downey.

Crime, Law and Social Science. By J. Michael and M. J. Adler.

Dialectic. By M. J. Adler.

Doctrine of Signatures. By Scott Buchanan.

Dynamics of Education. By Hilda Taba.

Effects of Music. By M. Schoen.

Eidetic Imagery. By E. R. Jaensch.

Emotion and Insanity. By S. Thalbitzer.

Emotions of Normal People. By W. M. Marston.

Ethical Relativity. By E. Westermarck.

Examination of Logical Positivism. By Julius Weinberg.

Growth of Reason. By F. Lorimer.

History of Chinese Political Thought. By Liang Chi-Chao.

How Animals Find their Way About. By E. Rabaud.

Human Speech. By Sir Richard Paget.

Infant Speech. By M. M. Lewis.

Integrative Psychology. By W. M. Marston *et al.*

Invention and the Unconscious. By J. M. Montmasson.

Law and the Social Sciences. By H. Cairns.

Laws of Feeling. By F. Paulhan.

Measurement of Emotion. By W. Whately Smith.

Medicine, Magic and Religion. By W. H. Rivers.

Mencius on the Mind. By I. A. Richards.

Mind and its Body. By Charles Fox.

Misuse of Mind. By K. Stephen.

Moral Judgment of the Child. By Jean Piaget.

Nature of Intelligence. By L. L. Thurstone.

Nature of Learning. By G. Humphrey.

Nature of Life. By E. Rignano.

Neural Basis of Thought. By G. G. Campion and Sir G. E. Smith.

Neurotic Personality. By R. G. Gordon.

Philosophy of Music. By W. Pole.

Physique and Character. By E. Kretschmer.

Pleasure and Instinct. By A. H. B. Allen.

Political Pluralism. By Kung Chuan Hsiao.

Possibity. By Scott Buchanan.

Primitive Mind and Modern Civilization. By C. R. Aldrich.

Principles of Experimental Psychology. By H. Pieron.

Problems in Psychopathology. By T. W. Mitchell.

Psychology and Ethnology. By W. H. R. Rivers.

17859. PRINTED BY HEADLEY BROTHERS LTD 109 KINGSWAY LONDON WC2 AND ASHFORD KENT